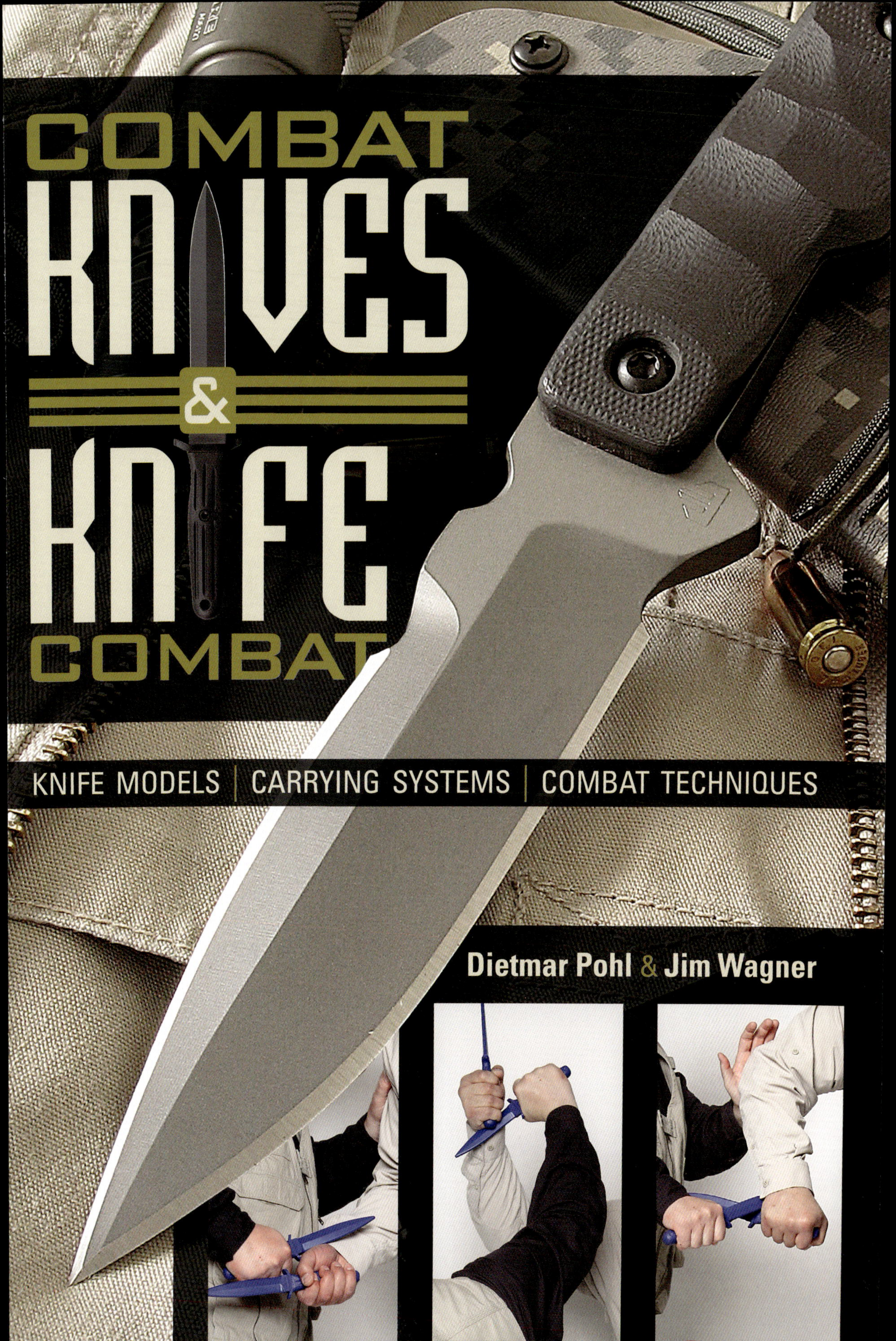

COMBAT KNIVES & KNIFE COMBAT

KNIFE MODELS | CARRYING SYSTEMS | COMBAT TECHNIQUES

Dietmar Pohl & Jim Wagner

Other Schiffer Books by the Author:
Modern Knives in Combat
978-0-7643-3766-6

Other Schiffer Books on Related Subjects:
The Fairbairn-Sykes Fighting Knife
978-0-7643-3763-5
Sharpening and Knife Making
978-0-88740-118-3

Originally published in German as:
Kampfmesser Messerkampf by Wieland, 2007.

Translated from German by Ingrid Elser, with Dr. John Guess as Editorial Advisor

Library of Congress Control Number: 2015932670

Type set in Badloc ICG/Georgia

ISBN: 978-0-7643-4834-1
Printed in China

Published by Schiffer Publishing, Ltd.
4880 Lower Valley Road
Atglen, PA 19310
Phone: (610) 593-1777; Fax: (610) 593-2002
E-mail: Info@schifferbooks.com

CONTENTS

Applegate-Fairbairn Custom Combat Knife of Bill Harsey.
Photo: Rex Applegate

"In close-quarters fighting there is no more deadly weapon than the knife."

- from "Get Tough" by W. I. "Dangerous Dan" Fairbairn

PREFACE

In the literal sense of the word, combat knives is a two-edged topic that has to be dealt with in a sensible and competent way, because the general public regards them as being suspect and politically incorrect. Actually, this is strange, because one of the oldest tools of humankind since time immemorial was used as a weapon, as well. Besides, no critical contemporary gets upset over Olympic fencing, though the common denominator is more than a layperson would guess. Furthermore, experts in this field know that skilled handling of a knife — because of its short constructional length — demands more dexterity, dynamics, and a higher reaction speed than you need for a rapier, epee, or a saber.

While working, I took several courses at home and abroad in self-defense with weapons such as sticks, knives, and all kinds of firearms. Thus, I freely admit that for me, knives are both tools and weapons. For many years, knives have been my everyday companions, and I even take one with me when I go to the bakery around the corner to pick up my buns for breakfast. Why? Well, the reports in print media and on TV prove day by day that this world can be rather bad — something you can see for yourself if you are at the wrong place at the wrong time. The psychic, physical, and legal consequences can be tragic if, for example, you want to protect members of your family in an exceptional situation but are bound to lose because of lack of knowledge. This is the reason why modern self-defense courses for the military, police, security personnel, and civilians with the necessary courage teach not merely combat techniques, but also how to avoid risks, early detection of danger, various steps of de-escalation, and the no less problematic debriefing regarding dealing with police and the legal system.

I have known Dietmar Pohl for about twenty years; I have watched his career as a successful knife designer and as author of the standard volumes *Taktische Einsatzmesser* and *Messer deutscher Spezialeinheiten* with interest. In addition, I honor

Dietmar Pohl as a straightforward, down-to-earth man who does not tend to exaggerate. All the more, I was surprised when he called me and almost enthusiastically told me about the competence and excellence of the American close combat instructor Jim Wagner. A few months later, I had the chance to get to know the charismatic US-instructor myself and to participate in one of his courses on "Reality-Based Knife Survival." From his professional background and experience in martial arts, Jim has acquired a profound basis of knowledge and training skills. This is mirrored in his complex training program, which he manages to make entertaining while always keeping practice in the foreground.

This said, I wish the reader much enjoyment with this book, accompanied by necessary vigilance in dealing with the challenges of life.

Stefan Perey
Cologne, Germany,
November 2006

Stefan Perey is chief editor of the German weapons magazine *CALIBER*.

INTRODUCTION

When I was asked a few years ago whether I would want to participate in writing a book on knife combat, I rejected the offer without hesitation. First of all, because knife combat in the public view has always had the connotation of assassination; and second, because the authors—especially the English-speaking ones, with the exception of a few—have a very dubious fame in public. Writing about this topic in a serious and open way without any pathos seemed at that time to be utterly impossible. The facts I knew about using knives in combat—which I mostly learned from Colonel Rex Applegate and various special units of the military—were mostly limited to mission techniques that should not be the topic of a civilian book. These should be limited to experts who use them within the domain of their official orders. In general, these techniques are offensive and do not belong to the realm of self-defense. Whoever hopes to find commando techniques in this book that would enable him to take down an opponent in an ambush without making noise will be disappointed.

What finally motivated me to participate in this book? First, the challenge to create a piece of work that erases common prejudices against knives and self-defense. On the other hand, there is my acquaintance with co-author Jim Wagner. Our first meeting dates back to 2000, when he taught the GSG 9 in armed and unarmed self-defense. In spring 2005, I successfully completed his *Knife Survival Instructors Course* in London and was impressed by his charismatic teaching style. I was

Among other things, Dietmar Pohl's job is the development of tactical knives for police and special forces. Here he is seen after diving with commando frogmen of the *Spezialisierte Einsatzkräfte* Marine (SEK M, special forces of the German navy) in Eckernförde.
Photo: dp

Jim Wagner with members of GSG 9 during his CQB seminar given in Hangelar, Germany, in 2000.
Photo: jw

especially convinced by the content of his seminar, which fully focuses on realistic self-defense with a knife. In Jim Wagner, I found a co-author whose reputation as an internationally acknowledged expert on close combat is beyond any doubt. He competently wrote the part of this book on tactical knife combat (beginning with Chapter 8).

How quickly and unexpectedly you can become the victim of a crime is proven by daily newspaper reports. Using a knife (or any other weapon) for self-defense can protect your very life, but should always be the last option, when all other possibilities have been exhausted. Many assailants will rethink their actions when they realize they have to face serious resistance. Quite often, this threat potential is already enough to de-escalate the situation. This is analogous to Jim Wagner's philosophy. His Reality-Based Personal Protection System is founded on stopping an opponent while taking into account the principle of proportionality with respect to the used means. How far these means have to be taken depends solely on the opponent's actions.

Unfortunately, there exists a widespread aversion towards people carrying knives and many people associate them with common criminals. This, too, should influence your thoughts about whether and which knife you want to carry for self-defense. For this reason, the concealed carrying of knives is not insignificant, not only because of the tactical advantage over an assailant, but also with respect to your personal reputation. Ultimately, I can only hope that no reader will have to use his or her knife for self-defense in a life-threatening situation.

My special thanks to all who helped to finish this book so rapidly in its current form. Their names are listed in the Appendix. But I especially want to mention Frank Soens and Thomas Fleitman, whose photographic support was invaluable. I also want to wholeheartedly thank guest authors Michael Janich, Bill Newman, Frank Metzner, Joachim Friedrich, Sal Glesser, Dieter Knüttel, and Sohny for their competent contributions.

Dietmar Pohl
Solingen, Germany
November 2006

Authors Dietmar Pohl (left) and Jim Wagner (right).

CHAPTER 1

KNIVES FOR SELF-DEFENSE (SD KNIVES)

Handmade sub-hilt combat knives of knifemaker Gil Hibben (top) and Peter Herbst.
Photo Peter Knoche

To defend yourself or someone else with a knife presupposes you are carrying it with you. A knife is of no use at all if it is at home in your desk drawer or in a display cabinet. But which knives are suitable for self-defense at all? Depending on where you are at the moment, this is any knife you can get hold of in a combat situation. If a violent burglar surprises you in the kitchen, grabbing a kitchen knife is surely the obvious choice. But apart from misusing this household tool, knives that can be professionally used in combat can be divided into three main groups: combat or fighting knives, tactical knives, and actual self-defense knives.

Kitchens by nature have a lot of household knives that you can use for self-defense in an emergency, even though it means misusing them.

Combat or Fighting Knives

This type is classically representative of military use. Usually, combat knives are ground with two edges as daggers. Their blades are long enough to cause fatal wounds to vital organs even after pushing through thick gear and clothing. As pure weapons, combat knives are primarily used for disabling opponents with cuts and stabs. Use as a tool plays only a minor role. In general, daggers are not constructed to be used as tools at all. To avoid suspicious reflections during night missions, combat knives have dull surfaces.

Because soldiers are allowed to or even have to wear combat knives openly while on duty, the possibilities for attaching them are configured accordingly. Besides securing knives to the waist belt—its configured carrying system—or the leg strap of a pistol holster, the MOLLE system, which is attached to a ballistic or tactical vest, is becoming increasingly important. With this system, the sheath is simply attached to the belt system of the vest by a strap sewed to the sheath's backside.

The weapons arsenals of military special forces can't possibly be imagined without containing combat knives. Here you can see a double-edged prototype of such a knife (infantry dagger 2000) of Eickhorn Ltd., located at Solingen.

SD knives are characterized by their concealed carry. Here is the Persian Fighter of the Montana-based knifemaker James Piorek ("Bladerigger").

Piorek's Jashido Compact is the best example of an SD knife with a fixed blade.
Photo dp

Nealy Battle Dagger: a handmade combat dagger by knifemaker Bud Nealy with a black-coated blade, micarta handle scales, and kydex sheath.

Marauder Folder. This SD folder was designed by Walter Brend and was produced in cooperation with knifemaker Bobby Branton. Photo Peter Fronteddu

Typical example of a tactical knife: the Microtech Currahee with tanto and drop point blade.
Photo Microtech Knives

For special police forces, tactical knives are mainly tools. This photo shows Mission Knives's MPK-S.

Military close combat training with combat knives is offensive and includes techniques such as taking down a sentry silently (sentry removal), although this is hardly ever done during modern special missions. Weapons with sound suppressors are taking over this task with far-ranging and deadly precision. Combat knives shaped as daggers are primarily found with special forces, as with German forces. Here, only the *Bundeswehr* (German Federal Armed Forces) specialists of the *Kommando Spezialkräfte*, the *Fernspäher* (Long Range Reconnaissance unit of the German Armed Forces), and the *Kampfschwimmer* (commando frogmen) are issued with the KSK combat knife (Böker Applegate Fairbairn Black). The late Colonel Rex Applegate was one of the most enthusiastic advocates of daggers in combat situations. Everything else for him was not a combat knife at all, only outdoor and utility knives.

Tactical Knives

Since the 1990s, this expression has stood for a type of knife that is supposed to be a tool and a weapon, with an emphasis on nonlethal use. Reality shows that during missions, most of these knives are used for tasks such as overcoming obstacles, saving someone in a life-threatening situation, or for general tasks, such as opening crates. Thus, tactical knives are optionally made with tanto, spear point, or Bowie blades which, compared to daggers, are more resilient. Of course, depending on the situation, all the above mentioned blade shapes are also suitable for combat.

Tactical knives are not only found in the arsenals of military units, but also with special police forces, where use during operations is highly regulated. In Germany, as well as in most other Western countries, their utilization as weapons is completely out of the question. Military units, however, are free to employ them as weapons within the limits of their mission. As with combat knives, the surfaces of tactical knives are nonreflective.

Because of their official use, this knife type is also normally carried openly and is thus easily accessible. To support the knife's function as a tool, many tactical knives are partially serrated, enabling quick cutting of straps or cords. Quite often, you can find a protruding glass breaker at the end of the handle. Tactical knives are offered as fixed as well as folding blades. An example of a tactical knife with a fixed blade is the CQD Mark V made by Masters of Defense®. It was acquired for the Austrian *Jagdkommando*. The special commando unit stationed in Potsdam, Brandenburg, Germany, procured the CQD Mark I as a tactical folder from the same manufacturer.

Self-Defense Knives

These are knives which are specifically used in defensive combat situations. The most important quality of a self-defense knife (called an SD knife in the book from now on) is its concealed carry. Contrary to combat knives and tactical knives, SD knives are not worn openly. Part of the tactical strategy with SD knives is the unarmed appearance of the user. The knife is only drawn when a confrontation is imminent. Here, it is not important whether the user is on an official mission, acting as a bodyguard, or is just a civilian.

In use, the SD knife is clearly defined as a weapon that helps you to protect yourself against an attack in an emergency situation. Of course, SD knives can also be used for everyday tasks or during your spare time.

SD knives do not necessarily need to have a dull surface, because reflecting metal parts are only of secondary importance and play little or no role in a defensive situation. The surface is solely to protect against corrosion, but more about this later. SD knives can have a fixed or foldable blade. Here, only the personal preference of the user is decisive. But with both knife systems, it is important the knife can be drawn quickly and is ready for action without any delay.

An SD knife with a fixed blade has to be constructed in such a way that it can be carried concealed comfortably, or at least under tolerable conditions. Here, many everyday situations should be considered in advance, such as how to comfortably carry the knife while driving a car or while jogging. Thus, the knife should not be too long. SD knives include those with a foldable blade that can be locked, which can be opened single-handedly, and either have a pocket clip or a sheath-carrying system that allows a multitude of ways to carry the knife. These qualities can also include tactical folders, which therefore are equally suitable for police/military/tactical use, as well as for self-defense. SD knives with foldable blades should also not exceed a certain length when closed so they can be carried comfortably.

1.1 The Development of Modern SD Knives

The development of modern SD knives would not be complete without the history of the British close combat trainer William Ewart "Dangerous Dan" Fairbairn during the Second World War. Almost no other person has influenced the development of modern combat knives in the twentieth century and their application as much as Fairbairn. He was born in England in 1855 and spent almost half of his life (1907 to 1940) as a member of the Shanghai city police—Shanghai was still part of the British Empire. After finishing his active duty in Shanghai, he returned to England in 1940, together with his colleague Eric Anthony Sykes, in order to offer his skills as a close combat trainer to the War Office. He was recruited into military service as a captain, and his duties included training the Home Guard, as well as the Commando and Special Operations Executive units, in military close combat.

Besides instinctive shooting and unarmed combat, Fairbairn put special emphasis on the use of knives. To provide the units with adequate and urgently needed melee weapons, he and Sykes designed a commando dagger that effectively changed the development of military combat knives. The templates for this dagger go back to Fairbairn's active police duty in Shanghai and are said to also include the input of American professionals. Today, the commando dagger named Fairbairn-Sykes (F-S, after its designers) is still the epitome for military special operations, but to a large degree is only the symbol in the emblems of special units.

But during World War II, the F-S commando dagger was not only in use in British special units—such as the Commandos, the Special Air Service , or the Airborne units—as a military combat knife in the field. Fairbairn experimented with the design and developed several variations for concealed operation with the Special Operations Executive (SOE). Agents of the SOE were provided with shortened F-S commando daggers that could be worn on the forearm or lower leg. Contrary to the F-S commando dagger, the shortened version for agents was never produced in large series. The company ESA today offers a copy that is very close to the original under the name Gung Ho Brand Knives. A modern cordura sheath with kydex inlay replaces the original leather sheath.

Fairbairn always carried the small version of his knife with him in a special trouser pocket sheath and loved to demonstrate how deadly this small melee weapon could be. Luckily, there still exist well-preserved images of this. His well-known student Rex Applegate, with whom he developed various combat knives during his time as a guest instructor at the Office for Strategic Services, reported an incident that took place in an officer's club in Washington. After drinking lots of alcohol, the small, wiry Fairbairn decided to give the attending officers a presentation of his close combat skills. When putting away his knife into his trouser pocket he missed the sheath. Typically British, he just commented about his blood-soaked trousers with the remark: "What a bloody mess!"

Fairbairn's most important contribution, besides developing the F-S commando dagger, without doubt is his training instruction for knife combat, which sometimes even went so far as to be medically exact in determining the time span between injury and point of death.

1.1.1 Fixed Blade SD Knives

Almost three decades passed until the knife industry focused on a new marketing segment: the knife for self-defense. The first models were created at the end of the 1960s under the names

During World War II, silent sentry removal belonged to the standard training of Allied special forces. Here a soldier of the free French 10th (Inter-Allied) Commando Unit trains thrusting at the carotid artery with the Fairbairn-Sykes combat knife.
Photo Imperial War Museum, H31429

Still a classic: the F-S combat knife of Wilkinson Sword. At right is a thumb dagger of the British SOE special forces, carried concealed.
Photo dp

Eickhorn Ltd. of Solingen, Germany, produces the latest model of the F-S combat knife as Dagger 2000. In the background, you can see the shoulder badge of the US special forces depicting a stylized F-S combat knife as part of the insignia.
Photo Eickhorn Solingen Ltd.

Group photo of OSS trainers taken in 1943. Bottom row, second from the right, is W. E. "Dangerous Dan" Fairbairn. In the top row Rex Applegate can be seen fourth from the left.
Photo Rex Applegate

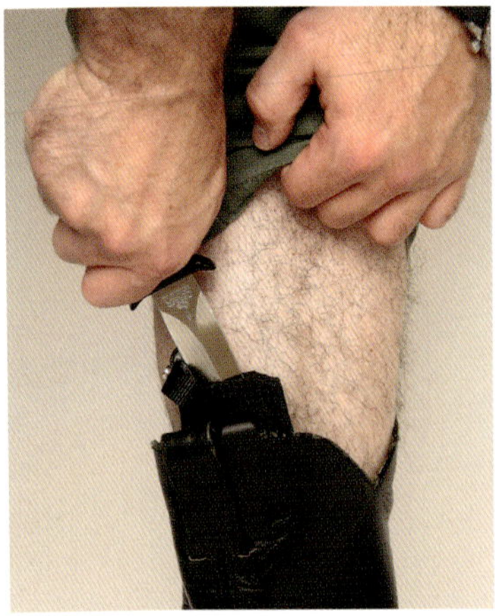

The Gerber Mark I was among the first well known boot knives in the early 1970s. Here is the version with a cordura sheath.

The production of Gerber boot knives stopped at the end of the 1990s. From left: Mark I Tactical, Command I, and Mark I.
Photo dp

Fairbairn experimented with the F-S combat knife; the result was a shortened and thus concealed-carry version for the SOE units. ESA-Sword produces a remake of the shortened F-S combat knife under the name "Gung Ho."
Photo dp

Representatives of the most favored, privately purchased combat knives of the Vietnam War: a Gerber Mark II from 1973 and Randall Knives's current production Model 2 with a handmade leather sheath by Floyd Byrd.

The Gerber TAC II, by knife designer Blackie Collins, was convincing because of its sophisticated sheath locking mechanism. Today, the TAC II is produced by Bear Cutlery & Sons.
Photo dp

boot knife and boot dagger, respectively. They designated a compact, fixed-bladed knife that could be attached to one's clothing by means of a metal clip on the backside of the sheath. Attaching the knife to the rim of a boot was well-suited for the American market, because military and cowboy boots were popular in the U.S. At this time, knives for self-defense with foldable blades were seen as totally inapplicable, as seen in publications of that time. This was mainly a result of the still-inadequate locking of the blade against snapping shut inadvertently. Single-handed opening mechanisms were also not in use, apart from automatic knives of Italian design and gravity knives.

Among the first companies marketing a convincing SD knife was Gerber of Portland, Oregon. Pete Gerber had a unique feel for new knife development and manufacturing techniques. Thus, with the Gerber model Mark II, a military combat knife was created at the time of the Vietnam War that is still very popular today. Besides Randall Knives in Orlando, Florida, the Mark II was then among the combat knives most bought for private use. As a counterpart to the Mark II, the designers at Gerber created the Mark I for concealed operation. Also provided with a dagger blade, it was a smaller version of the Mark II. The design of the aluminum handle was adapted to fit the new and more compact size of the knife. Many users later lamented that the pommel of the larger model, which was designed for striking, was unluckily a victim of these changes. Nevertheless, the Mark I was so successful that it was one of the most-copied knives of its time in the U.S., Japan, and Germany.

Over the decades, the Mark I was only insignificantly modified. For example, in the 1990s, the initial leather sheath was replaced by a cordura sheath. The rest remained the same. As variants, Gerber offered the Mark I with serrations on both sides as the Tactical, or with the back only partly sharpened as the Command I. Unfortunately, the production of the Mark I—as well as that of its big brother, the Mark II—was stopped at the end of the 1990s. According

Randall Knives of Orlando, Florida, participated in the 1970s boot knife boom with their Model 24 Guardian.
Photos dp

William "Bo" Randall, the founder of Randall Knives, presents different production steps from Model 2 combat knife, from forging billet to finished knife.
Photo Randall Knives

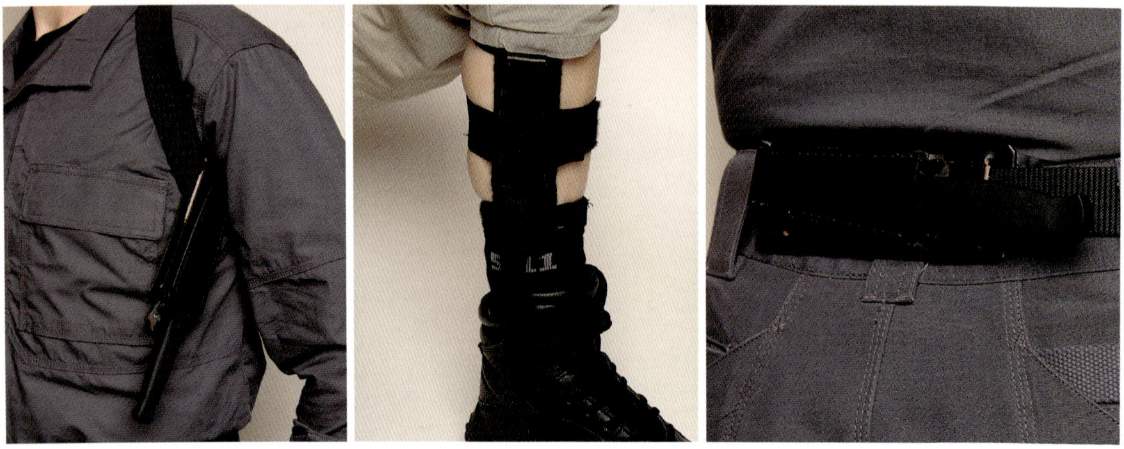

By means of their optional carrying system, the Gerber Guardian and Guardian I models could be worn in three positions.

A. G. Russell searched for a long time to find a new manufacturer for the Sting. Since 2006, it is produced again by Columbia River Knife & Tool.
Photo CRKT

Bob Loveless was responsible for the design of the Gerber Guardian I. At left is the standard version with satin-finished blade and black handle. The camo version (right), with black-coated blade and camouflage woodland pattern, failed to win customer favor.
Photo dp

American design made in Solingen; A. G. Russell had his Sting produced by Anton Wingen for many years. After the company was closed, the Sting became a sought-after collector's item.
Photo dp

The Kershaw Trooper belongs to the most beautifully mass-produced boot knives. The included leather sheath is provided with a boot clip.

From left: The Guardian Camo, Standard, and Presidential Collection models.
Photo dp

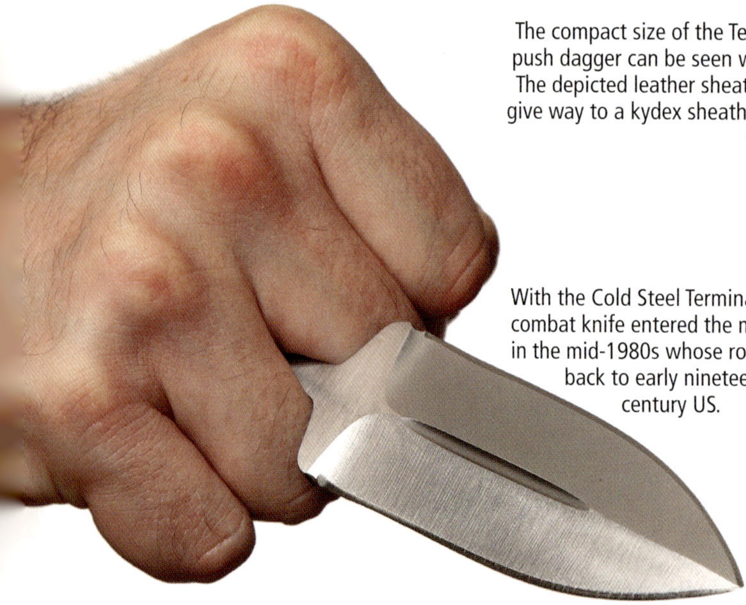

With the Cold Steel Terminator, a combat knife entered the market in the mid-1980s whose roots date back to early nineteenth century US.

The compact size of the Terminator push dagger can be seen well here. The depicted leather sheath had to give way to a kydex sheath for later versions.

to the manufacturer, the die casting tools for the handles were worn and an expensive acquisition of new tools was unwarranted, considering unknown sales numbers.

The 1970s were also shaped by innovative ideas of the ingenious knife designer Blackie Collins. Many of his designs were at first serialized by the U.S. company Benchmark. Later, Gerber produced many of his designs. His designs were convincing not only because of their shape, but also because of their technical finesse. For example, Collins provided his knife sheaths with a multitude of different securing systems. Among the most well known of his boot daggers are the Frisco Shiv and Ninja models. His TAC II model crossed the border between military combat knife and SD knife. While the Frisco Shiv is no longer produced today, the Ninja and TAC II are again available from Bear Cutlery & Son.

The new boot knife market in the 1970s was discovered by other manufacturers as well. Randall Knives, for example, launched a small SD knife based on specifications of the concessionaire Charles L. Alden, who mainly sold knives to the employees of security companies and units of special forces participating in U.S. operations abroad. His Maximum Concealment Knife ought to give the user a last chance as a backup weapon in case he or she got into a situation where their firearm was either emptied or lost. Luckily, this weapon is still available as the Model 24 Guardian (not to be confused with the Gerber model of the same name).

In the 1970s, the American knifemaker and designer A.G. Russell authorized the company Anton Winger ("Othello"), formerly of Solingen, Germany, to mass-produce the Sting. This was an integral knife forged of a single piece of steel and provided with a mirror-polished surface. The customer could choose among three different handle materials: rosewood, stag, or ruby-colored micarta. The production of Sting in its original version stopped when Anton Winger was closed at the end of the 1990s. For many years Russell tried unsuccessfully to find a new manufacturer for his beloved design. Since 2006, a new, all-metal version of coated carbon steel with a multi-functional plastic sheath is available from the Columbia River Knife & Tool.

In the 1980s, a multitude of new SD knives were created, such as the designs of knifemaker legend Bob Loveless that were mass-produced by Gerber. While the Guardian II was primarily for use in military combat, the Guardian I and Guardian supplemented the already tried and tested Mark I in the area of SD knives. Besides the knives, Gerber offered an optional carrying system with cordura straps and velcro connections. With this, the Guardian I and its little brother, the Guardian, could also be worn concealed underneath a jacket and upside-down, with the handle facing downwards.

With the Guardian series, Gerber also started to create a new trend with respect to colors. Besides the standard version with satin-finished blades and black handles, Gerber also tested the production of handles and sheaths in camouflage colors fitting for the woodland camouflage of the American armed forces. Probably the time was not yet ready for this idea, because these knives did not win customer favor. The Guardians faced the same fate as the Mark models: after a few years, production of the series was stopped. During the early 1990s, Gerber once more released a strongly modified Guardian model with a plastic handle and sheath that could be attached in multiple ways. This model can still be found in the Gerber catalog today. It is especially interesting because of the individually adjustable resistance for the pull of the sheath.

Kershaw also participated in the boot knife trend, presenting the Trooper with a polished dagger blade, stainless steel mountings, and wooden handle scales. It is still one of the most beautiful SD daggers. Even Rex Applegate is said to have admired this model, according to author Leroy Thompson, and to have promoted it until his own models were mass-produced. Luckily, Kershaw never ceased production this flagship SD knife; the Trooper is still available in its original form today. The successful follow-up of this model by Kershaw is the Amphibian, which is also one of the classic SD knives.

Lynn Thompson, CEO of the American company Cold Steel, created a new trend in the mid-1980s with his thermoplastic handles. Soft, rubber-like plastic (Kraton) in combination with a diamond-shaped surface structure provides an almost inseparable connection between hand and handle. While in the beginning this material was only used for Thompson's legendary Tanto model, he later used Kraton for the new version of his push dagger, as well.

The big advantage of a push dagger is its compact size. The handle is turned around ninety degrees and cuts the overall length of the knife down by almost half. For its use as an SD knife there are various judgments, ranging from "ideal pushing weapon" to "hard-to-handle knife for other tactical maneuvers." Push daggers are prohibited in many countries. This doesn't hinder Cold Steel from producing this knife type in its third generation. The simple boot leather sheath of the Terminator model was exchanged in the second generation to the Safekeeper model with kydex sheath. The current version is the Safemaker and, according to Thompson, was once more improved in design.

On the outside are belt buckle knives, although Bowen Knives, in Arkansas, still exists and offers various models. The idea behind these knives, which are worn concealed behind the belt buckle, is surely interesting at first glance, but is questionable with respect to their practical use. Of course, with such a knife you always have a weapon for self-defense at your side that is quite comfortable to carry. But practice reveals that a belt buckle knife can only be used inadequately in combat. Even worse, trousers that are no longer in place but have slipped down may be an obstacle to defending yourself effectively.

1.1.2 Foldable SD Knives

Knife developments in the 1980s made folders increasingly interesting for self-defense. One of these developments was the butterfly or balisong knife, whose principle is based on rotating both handle halves about 180 degrees. While opened, both handle halves prevent the blade from inadvertently retracting during use. When closed, the blade is secured inside the handle. Self-defense experts trained in martial arts were very interested in this knife type from the Philippines. They loved to show how to open this knife quickly with one hand in front of an amazed audience. The balisong was part of many movie and TV productions, most times seen in the hands of the villains. Thus, balisongs quickly received a bad reputation.

One of the most successful manufacturers of this knife type is Benchmade, based in Oregon. Because of its quick success, dozens of knife manufacturers jumped on the bandwagon with their own butterfly models. Knife manufacturers from Asia proved to be very creative and offered balisongs for even the smallest wallet. The other side of the coin was that because of the dramatic look when opened by skilled hands and because of their low price, young people were especially attracted to balisongs. At times, this knife type was seen used in schoolyards.

The company's Spyderco is especially connected to one-handed folders. In the early 1980s, the founder of the company, Sal Glesser, had the ingenious idea to add a hole to the blade as a means for opening the blade with the thumb. This way, laboriously opening the knife with two hands was no longer necessary and folders advanced more and more into the realm of SD knives. The increased spread of a locking mechanism with backspring and hammer (back lock) also contributed to the safe use of folders. Now the restraint had to be unlocked deliberately to close the folder. This means for use in self-defense you now had a knife at hand that could be carried comfortably and could be turned into a weapon with a lockable blade lightning quick and with one hand.

Another important innovation by Spyderco was the pocket or belt clip screwed onto the handle. This allows the knife to be carried without an obvious belt pouch concealed and at various positions—a decisive tactical advantage with an SD knife. In addition, the flat handle scales of Spyderco knives increase their carrying comfort. Spyderco can also claim to be the first company to provide a folder blade with scary-sharp serrations. These are all self-evident qualities for tactical and SD knives today.

At the end of the 1980s, another locking mechanism for blades drew attention: the liner lock. Although this mechanism was generally known in the knife industry for many years

Contrary opinions exist about the value of the Bowen Belt Knife with respect to its use in action; many claim it is of absolutely no use in SD situations.
Photo Michael Janich

The Kershaw Amphibian is especially convincing because of its functionality and can be delivered with various sheaths for different uses.
Photo Kershaw Knives

In product evolution, the Cold Steel models Safekeeper (left) and Safemaker replaced the original model Terminator.
Photo ACMA Reus, Cold Steel Knives

previous, knifemaker Michael Walker deserves the credit for helping the liner lock making its decisive breakthrough. The advantage of this mechanism on the one hand is that the knife can be opened much easier because the permanent pressure of the backspring onto the blade for the back lock is dispensed with. On the other hand, the folder can also be closed comfortably with one hand and without the need to change one's grip—advantages that other knifemakers and especially the knife industry quickly realized.

The clip at the handle scale allows fixing the knife to the rim of a trouser pocket.

The hole as an aid for opening is a trait of Spyderco's Clipit models.

The US company Benchmade can claim to be the first company to successfully establish balisong knives on the market. It still produces balisong knives today.
Photo Benchmade Knives

Handles of titanium 6Al4V made by different companies (from top):
Walter Brend (Model # 2 Folder), Bob Terzuola (ATCF), and Chris Reeve (Sebenza).

Eugene M. Stoner
1922
1997
MAXPEDITION
TM
HARD-USE GEAR

Ron Miller's Black Knife switchblade design as it is still offered by knifemaker Charles Ochs.

Photo Charles Ochs, Point Seven Studios

Microtech Knives is still the frontrunner with respect to manufacturing switchblades with CNC-milled aluminum handle scales. Here are the H.A.L.O II (top) and H.A.L.O. III models.

Photo Microtech Knives

With the AFO, Benchmade turned the switchblade surge of the early 1990s into an outright boom.

Photo. ACMA Reus, Benchmade Knives

SPYDERCO CHANGES THE KNIFE WORLD: SAL GLESSER REMEMBERS

Spyderco's first invention in the knife industry was our sharpener named the Sharpmaker, which was introduced to the market in 1978. I was always interested in knives; throughout my entire life I was fascinated by them. When the first lockback folders entered the market in the mid-1960s, I quickly learned how to open these knives with one hand, using my thumb to rotate the blade.

In 1980, I searched for a way to transfer this concept to a knife so everyone would be able to open the blade with one hand. My developments started with attaching small things to the blade that could be gripped by the thumb to open the folder. Pins and disks were quite functional but had other disadvantages. There was also another product on the market called "Flick-it" that helped opening the folder. But for me, it had the same disadvantages as pins or other attachments, which can get caught on trouser pockets, are in the way when cutting things, and so on.

At this point, I developed a means to modify the blade itself to open it with one hand. At first, I began providing the surface of the blade with a rough structure on which I could anchor my thumb, but this remained difficult. Then I ground a dent into the blade onto which the thumb could hook. When I started to grind dents on both sides of the blade for the knife to be opened by right- and left-handed people, I realized it worked even better when I cut a complete hole instead of grinding two dents. The original design allowed for a round hole, because we believed it would work better than other shapes.

The concept of mounting a clip to the side of the knife to attach it to the upper rim of the trouser pocket came into being because of a key chain with hooks I always carried on the rim of my trouser pocket. The key chain prevented my keys from falling to the bottom of the pocket and thus becoming uncomfortable while carrying. This was a well-known problem for pocket knives. I worked on a whole series of clips, but finally, we decided on a shape that can still be found on almost every Spyderco knife.

Our knives only started becoming really popular in the early 1990s, after we had already produced them for ten years. Our opening system could be patented, but no industrial property rights existed for our clip. By the mid-'90s, the clip was already a common appearance with many knives. Our invention had taken root and founded a lively competition.

In the mid-1990s, another knife manufacturer found a loophole in our opening hole patent and, by the end of the 1990s, a multitude of opening holes with all kinds of shapes existed. We believed in a larger success of the round opening hole because it worked equally well as other shapes and could be integrated into the knife design much easier. When we realized that nobody else used

Company founder Sal Glesser, together with his wife Gail. Without her, Sal states, Spyderco wouldn't exist. Photo Spyderco

round opening holes, we applied for and were granted a trademark for the round shape of the hole, distinguishing ourselves from all other shapes.

I first dealt with serrations during the development of our Sharpmaker sharpener. We realized the necessity of sharpening serrations and the Sharpmaker was well suited for this task. Our R&D team quickly realized that sharp serrations were very effective in various situations, such as cutting ropes or other materials containing fibers. At the beginning of the 1980s, we first introduced the serrations on our rescue knives, later on providing almost all our models with serrations. Today, Spyderco offers many models with serrated blades.

Sal Glesser is founder and owner of Spyderco. With his innovative designs he provided the knife world with many new ideas.

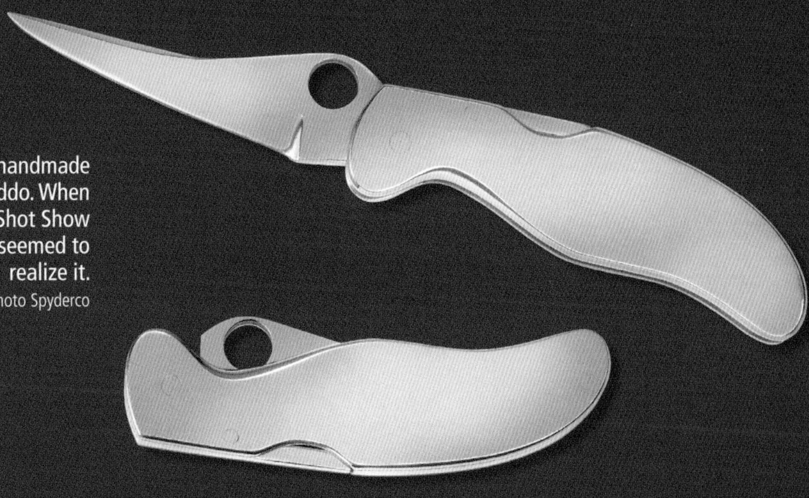

The first Spyderco prototype handmade by Sal's brother-in-law, Jim Oddo. When the knife was shown at the Shot Show in Las Vegas in 1980, nobody seemed to realize it.
Photo Spyderco

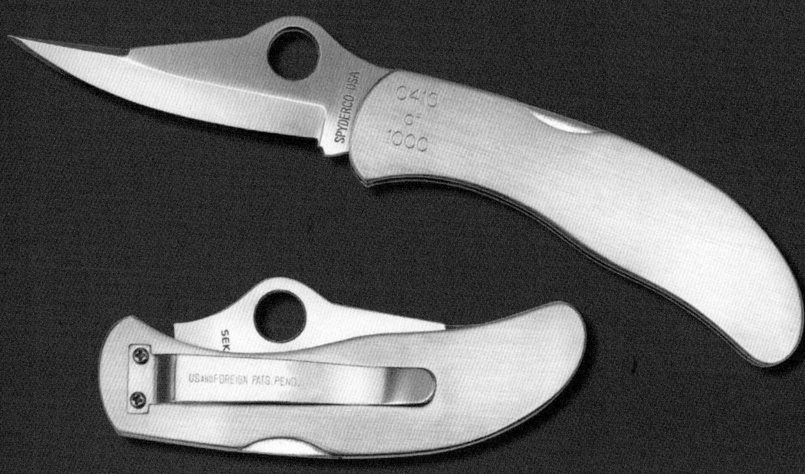

Based on this prototype, in 1981, an initial batch of C01 Worker was produced, called the 2-screw-clip model. Later, Spyderco Clipits used three screws for fastening the clip.
Photo Spyderco

1.1.3 Modern Materials

With the trend of tactical knives during the early 1990s, high-tech materials and modern production methods became increasingly accepted in the knife industry. Folder handles were now cut from titanium or aircraft aluminum by computer-controlled milling machines. The charm of hand-finished wooden handles made way for clinical-looking metal surfaces, usually satined by sandblasting or coated with a dark color. Apart from aesthetic aspects, the biggest advantage of this production method lies in its small tolerances. Benchmade and Microtech especially make use of this.

Besides metal, from the mid-1990s onward, new plastic materials were increasingly used. Because of their stability, they are especially well suited for handle scales. Particularly carbon fibers and G-10 composite materials are still in great demand today.

New production techniques also enabled the unthinkable in serial knife production. For example, knifemaker Ron Miller of Largo, Florida, developed an automatic knife with a new spring mechanism; the self-supporting handle was cut with a CNC milling machine. This guaranteed necessary tolerances, while on the other it reduced the mounting time because less manual work was necessary. Because the parts were screwed together, fewer elaborate, traditional production steps were required and the knife could be taken apart easily for cleaning and repair.

Together with knifemaker Charles Ochs, Miller marketed the knife under the name "Black Knife" until his death in 1995. Although it looked as if the knife would never be produced again, Ochs quickly decided to offer a modified version of the Black Knife himself. Its size and the possibility of opening the knife with one hand made this knife interesting for self-defense from the very beginning—which did not fail to catch the attention of other manufacturers. Miller missed the opportunity to patent the spring mechanism in time and more and more manufacturers produced automatic knives based on his design.

In the area of SD knives with fixed blades, kydex as a sheath material was only slowly accepted. Although it was known since the 1980s and was also used by a few US knifemakers, this thermoplastic started its triumphant success at the beginning of the '90s. The advantages of sheaths made from this material were especially interesting for use as SD knives. In addition to secure carrying, kydex sheaths were especially convincing because they allowed quick drawing of the knife without having to open a safety latch first.

Among the first industrial suppliers of kydex sheaths was Cold Steel. Here is their Mastertanto model.
Photo dp

Knifemaker Bud Nealy of Stroudsburg, Pennsylvania, first recognized the potential of this raw material and developed the Multi Concealment Sheath (MCS) System. With an entire system of

Close combat expert Duane Dieter provided his Masters-of-Defense CQB Mark V model with a multitude of possible applications, such as opening a door latch with the claw-like guard, as shown here.
Photo Masters of Defense

In 1989, Bud Nealy first presented his MCS system at the East Coast Custom Knife Show. His Kinzhal model of the late 1990s is shown here.
Photo dp

add-ons made of kydex, the MCS can be carried at almost any position on the body or clothing. Because of the flat and compact construction of his knives comfortable carrying is possible. According to Nealy, among his customers are officers of the FBI, Secret Service, and other US government agencies. For a few years now, Nealy has offered an improved version of his MCS system. Instead of screws, for his MCS II he uses a very stable hook-and-loop tape from 3M. This allows even more possibilities for attachment and angles for drawing the knife.

Since the mid-1990s, knife manufacturers have increasingly employed experts on military close combat and self-defense as designers for their SD knives. Among the most well-known of these are Rex Applegate, Michael Janich, Duane Dieter, Kelly Worden, Bram Frank, and even the actor Steven Seagal, who became famous for his action and martial arts movies. This was done not only for the purpose of making the designs more practice oriented, but also as an argument to improve sales.

Nomenclature of knives with a fixed blade:

1. main edge
2. back edge
3. fuller (blood groove)
4. guard
5. handle scale
6. tang
7. smash point
8. handle butt, pommel
9. handle screw
10. lanyard hole

Graphics: Böker Baumwerk, Rainer Klein

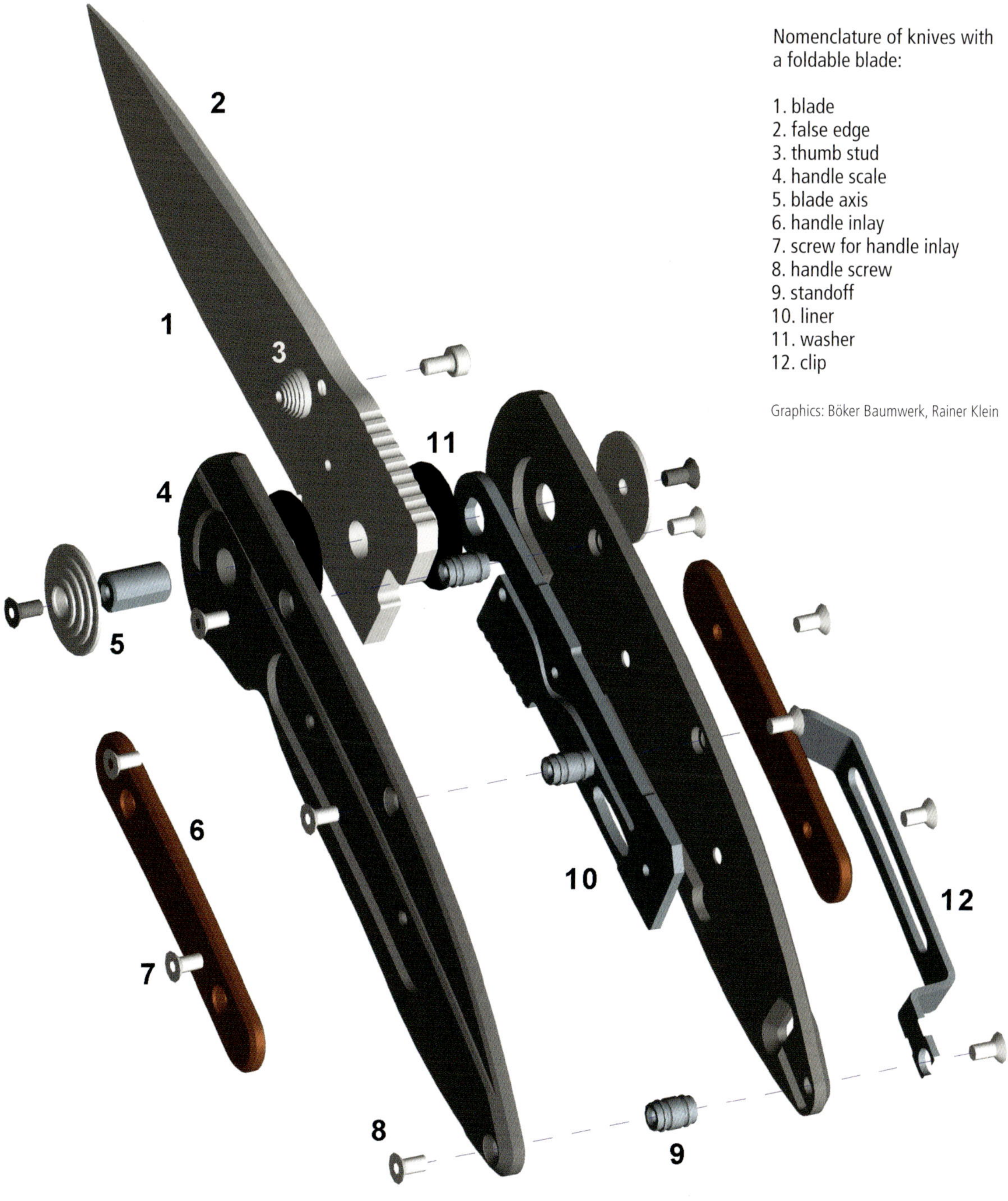

Nomenclature of knives with a foldable blade:

1. blade
2. false edge
3. thumb stud
4. handle scale
5. blade axis
6. handle inlay
7. screw for handle inlay
8. handle screw
9. standoff
10. liner
11. washer
12. clip

Graphics: Böker Baumwerk, Rainer Klein

THE PHILIPPINE BALISONG: A TRADITIONAL TACTICAL FOLDER

by Michael Janich

The balisong, or Philippine butterfly knife, is one of the most unique and dynamic knife designs ever developed. Contrary to traditional folders with the blade folding back into a single handle, the balisong is distinguished by a double handle design. The handles rotate around the blade axis and in closed position cover half the blade each, while releasing it in the open position. This unusual design has a number of advantages not possessed by conventional folders, especially as a tactical operational tool for combat.

To begin with, the extremely simple construction of a balisong means fewer movable parts. When the knife is well made, there is practically nothing that can break or work badly. The locking mechanism of a balisong is extremely strong and reliable. The lock is available in three variants: the original version you know from traditional Philippine balisongs consists of a pin that runs through the tang. This version has U-shaped metal handles that hold the blade in the closed position. If the knife is open, the handles touch the blade pin and clamp it tightly. As long as permanent pressure is exerted either with the hand or by means of a safety latch, the blade stays securely in the open position. The triangular positioning of the blade pin and both blade axes in general make up one of the strongest locking mechanisms of folders.

Another balisong locking mechanism comprises two blade pins inserted above and below the blade axes, respectively. This construction can usually be found on balisongs with sandwich-style handles. With this knife type, the second blade pin is needed to fix the blade in the closed position, preventing the sharp blade from punching through the slits in the handle.

The third locking mechanism consists of two hardened steel pins running through each of the handles and an elongated tang at the blade. If the knife is opened, both pins touch the elongated tang from both sides and secure the blade in the open position by means of pressure. This type of balisong mechanism is commonly known as zen pin construction.

Balisong construction is also unique because it is one of the few folders that allow the use of dagger blades ground sharp on both sides. Since both handle halves surround the blade completely in their closed position, such a dagger can be carried without danger of injury. The biggest advantage of a balisong, however, is that it can be opened very quickly with only one hand. If you hold one handle half and swing the other, there are countless possibilities for opening and closing the knife at high speed. Some balisong experts are proud to point out how many combinations of impressive opening techniques have been developed by them.

The balisong is an excellent choice for tactical knife users. It can be used the same way as other tactical knives. It is functional, can be carried comfortably, and can be opened quickly and reliably with one hand. If the knife is considered with respect to these basic principles, the balisong is an excellent combat knife.

The next question is: "How do I fight with it?" In my view, practical self-defense and martial arts follow two different methods. In a real self-defense situation you go through high stress levels, because the attacker has the intention to hurt or even kill you. In such situations, the body is programmed to react instinctively in order to maximize your chances of survival. To say it more simply: under life-threatening circumstances, the gross motor skills prevail and the fine, complex skills become very difficult to perform. This means complicated action patterns that require a high level of skill, such as fanciful balisong opening techniques, won't work really well under these circumstances.

Thus, it is recommended one keeps the opening technique as simple as possible. In addition, you ought to take care to grab as much of the handle as possible prior to swinging it open. This enhances control over the weapon and reduces the probability of dropping the knife, or not being able to open it completely. For example, latch opening (a technique where you hold the safety latch between thumb and forefinger and open the free-swinging handle half with a throwing movement) is a simple opening technique and does not need a complex series of movements. But the fact that you hold the knife only at a very restricted area makes this technique less reliable than the handle throw or ice pick spin, with which you can hold the handle itself.

With convincing design and finish: Spyderco's Spyderfly with titanium handles and four different possibilities for clip positioning.
Photo Spyderco Knives

Balisong knives in capable hands impress by means of their lightning-quick opening technique.
Photo Michael Janich

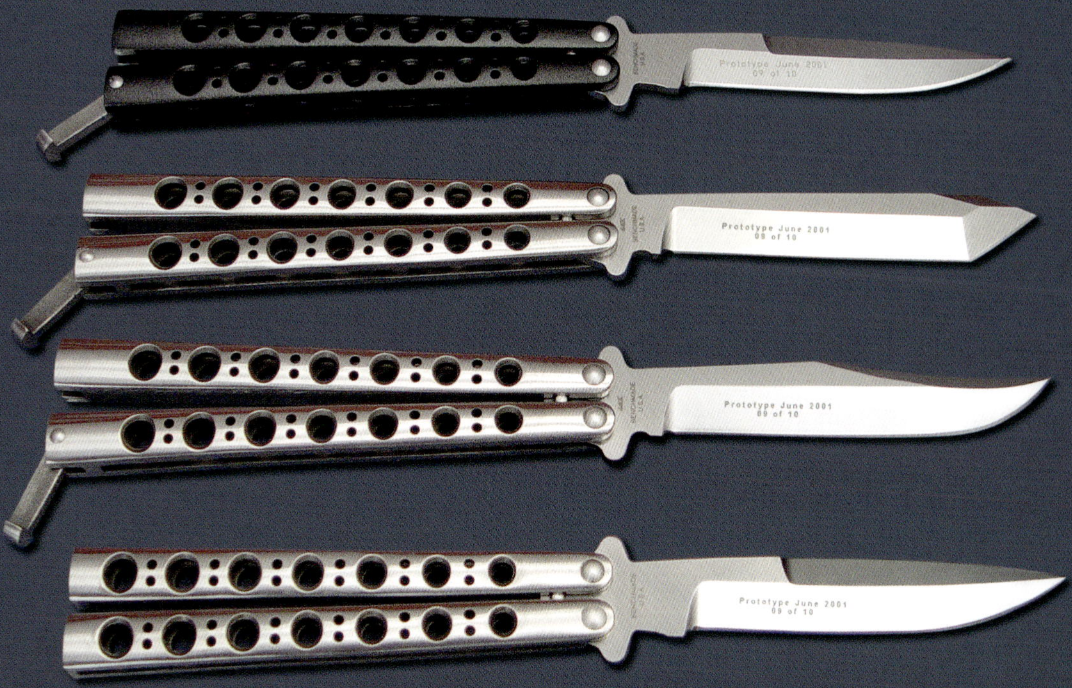

Benchmade's Model 42 still sets the international standard others have to compete against. The photo shows different versions of Benchmade prototypes from the collection of Michael Janich.
Photo Michael Janich

An assortment of traditional balisong knives from Michael Janich's collection.
Photo Michael Janich

Another tactic often seen in the movies and also recommended by some martial arts experts is to perform a whole series of opening and closing techniques in order to confuse the attacker and maybe even convince him to retreat. Personally, I think this is absolute nonsense. If I have to draw my knife, I assume I will have to use it to protect my life. If this is the case, I also face a threat and, with high probability, stress will occur immediately. At this stage, the balisong "dance" will probably be difficult to perform or won't work at all.

There is a whole series of other balisong techniques recommended by martial arts experts but, in my opinion, they don't make any sense at all in real combat. To these belong hitting the opponent with the handle half swinging upwards or pinching skin or fingers between both handle halves.

Hits with the closed handle halves or other firm objects are preferred anytime. It only creates a small impact force if you hold one handle half and hit with the other, swinging part of the handle. You always have to keep in mind that you drew the knife for a specific reason: to protect your life. To only give a little "pat" with one half of the handle when you could have given a big hit or could have used the blade for cutting or stabbing is wasted effort. The same goes for the idea of pinching skin, fingers, or other body parts within reach between the handle halves, as if it were a nutcracker. In a fight of life and death there is no room for such things.

Finally, many balisong artists recommend opening the knife only partially, to assist the blade's back with the thumb and to use this position for cutting. I believe if you have the possibility to place a decisive cut during a counterattack, then it should show results! But the knife has to be opened completely, because otherwise the blade can't be stabilized. With the right opening technique, it takes as much time to open a knife entirely as it takes to open only half of it. Thus, there is no rational reason to use the thumb braking technique.

Regarding securing the knife in the open position, some balisong fans state the knife is not completely secured as long as the safety latch is still open. But from a purely functional viewpoint, the balisong is secured as soon as both handle halves are pressed together with a firm grip when the knife is open. You can make powerful cuts or stabs without fearing the blade will snap shut. There exist quite a number of balisongs that were intentionally produced without any safety latch.

The use of a balisong basically does not differ from a conventional knife. As soon as it is opened and secured, the techniques and tactics are exactly the same as with any other knife. A balisong only differs from a conventional knife in its ability to change from the closed to the open position at a decisive moment. In other words, the design and characteristics of a balisong allow the knife to be used as a striking tool and opening the blade while this maneuver is still being executed. In the ideal case, you strike several times with the closed knife and then use the chance to open it.

The balisong is a unique and versatile knife design, but to use it the right way, you need continuous training. Preparation is required to use it in a stressful, real self-defense situation. As with any other weapon you want to trust your life to, you have to invest time and effort to achieve applicable skills. In any case, you also have to sharpen and refine these skills under challenging training conditions in order for you to function under stress. If you are ready to take on these efforts, then you will be able to exploit the potential hidden behind this elegant and simple knife design.

Michael Janich belongs to the worldwide leading experts in close combat and has already published a number of books and videos on the topics of knives and knife combat. In addition, he has made various knife designs for companies such as Spyderco and Masters of Defense. More information on Michael Janich is available at www.martialbladeconcepts.com.

Top-class balisongs (from top): a custom Benchmade model with ivory micarta handle inlays and a unique, handmade piece by knifemaker Darrel Ralph.

Photo Michael Janich

This series of balisong techniques illustrates their use as an impact weapon, as well as the opening technique during the climax of the fight. When Michael Rigg (right) attacked Michael Janich with his forehand, Janich blocked with a two-step left-right combination. Then he grabbed Rigg's elbow to subsequently hit his face forcefully with the closed balisong.

While Rigg's head is thrown backwards by the blow's force, Janich fixes his arm with his left hand and opens the balisong. After the opening is completed, Janich makes a deep cut into Rigg's right thigh and renders him immobile. Afterwards, Janich moves away from Rigg's sphere of action in order to reach a safe distance. Photos: Michael Janich, Michael Rigg

1.2 Choosing An SD Knife

Choosing an SD knife requires a number of basic considerations, because not every knife is well suited to self-defense. Five factors should be considered for an SD knife: blade length, blade shape, safe use of the handle, stability of the knife, and the ability to quickly use it. All five factors build on each other and are not independent.

How long should the blade be?

This question depends on the target you want to hit and how comfortably you want to carry the knife if concealed. A military combat knife has a blade length that can easily hit any vitally essential target on your opponent's body. But with a blade length of about six to seven inches (fifteen to seventeen centimeters), these knives are usually much too large to carry comfortably concealed. A small folding knife (folder) with a blade length of about two inches (five centimeters) can cause severely bleeding cuts or hit an artery underneath the skin, but the blade length isn't sufficient for effectively stabbing vital body parts. Thus, a blade length between three and five inches (eight and thirteen centimeters) is recommended, combining effectiveness with carrying comfort. Fixed and folding blades are easily found in this size range.

How should the blade be shaped?

There are two primary tactical actions in knife combat: stabbing and cutting. The blade has to be shaped accordingly, regardless of how the designer does this. The blade tip should be sufficiently long enough to penetrate deeply, but it also has to be shaped in such a way as not to break if a soft target is missed and hard metal parts (buttons, belt, keys, coins in a wallet) or the bones of the opponent are hit instead. The blade shape should also allow effective cuts through clothing and human tissue. How different the blade designs can be is shown in detail in the next chapter.

What should the properties of the handle be?

The handle should protect the user from his own blade during combat. One can imagine how fatal it would be to slip down to the blade in the middle of a fight. This can happen easily, all the more if sweat or blood come into play. Unfortunately, many designs do not consider this. Many designers believe fluting and finger grooves are sufficient, but a real guard is necessary. On the other hand, the guard should not project too much and get caught in one's clothing when drawing a concealed knife.

The handle should be shaped so that you immediately hold the knife in the right position without having to think about it. The user has to instinctively know where the blade edge is located. This is especially difficult for knives with round handles. In addition, the handle surface—its material and shape—should always allow safe guiding of the knife during pushing or pulling movements.

What should the knife be able to endure?

The stability of a knife in its entirety should be sufficient to meet the extreme requirements it may have to face in any individual case. For a folder, this especially concerns the locking mechanism. If the blade snaps shut as soon as it hits an obstacle, the user may suffer injuries that render him unable to fight. Loss or impairment of fighting ability could possibly be a death sentence, so you have to be able to blindly trust the locking mechanism.

It is also important to not inadvertently unlock the blade in the heat of battle, which may happen with locking systems that protrude too much, or that have to withstand different pressure ratios of the hand or fingers for different grip positions. Thus, one ought to check whether the locking mechanism is sturdy in all possible grip positions before purchasing a knife.

The length of the blade is decisive as to which targets can be effectively reached. Top: the Boker Plus Subcom FB model with a blade length of 1.85 inches (4.7 centimeters). Bottom: the Harsey Tactical Folder model of Lone Wolf Knives with a blade length of 4.72 inches (12 centimeters).

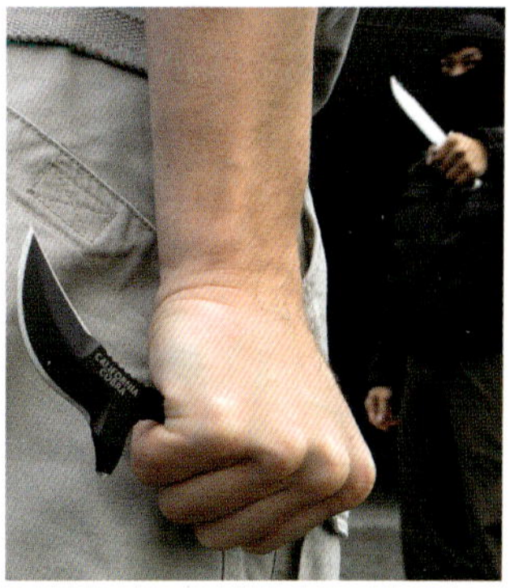

SD knives with compact blades can usually be readied for action concealed. This is a tactical advantage that shouldn't be underestimated. The photo shows the California Cobra of TOPS Knives.
Photo Marc Götzmann

The handle has to allow a secure grip at all times. A very pronounced index finger groove prevents one's hand from slipping onto the blade. The photo shows the Air Marshall of TOPS Knives.

The blade shape has a decisive influence on fighting style. On top is the Karambit model with hawkbill blade and at the bottom, the Sniper with spear point blade. Both knives are made by US company Strider.

A massive tang that runs throughout the entire handle, such as the one in this ST-01 of Crusader, doesn't give way even under extreme loads.

In SD use, the knife should be drawn and ready for action without losing time. With a suitably functioning sheath system, this is possible even with large knives, such as the sub-hilt fighter by Gil Hibben, which is enabled through its Kytac/Blackhawk shoulder carry system.

Closed knife pouches protect the knife from being lost. At the same time, they reduce the knife's ability to be ready for action immediately.

Changing from a folder to a fixed blade with its carry system can lead to a tactical mistake due to habit. This has to be considered before any change and must be trained for accordingly.

For knives with a fixed blade, the tang should reach as far into the handle as possible to enhance stability. The knife has to tolerate extreme lateral loads, as the blade breaking could be fatal.

How quickly do you have to be able to draw the knife?

As quickly and as controlled as possible! The probability of an unexpected attack while you are in a tactically unfavorable position is quite high. You have to be able to draw the knife instinctively from any thinkable position and make it ready for action, attacking with effective stabs and cuts. This has to be done single-handedly and with each of your hands, so if your right hand gets injured and can't be used, the left hand can still reach your weapon for defense.

Thus, when choosing an SD knife with a fixed blade, optimum knife and sheath matching has to be taken into consideration. Today, it is possible to refit a good knife with a matching sheath acquired from a kydex sheathmaker. Accordingly, if a knife fulfills all the requirements, you ought to buy it even if the sheath is bad or doesn't offer all the desired possibilities for carrying the knife.

With drawing a folder another factor comes into play: opening the blade takes additional movement and the knife has to be readied for action. Here, opening it with one hand has to be flowing and quick as lightning. Folders whose blades have to be opened with two hands don't fall under the SD knife category and should not be used. Models that have to be extracted laboriously from a holster or pouch should also be avoided.

For many years, a great number of knives have been on the market that comply with these five basic requirements. But in the end, what does the choice of the right knife depend on? How can you reduce the assortment to choose from even more? The answer to this is found in your wardrobe. If the knife doesn't fit in your regular clothing, or if it can't be worn comfortably on the job or during your spare time, then it will usually stay at home or in the car and won't be at hand when you need it most. Unfortunately, this happens whenever the choice is made with only the weapon in mind and a large combat knife or tactical knife is chosen. Soon, you'll find either that a large knife is not really comfortable to carry in everyday life, or it draws unwanted attention from acquaintances and colleagues.

Thus, your first glance should not be at the catalog of a knife manufacturer, but at your closet. The most important goal is to find an SD knife that fits with all your clothing and can be worn all the time. Only then will you always be armed. Of course, you can buy several SD knives that you can carry in different places, depending on the clothing you wear. For example, during summer, you can comfortably wear a folder with a clip attached to your trousers. In winter, you could change to a knife with a fixed blade and kydex sheath underneath a jacket.

But such a change can also cause problems: in a confrontation in which you may draw your weapon, the movements should be carried out quickly and automatically. If you are used to having a folder in your trouser pocket but your knife is now in a holster underneath your arm, there is a high probability that you will reflexively grab for your weapon at the wrong place.

Body size and stature also play a decisive role in deciding on the right SD knife. For example, a knife with a fixed blade that is carried in a shoulder or back holster is more problematic for a small person than for a large one. Similarly, the circumference of an individual matters, as well. A broad person can wear a belt sheath horizontally or oblique on their back, while for those of smaller stature, the handle and sheath will conspicuously poke out on both sides. In these cases, carry a folder with a clip or use a holster for quick drawing.

The way you carry a knife also determines the appearance of a person. If you decide on carrying a folder in a belt holster, you show the world you are armed with a knife. Even a folder clip in your trouser pocket can be obvious if its color stands out. In the workshop of a craftsman or on a construction site a folder will be seen as a tool, and thus totally normal. But if you work in an office, the shown knife is sometimes seen negatively. The way of carrying should not be changed when you change from your work clothes to casual wear after work is over.

It is also important to take a look at your everyday activities. A fixed blade in your trouser waistband is quite convenient while standing, but after sitting in a car for some time, the knife will press uncomfortably on your spine, not to mention the difficulty drawing the knife with your seat belt fastened. In this case, a knife in a shoulder holster is surely the better solution.

Another question is whether the knife is used only for self-defense or for other tasks as well, such as opening a letter, cutting fruit, or simply cutting off a bothersome thread from your clothes—there are hundreds of possibilities for using a knife for totally peaceful tasks on the job or in your spare time. Of course, there is the advantage that by frequent use of a knife you'll also become more trained in drawing and handling it. The routine you achieve using a knife will be helpful in a self-defense situation under stress.

Finally, the knife should fit your personal style of knife combat. During training, you should watch very closely how you fight with the knife and which techniques you tend to prefer. If you prefer holding the knife in a fencing grip, you ought to have a knife that has a guard angled towards the front or a fluted thumb ramp ("with jimping"). If you want to use the handle end for striking, a knife with a suitably shaped pommel is the right thing. This part of the knife is often martially called a skull crusher or smash point.

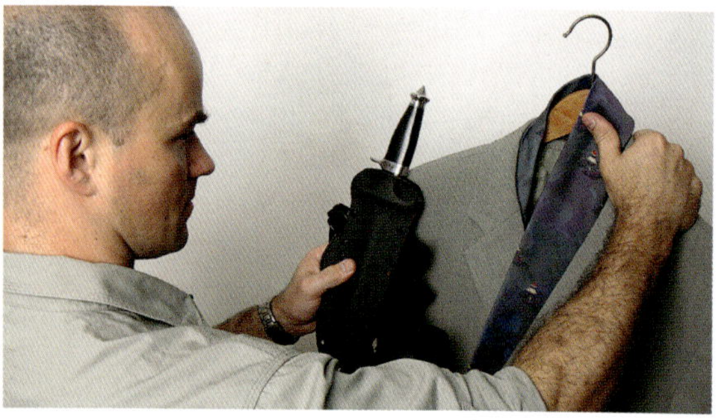

Prior to visiting a knife shop or studying a knife catalog, you ought to think about which clothes the knife has to fit in during daily use.

In a cramped space, such as inside a car, a knife can best be drawn from a shoulder carry system, such as the Execulite system by knifemaker James Piorek.

It is favorable if the clip's color is the same as the trousers, or even identical. This way, the knife is less obvious in everyday life.

The sheath carry system should provide a certain comfort in daily use and, if possible, not be seen by persons around you. This is hardly possible with the kydex sheath of Survival Sheath System for the Cold Steel Tai Pan shown here carried diagonally on the back.

Not recommended for imitation: whoever draws a Harsey A-F combat knife with its seven inch (18-centimeter) dagger blade in the office to open a letter can count on being ostracized by colleagues and is announcing that he is armed.

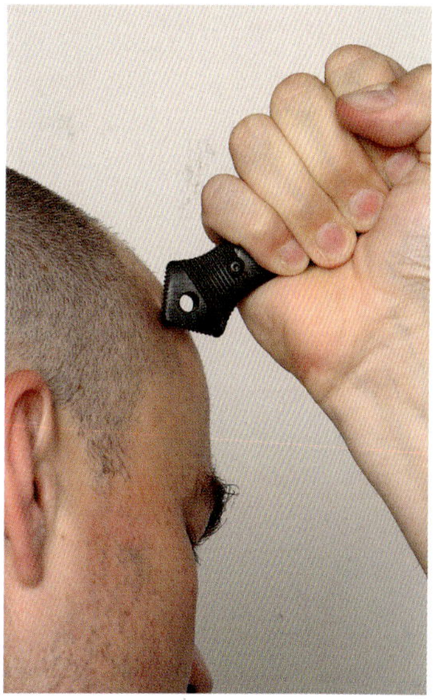

The handle butt can be used for striking, as shown here with the Battle Dagger of Bud Nealy.

PALMSTICK USE: HITTING INSTEAD OF STABBING

by Frank Metzner and Joachim Friedrich

ESCRIMA HISTORY

Escrima is a martial art that almost exclusively deals with armed combat and is of European ancestry. From time unknown, humans have tried to enhance their body strength by using tools and weapons. Understandably, a great variety of techniques and tactics have been developed and used. Germanic warriors had very sophisticated techniques for swordplay that quite often led to victory. The teacher of these thrusting and slashing techniques—the weapons master—was one of the first approved professions. At the time of the Romans, a sword master could even receive the coveted title of doctor—the doctor *gladiatorum*.

ESCRIMA TODAY

Today, Escrima is a leisure exercise, a martial art, and a philosophy of life. It can be used for body fitness and for self-defense. For a couple of years it has been spreading, especially in the police sector, because it trains in handling a variety of police weapons (truncheon, tonfa/MES, shield, etc.). In Germany, Escrima is taught in more than a hundred schools belonging to the EWTO (European Wing Tsun Organisation). The section leader is the renowned grandmaster William Newman ("Master Bill") of Great Britain. German police officers are often organized in the DKO (Deutsche Kyokushinkai Organisation).

ESCRIMA WEAPONS

Because of the "transition principle," Escrima can be practiced with many different weapons without a significant change in movement. The escrimador only has to adapt to each weapon with respect to striking, cutting, and stabbing techniques. A weapon well suited for self-defense in a confined space is the so-called palmstick. The palmstick is a weapon that sticks out a few inches when carried in a closed fist, with its lower end on the side of the little finger and its upper end on the thumb side. Various offensive and defensive techniques can be executed with it. Many everyday things can be used as palmsticks, including pens, a bunch of keys, or even a mobile phone.

ESCRIMA AND KNIVES

A closed folder can also be used as a palmstick. In addition, there is always the possibility of "upping the ante," i.e, to open the knife in case the attacker draws a (superior) weapon or the situation turns to your disadvantage. An ideal palmstick is the EFD (Escrima Folding Dagger) by Böker, in Solingen, Germany. Its basic design took close combat qualities into account and special emphasis was put on lateral safeguards, which not only prevent slipping towards the blade edge when the knife is open, but guarantee a secure grip while striking with the knife in the closed position. In addition, the EFD has a rounded handle and a tapered pommel meant for potentially lethal techniques. Depending on the user's judgment, one or the other end may be used.

ESCRIMA TECHNIQUES

Depending on the initial situation, the use of the palmstick begins concealed or from a combat stance. The concealed position has the advantage that the assailant is not aware of the weapon. The closed folder here is either carried with the right hand (for right-handed persons) in a pocket of the jacket, behind one's back, or behind the thigh. The left hand—the so-called check hand—is up at chest level to counter fast attacks. If the assailant is within reach and attacks with a hand or foot technique, the palmstick is brought in front of the body and used in a direct move against him.

To show the weapon to the assailant, to let him see the closed knife in a combat stance—e.g., classic boxer coverage—can have advantages as well as disadvantages. From a legal point of view, such a threat—best made verbally—can have additional advantages in a possible

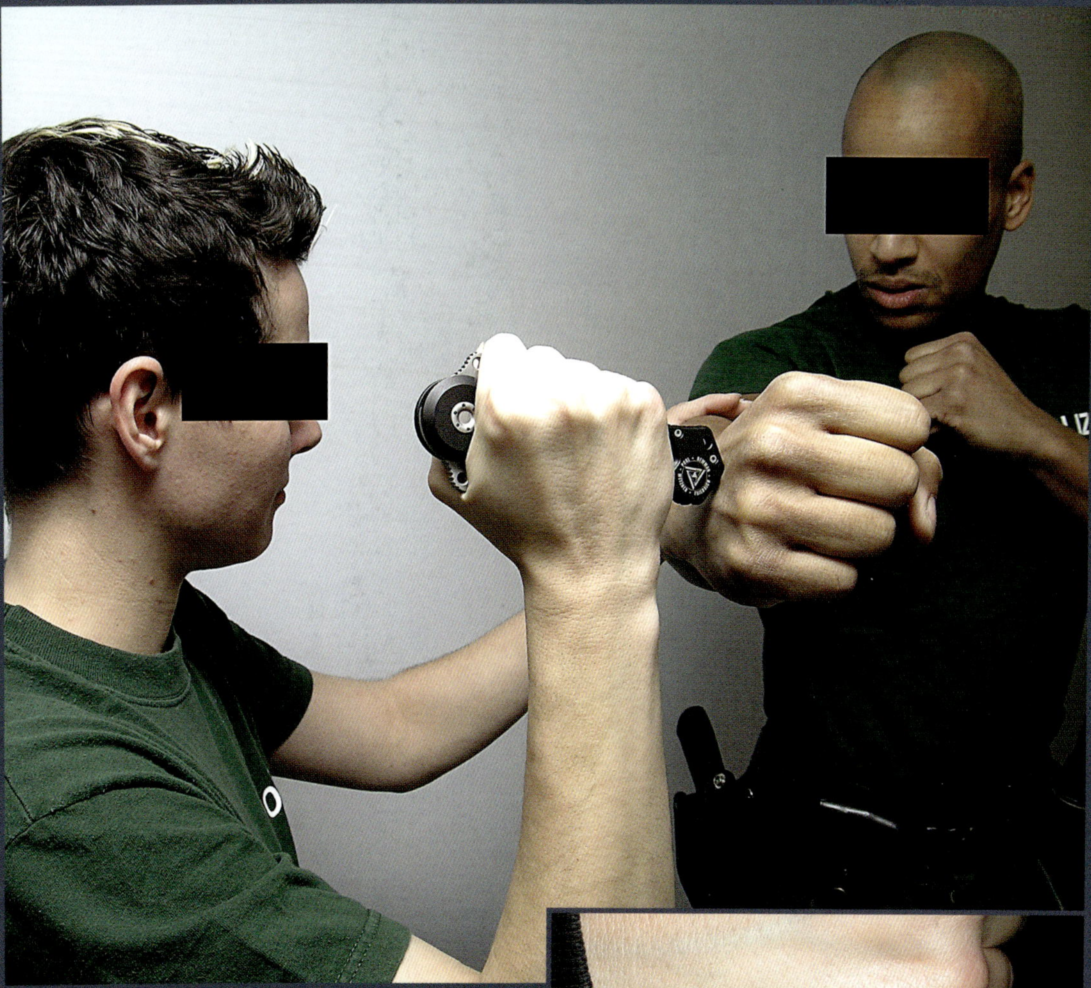

Strike against the backside of a fist with the smash point.
Photo Frank Metzner

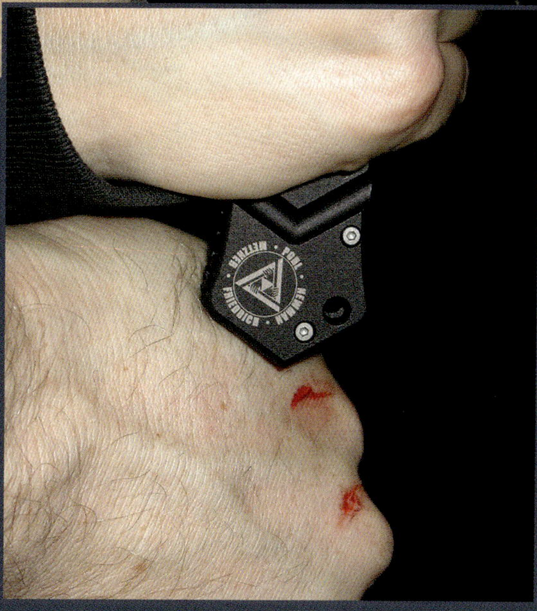

Using the Böker EFD model as a palmstick causes injuries, as this photo undoubtedly shows.
Photo Frank Metzner

subsequent court case. On the other hand, the shown weapon may prompt bystanders to "mix in" or challenge the assailant to use his own weapon.

ESCRIMA RISKS

Strikes and blows with a palmstick can be made against lethal targets—mainly the head and neck—but also against groups of muscles and bone areas, achieving a nonlethal result. Techniques against groups of muscles usually lead to slight crippling and a strong restraint regarding motivity. With this, a decision in combat can be achieved. The lethal targets at the head incur incalculable risks. In addition to insignificant lacerations, bone fractures or brain bleeding with unforeseeable developments may be caused. Legally, they are only sanctioned if the actions stay within the frame of proportionality. Here the law with respect to self-defense has to be considered.

Frank Metzner and Joachim Friedrich are leading police trainers in Germany and have already published several books on the topics of special units and combat shooting. They operate two sport academies in Maintal and Eschwege (www.wt-maintal.de and www.wt-eschwege.de). Both participated significantly in the development of the Böker Escrima Folding Dagger (EFD) and Escrima Fighting Knife (EFK).

Not only the handle butt of a knife can be used as a palmstick, as demonstrated with this Tactical Defense Pen (TDP) of American knife manufacturer Mil-Tac. The biggest advantage: since it is not a knife, you can take it with you on board an airplane without trouble.
Photo Mil-Tac Knives & Tools

The Escrima Folding Dagger of Professor "Master Bill" Newman, Frank Metzner, Joachim Friedrich, and Dietmar Pohl.
Photo Böker Baumwerk

Series of techniques with Professor "Master Bill" Newman (9th grandmaster rank of Escrima). Here he shows a very impressive way to use an EFD as a palmstick against an opponent armed with a baseball bat.
Photos Frank Metzner

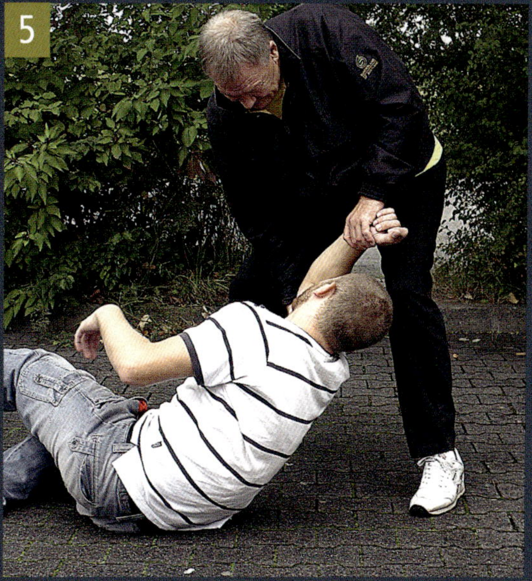

Brent Beshara's SF-1 Micro is made of non-stainless O-1 carbon steel and covered with a typical Japanese handle wrapping—an SD knife that surely doesn't meet everyone's taste.

Photo Besh Knives, Point Seven Studios

CHAPTER 2

DESIGN AND MATERIALS

Many aspects of design and materials have to be taken into account when choosing the right SD knife. For example, a nylon cord or cloth band wrapped around the handle may be right for one user, while another swears by a soft handle of kraton. The same goes for the blade shape. Some prefer blades shaped as daggers, while others have a strong affinity towards tanto blades. Personal taste and style of fighting are decisive.

A double guard today is even possible for folders and reliably protects the hand from the blade. The photo shows the Böker model EFD.

2.1 The Handle Shape

As described previously, the handle ought to be shaped in such a way to reliably protect the user from the blade. This is easily done by means of a guard located on one side (single guard) or on both sides (crossguard). It is interesting that folders with crossguards are increasingly offered, such as the special forces models of Columbia River Knife & Tool or the Escrima Folding Dagger of Böker. Knives without a protective guard are not necessarily excluded, but they ought to be held with the modified ice pick grip. The thumb on the butt prevents the hand from slipping towards the blade when hitting a hard target. A supporting loop is also useful for securing the hand. A prerequisite is a hole in the handle to fasten the lanyard.

A well defined groove for the forefinger also contributes to a safe position of the hand. But for handles with four finger grooves, care must be taken that these fit the individual size of the hand. Too big or too small grooves are quite annoying when holding a knife. In addition, these grooves are not favorable to changing to another grip position.

A real exotic among handle designs is the sub-hilt. It ought to prevent the hand from slipping during pulling movements. The disadvantage: you are restricted to only a few grip variations. Thus, use the sub-hilt in combination with double-edged blades, which again provide you with all the options in a fight.

In general, you ought to take care that the SD knife rests safely and securely in your hand, not only when pushing, but also when pulling the knife. One means of doing this is having

A knife without a guard, such as the CRKT Hissatu shown here, always carries the risk of your fingers slipping onto the blade in case you hit a hindrance when striking, or the handle is moist due to blood or sweat.

Jimping/Fluting in the area of the thumb rest provides additional grip for the Harsey Tactical Folder of Lone Wolf Knives.

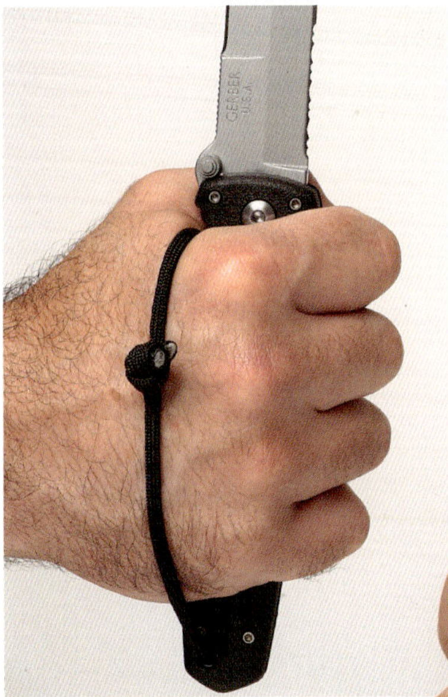

A lanyard loop also prevents the hand from slipping onto the blade. Visible in the photo is the Gerber A-F combat folder.

Knives without sufficient guard can best be guided with the thumb resting on the handle butt. This grip is known as the "modified ice pick grip." Here is the Strider MG model.

The sub hilt of this knife by Peter Herbst literally ties the hand to the handle for pulling movements.
Photo dp

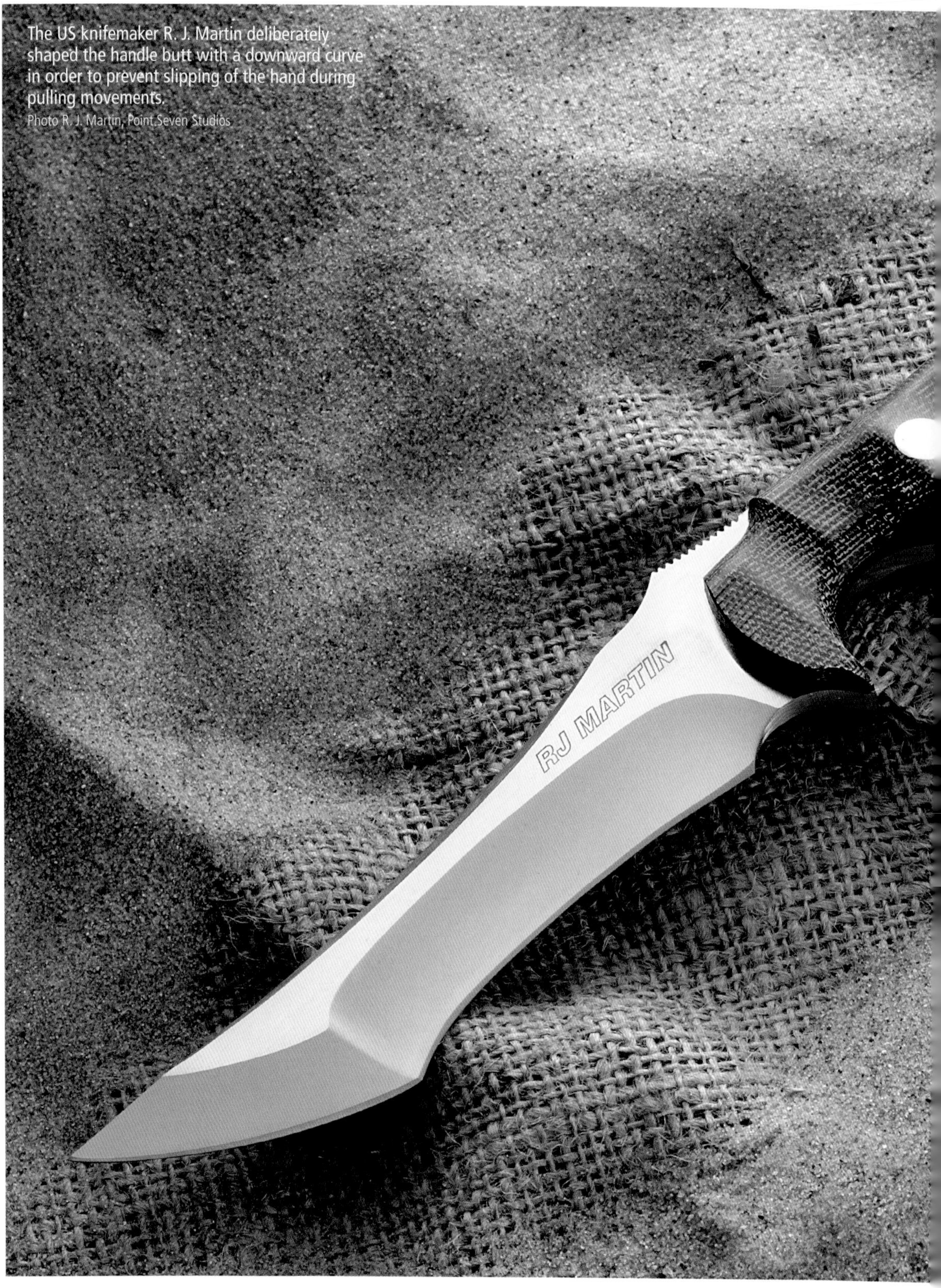

The US knifemaker R. J. Martin deliberately shaped the handle butt with a downward curve in order to prevent slipping of the hand during pulling movements.
Photo R. J. Martin, Point Seven Studios

a handle butt that curves downward. Here, the little finger is retained easily during pulls. Milled fluting or fluting recessed in plastics in the areas of the thumb and forefinger are also expedient. But here, it is important to assure that the fluting is not too coarse or sharp-edged, because otherwise unpleasant abrasions may occur, although quite often the annoying burr can be removed with fine-grained abrasive paper.

The handle shape also usually determines the best grip, as intended by its designer. An often quoted example is the handle of the Applegate-Fairbairn (A-F) combat knife. Because of the recesses in the area of the forefinger and thumb, a guard angled towards the front, and an increasing diameter towards the center, one automatically tends to use a fencing grip. All these details were specifically implemented by the designers, Applegate and Fairbairn. Applegate was convinced throughout his entire life that a blindfolded soldier would always choose the handle of an A-F combat knife from an assortment of knife handles.

2.2 The Handle Material

The best recommendations are of no use at all if the knife handle doesn't fit the hand well and doesn't fit to the preferred style of fighting. Here, the surface quality of the handle also plays a decisive role. Knife handles can be made from a wide variety of materials with a decisive influence on feel. For combat knives, tactical knives, and SD knives, mostly metals and plastics prevail. The reason for this is the toughness and ruggedness of these materials. Natural materials, such as wood, stag, bone, and leather, are principally suited for SD knives, too. But these materials don't have the same resistance to environmental influences, such as moisture, temperature fluctuations, or brute force. Since SD knives are not carried openly and also don't have to have a given appearance, their handle materials may differ from that of knives used in police or military operations. In daily use, a handle made of natural material usually doesn't appear especially martial to the people in your business or personal environment.

Rex Applegate, at more than 80 years, demonstrates the type of fencing stance he favors.
Photo Rex Applegate

The handle of the A-F Tactical Smatchet was shaped according to Applegate's ideas and was optimized by knifemaker Bill Harsey.
Photo Thomas Philippi

With all materials, special emphasis should be put on resistance to slipping, because it is very probable that the handle will come into contact with blood and sweat. A slip of the hand can have dramatic consequences. The slip resistance of a handle can be improved to a limited extent. For example, sandblasting can roughen a smooth metal or plastic surface. With some manual skills you can create a similar effect with abrasive paper.

It is easier to use non-slip tape adhesives, such as for stairs or aircraft wings. For years, many knifemakers have been using this kind of material for handle inlays. Since subsequent attachment of the tape creates protrusions at the edges and the tape is not recessed in the handle, the tape has to be relaced every now and then. Nevertheless, the effect of this adhesive is amazing. Non-slip tape adhesives are available in various degrees of surface roughness. In any case, you should touch the adhesive at least once prior to buying any, to see whether you feel comfortable with this type of surface, which is similar to that of abrasive paper. Of course, your clothing will suffer as well, depending on how and where you wear the knife.

Finally, a professional shop or knifemaker can emboss the handle surface or add fluting by milling; however, these measures are some of the most expensive improvements to a knife.

What are the differences between the individual materials; what are their advantages and disadvantages? With respect to metals, three types have become prevalent: steel, titanium, and aluminum. Because of its enormous stability, stainless steel is mostly used for folders. The company Spyderco was one of the pioneers. In 1981, Spyderco released the first folder with a flat steel handle under the name "Worker." Today, the company remains true to this philosophy. The biggest disadvantage of handle scales made from steel is their heavy weight and slippery surface. Using drill holes in the handle, the weight disadvantage can be compensated without reducing the overall stability. The weight of a knife with steel handles also provides a reassuring feeling, having the knife located at its proper place. Interestingly,

Typical EK Knives handle design with a one-directional wrap of nylon cord.
Photo dp

Wooden handles in general are also suited for SD knives, especially in case the surface—such as with the EK Knives shown here—is provided with a slip-resistant surface.
Photo dp

Strider twists the nylon cord wrapping and achieves a larger handle diameter.
Photo dp

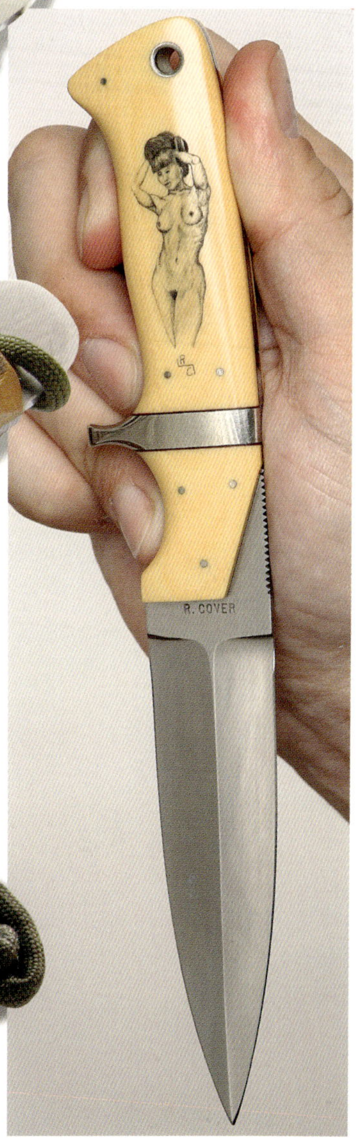

A sub-hilt combat knife by Ray Cover with ivory micarta handle scales and scrimshaw motif. In some cases, less martial-looking handles can soften the impression of a weapon (though this knife may cause indignation among ladies).

Microtech was one of the first manufacturers using non-slip tape adhesives for their aluminum knife handles and still uses them today, as shown here with the Magora OTF model.
Photo Microtech Knives

Because titanium weighs about forty percent less compared to steel, knifemaker Allen Elishewitz decided on this handle material for his Piratage model.
Photo Allen Elishewitz

Spyderco uses the steel type 420J2 (material number 1.4034), which is primarily used for making knife blades.

Steel handles for fixed blades can usually only be found with skeletonized versions, meaning the knife is made from solid stock. The stability of such a knife is enormous, while the comfort of handling it is quite often just mediocre. If you want to increase the handle volume, the knife has to be die-forged, as with the new version of the Sting model designed by A.G. Russell. It is manufactured from carbon steel by Columbia River Knife & Tool and has a corrosion-resistant coating. Caution is recommended with respect to steel handles with a sandblasted surface; the surface is roughened to such an extent that body heat and moisture from concealed carry can quickly cause pitting.

Titanium is one of the most challenging materials with respect to its price and processing. Compared to steel and aluminum, the price of titanium is many times higher. Because of its enormous toughness, it takes much longer to mill handle scales of titanium; accordingly, the tools show much more wear and tear. But titanium has decisive advantages: it is about forty percent lighter than steel, not allergenic at all, and is absolutely stainless. Among the first people to use titanium as handle material for tactical folders was knifemaker Bob Terzuola. At the end of the 1980s, his ATCF model became the basis for many later developments worldwide.

Knifemakers like Brent Beshara (knife on the left) and James Piorek design their handles based on Japanese patterns and models. To make the wrapping more durable, both seal their handles with epoxy resin.
Photo dp

STAINLESS OR NOT?

Most stainless steels are not really stainless, but are just not prone to rust. From a chromium content of 13.5 percent onwards a steel is called stainless, but under adverse conditions (moisture, salt, etc.) corrosion can nevertheless occur. This is true for all "stainless" steels, as well as handles of the same material (such as 420J2 for Spyderco handles). Complete stainlessness is generally only achieved by really high quality steels. Usually, these are chromium-nickel steels (eighteen percent chromium, eight to ten percent nickel) such as used for cooking pots. But these steel types can't be hardened and are not suited for knife blades. The expression high quality steel should only be used for steel types that fall into this category; for knife blades, it is better to use the expression stainless or rust-resistant steel.

To make knives with steel handles safer and save weight at the same time, they are usually provided with a lot of drill holes. Knifemaker Raimund Lothak followed this maxim, as seen here.
Photo Peter Fronteddu

Aluminum has been used for decades as handle material for combat knives, such as this Gerber Mark II. To enhance the handle's slip resistance, molten metal particles are sprayed onto the surface.
Photo dp

The most commonly used titanium alloy in the knife industry is 6Al-4V (6% aluminum, 4% vanadium), which, with a Mohs hardness of 5, belongs to the most robust titanium alloys. In addition to its use for handle scales, this alloy is also used for the liners of linerlock folders. Some knifemakers and manufacturers use this material for a combination handle scale and lock. This so-called frame lock is extremely effective and saves even more weight. Generally, titanium handles on SD knives are provided with a sandblasted, brushed, or anodized surface.

For many decades, aluminum has been one of the most successful handle materials. As early as 1967, Gerber used aluminum for the legendary Mark II combat knife and, during later years, the smaller Mark I boot knife version, as well as for the Guardian series of Bob Loveless. In order to enhance the grip of the aluminum handle manufactured by pressure casting, the surface was additionally sprayed with molten metal particles, leading to the name cat tongue for this extremely rough knife handle. In later versions, the rough surface was smoothed by means of a special, electrostatically applied and baked coating based on epoxy powder.

In the early 1990s, many knife companies produced their tactical folder knife handles from aluminum alloys such as those used by the aircraft industry. Here, the aluminum is not processed by means of pressure casting, but is milled from solid material using CNC technology. The most common aluminum alloy is 6061-T6, which belongs to the group of hardenable AlMgSi alloys. While the handles were quite angular in the beginning, nowadays they can be milled to almost any three-dimensional shape with fast, modern production machines. This results in enhanced handling comfort, as demonstrated by knife models from Benchmade and Microtech.

To protect surfaces from exterior influences, the handle scales are usually anodized or provided with an extremely abrasive-resistant hard coating. Nevertheless, aluminum is a good deal more sensitive to damage than titanium, a fact that has to be taken into account for its use with SD knives. But for folders used in SD that are also used in everyday life (Every Day Carry Folder, EDC-folder), the very light material's weight advantage is unsurpassed.

Among the most popular SD knife materials are plastics, regardless of whether they are extremely hard and stress-resistant, such as G10, or soft and nonslip, such as Kraton. Their biggest advantage: they are almost impervious to external influences, such as the heat and moisture a knife is exposed by carrying it concealed on the body. Plastics can't rust, either.

Plastics can be divided into two groups: thermoplastics and thermosetting materials. Thermoplastics are shaped by means of heat and keep their shape after cooling down, but a mold is needed for injection die casting. Producing high numbers of handles made from such materials is very economical, because they can be reproduced exactly; and surface structures, such as diamond patterns or grooves, can be implemented in the mold. If the material is injected directly onto the tang, the handles don't have to be assembled later on. With a few exceptions, today thermoplastics such as polyamide (Zytel or PA6), polycarbonate (Lexan), and elastomer (Kraton or Santoprene) are used almost exclusively for SD knives. By adding glass, carbon, or Kevlar fibers, the toughness of the plastics can be changed.

Thermosetting plastics are used whenever the handle should be shaped further by milling or grinding. In a chemical process, the thermosetting plastics are combined with epoxy resin and reinforcing fibers, giving the final material its special qualities. These reinforcing fibers can be glass, carbon, or natural fibers, such as linen. Contrary to thermoplastics, thermosetting plastics can't be molded into a new shape with heat; only mechanical processing is possible.

Among the most well known thermosetting plastics are carbon fiber, G10, and micarta. All three materials are very tough and are used for knife handles. Their surface treatment is

Knifemaker Darrel Ralph uses titanium for his frame locks, as well as other things.
Photo Peter Fronteddu

Hill Knives from the Netherlands uses thermoplastics for the handles of many combat knives; in this case Lexan was used.
Photo dp

Cold Steel introduced the rubber-like material Kraton (another thermoplastic) of DuPont to the knife industry as a handle material.
Photo dp

Knifemaker Bud Nealy uses handle scales from G10 plastics for his X-Cel model.
Photo dp

Micarta is a typical example of thermosetting plastics. Knifemaker Bill Harsey artfully shaped a handle of this material for his A-F Urban model.
Photo dp

essential to their later non-slip quality. If a handle scale of G10 or micarta is polished, its surface becomes very slippery, which is problematic use in self-defense. It is better if the handle is roughly polished or sandblasted. For G10, which is mostly used for flat handle scales, sandblasting is unavoidable to achieve the desired grip and look. Depending on its material strength, G10 can be used without steel or titanium stabilizing liners. Carbon fiber has become more and more rare as handle scale material. Although this material is very robust and lightweight, it is rather unsuited for use in SD because of its smooth and shiny surface. An exception is contoured carbon fibers ground to shape and provided with a satin-polished surface.

In recent years, nylon cords or braids of fabric have also increasingly been used for wrapping the handles of fixed blade knives, and the versions span from simple to artsy. For the simplest version of a nylon wrap, the cord is wrapped once around the tang in one layer. This way, you obtain a quite slip-resistant but also very flat handle. A bit more sophisticated version is provided by the company Strider. As a foundation, at first Strider only uses the outer hull of the nylon cord—without the inner strands, with their high tensile strength—and wraps it flat around the tang. This is primarily meant to cover the tang underneath the later main wrap. The wrap is done with two symmetrically twisted nylon cords from the guard to the handle butt. The twisted strings increase the cross section of the handle and thus its volume, so the handle fits the hand better.

Tactical and SD knives with handles inspired by Japanese cloth wrappings can be found from many well known knifemakers and manufacturers, such as Steve Corkum, James Piorek, R.J. Martin, Brent Beshara, Spyderco, and Columbia River Knife & Tool. Here, the tang is first covered with ray skin or string; afterwards, it's covered crosswise with a band in the traditional Japanese style. In order to make the wrappings more durable, many manufacturers seal them with epoxy glue. SD knives with such a wrapping are not prone to slip in your hand. With regular use and under various conditions of use, however, the wrappings lose their good looks and become quite shabby. In addition, the gaps between the individual turns are a refuge for dirt and dust. Thus, you ought to apply at least a regular minimum of care. If the handle wrapping comes loose completely, the homework of repairing this can turn into a real challenge. It is recommended to let the manufacturer do the professional repair.

2.3 The Blade Shape

The second part of an SD knife is the blade. Generally, no ultimate blade shape exists, even though some manufacturers time and again state there is with respect to their products. The blades of SD knives can be roughly divided into seven basic shapes that have quite a few variations.

Dagger

Certainly the most versatile blade shape in combat, because with its blade sharpened on both sides, the knife can be guided tactically upwards and downwards without having to turn it or your hand around. The dagger reveals its special qualities when stabbing. Because of its small cross-section and dual edges, the blade easily penetrates clothing and human tissue.

Until his death in 1998, Colonel Rex Applegate belonged to the most consistent advocates of dagger blades. Here you can see his personal OSS model from World War II made by Landes, Fray & Clark.

Photo dp, Rex Applegate

Author Dietmar Pohl (right) in 1996 was able to convince Rex Applegate to collaborate with the company Böker, which has mass-produced all combat knives designed by Applegate since.

Photo dp

The A-F boot knife models by Bill Harsey show how effective dagger blades can be with small knives. In the background is Applegate's classic book, *Kill or Get Killed*.

Photo dp

Tanto blades are massive and can endure extreme loads, especially if they are made—as shown here with Brent Beshara's Spec-1 Mini—with a chisel grind.
Photo Besh Knives, Point Seven Studios

Tanto blades can be shaped quite differently: at right is a classical tanto blade (Böker Turbine Tactical), while at left is a heavily modified blade shape influenced by Jim Wagner (Bernhard Zwicker, Reality-Based Blade Custom).
Photo Böker Baumwerk, Thomas Philippi

Spyderco uses Bowie blades time and again for their folder models. On top is the Chinook II model by designer James Keating; below is the A.T.R. model.
Photo Spyderco Knives

Some of the historical Bowie blades of the nineteenth century have an enormous blade length. Here is a well-made Bowie remake by knifemaker Joe Keeslar from Kentucky.

Knife designer Chad Los Banos decided on short, compact drop point blades for his Subcom models (Boker Plus).
Photo Böker Baumwerk

Tanto

The roots of the tanto shape are undoubtedly in its use as a weapon. The first tantos date back to the Japanese Heian period (794 to 1185 AD), during which similar shaped blades were mainly used for penetrating heavy body armor. At the beginning of the 1980s, Lynn Thompson—the founder of Lion Steel—reclaimed the tanto, starting the industrial rebirth of this unusually shaped blade. Its big advantage is its enormous stability. The blade back keeps its strength almost up to the tip, ensuring that high lateral stress can be endured without problems in the frontal area of the blade. The tanto blade is suited for stabbing and cutting. With respect to its geometry, hollow and flat grinds have become accepted, as well as chisel grinds. The latter can be found quite often on tanto knives, since the trend to tactical knives started in the early 1990s.

Drop Point

This shape initially stems from hunting, but it can be used as a weapon, too. Especially with short, compact SD knives, this blade reveals its advantages during forcefully and effectively led cuts. The drop point shape is less effective for stabbing.

Saber Point

The saber or Bowie blade is the brainchild of Texan national hero James Bowie (1796-1836). He is responsible for the legendary fame of this blade type. The blade tip is curved inward along the radius, and typically sharpened edge on the back is very effective for stabbing, similar to a dagger. But because of its entire construction, the Bowie's stability is higher compared to that of a dagger. Saber blades are either hollow ground up to the back or to the blade's center line; the blade ridge created provides additional stability and prevents the hollow grind from breaking easily.

Spear Point

Like tanto blades, spear point blades have high stability near the blade tip. Because of the curved shape of the edge on the back, it stays massive in the frontal part and can take high mechanical loads. In case the back edge is sharpened, the stabbing qualities of spear point knives are similar to those of a dagger. Many spear point blades are provided with a so-called recurve edge. Here, the drop-shaped, convex tip is followed by a concave edge curve. This shape provides a dynamic cutting effect for drawing cuts.

Knifemaker Brent Beshara combined a curved drop point blade with a typical Japanese handle design.
Photo Besh Knives, Point Seven Studios

Wharncliffe

This design dates to 1832. Lord Wharncliffe, owner of the British knife manufactory Joseph Rodgers & Son, absolutely wanted to have a pocketknife with a short but very stable blade and designed the shape named after him. It is highly probable that Lord Wharncliffe, at the beginning of the nineteenth century, did not think of using the knife for self-defense. Its geometry makes the blade effective, especially for deep cuts. A variation of the Wharncliffe design is the reverse tanto blade. Here, the tanto blade is ground mirror-inverted, which leads to it standing upside down optically.

Hawkbill

The hawkbill has its origins in a very peaceful use as the knife of a gardener for shortening branches. The design has also been used for hundreds of years on ships, where it is used to cut ropes. In SD, this blade shape was first used on the Spyderco Civilian, introduced in 1990 as an already modified hawkbill. A real boost for this shape came from the karambit models of the Far East, which traditionally have such a blade. The hawkbill blade is very unconventional and, for use in SD, requires special basic handling knowledge and a special style in combat.

Besides its shape, the grind of a blade is decisive for its stability and edge retention. Four different grind types are distinguished: hollow, flat, chisel, and spherical.

Mercworx adopted the Brend shape for their models. Here is the Atropos model of the Mercworx folder series.
Photo Ninjutsu Akademie, Mercworx Knives

Knifemaker Walter Brend designed one of the most beautiful spearpoint blade shapes for his Model # 2.
Photo dp

Different versions of wharncliffe blades: at the bottom is a design by Michael Janich (Spyderco Yojimbo), and above is one by Chad Los Banos (Boker Plus Wharcom).
Photo Spyderco Knives, Böker Baumwerk

Modified hawkbill blades by Spyderco (Civilian on top) and Cold Steel (Black Talon).
Photo Spyderco Knives, ACMA Reus, Cold Steel Knives

Phil Hartsfield (at right) was the first knifemaker in the US to provide handmade combat knives with a chisel grind. Unfortunately, this fact is not well known in the knife community. His son Phil (left) now continues the family's knifemaking tradition.
Photo Hartsfield Knives

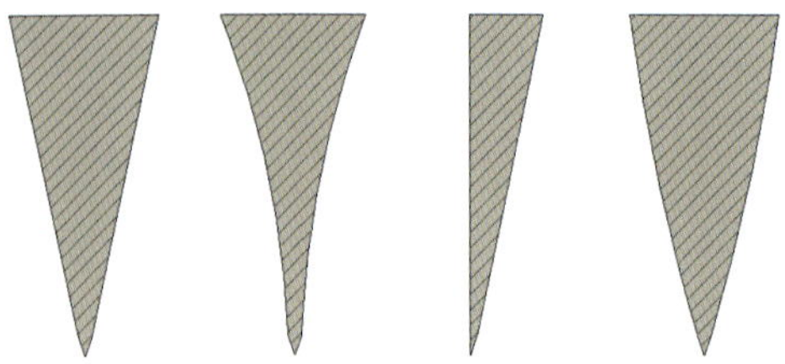

Depiction of different grind types in cross-section (from left): conical, hollow, chisel grind, and convex.
Graphic: Böker Baumwerk, Rainer Klein

Classic Hartsfield neck knife with a chisel-ground blade from tool steel, cord wrapping with underlying copper, and a typical leather-covered metal sheath.
Photo dp

The hollow grind—also called razor grind—is ground concavely, i.e., with a radius facing inwards. This means that relatively much material is removed from the blade to achieve a very thin and sharp blade that can be re-sharpened easily. The downside is that a hollow-ground blade is rather prone to break under extreme loads. However, most models are not ground completely up to the back, but only to about the blade's center, meaning the blade keeps its basic stability.

With conically or flat ground blades, less material is taken off, so generally these blades are more stable. The larger (more obtuse) the angle of the grind, the more difficult it is to re-sharpen the blade edge.

For the chisel grind only one side of the blade is ground flat, resulting in even more material left over. The load-carrying capacity of such blades is extremely high. Re-sharpening is also only done on one side. Phil Hartsfield and Ernest Emerson are some of the pioneers of this grind type for SD and tactical knives. Because of them, this grinding technique became widely accepted in the 1980s and '90s.

The convex grind (spherical grind) is mainly found on knives and axes used outdoors. Good examples for spherically ground blades are the knives of the Swedish company Fällkniven.

Basically, all four grind types are suited for SD knives, with the hollow, flat, and chisel grinds prevailing. However, the sharpness of a blade does not only depend on the grind itself, but also the sharpening angle, i.e., the ground bevel (usually between twenty and twenty-five degrees); the smaller (steeper) the angle, the sharper the blade is. Knife manufacturers can determine the bevel angle during grinding by means of the facet strength. The facet of a blade is its unsharpened edge. Usually the blade is ground to a facet strength of between 0.5 mm and 1.0 mm and only sharpened during the last work step. Some manufacturers grind their blades sharp from the beginning and only do some finalizing work on the edge with a leather wheel. You can easily see this with early Mark I and II models from Gerber; the combat knives of John Ek of Richmond, Virginia; and some of the models of knifemakers Phil Hartsfield, James Piorek, and Brent Beshara.

In addition to selecting the proper grinding angle, the effectiveness of a blade can also be enhanced with serrations and indentations. Today, hardly any knives can be found on the market that do not have at least partial serrations. But what is their advantage? First of all, adding the radii results in a longer linear edge. But more important is the fact that each tip of the serrations grabs the material to be cut and tears it. With respect to applied force, you can achieve a much larger cutting depth than with smooth blades. In case the material to be cut is some kind of clothing, such as thick jeans or a leather jacket, the advantages of serrations become obvious.

The shape and position of the serrations on a blade have almost become a question of faith within the last two decades. Some believe that serrations with pointed teeth cut better than ones with rounded tips. The next faction quarrels whether the serrations ought to be sharpened on the left or right side of the blade. For its use as an SD knife, it does not matter at all whether the blade's teeth are pointed or have a rather rounded appearance, nor whether the serrations are sharpened left or right. But there is mutual consent that up to now, no truly convincing method exists to re-sharpen serrations yourself. Depending on the method and sharpening tool, this works for better or for worse.

The sense and purpose of blood grooves (also called fluting) on a blade have already heated knife experts' tempers over generations. One theory claims the elongated depressions on both sides of the blade have nothing to do with blood at all, only making the blade lighter, more elastic, and also more stable. The other theory states blood grooves ease pulling the blade from an opponent's wound because they counteract the low pressure caused by contracting muscle tissue. Time and again, you may also hear the argument that blood grooves ought to speed up the blood flow in case the knife is stuck in the enemy's body. Whether these theories are right or wrong cannot be determined within the scope of this book. As with serrations, these are questions of faith. Only one thing is certain: blood grooves are still in use on combat knives and bayonets today.

In order to minimize the risk of cracks at the blade tip while at the same time enhancing its penetration effect, various knife manufacturers and knifemakers have developed special tip geometries, trying to mitigate the thin tip with additionally ground, flat angles, giving it more mass at the same time. This can be seen especially well on the Pentagon Elite model from SOG, Spyderco's A.T.R., and the Spec Recon II of knifemaker James Piorek. Quite often, tanto knives are also provided with an almost blunt tip to prevent breaking when they suddenly hit a hard obstruction after a forceful stab misses the target. In general, this leads to a design that restricts its use as an EDC knife for general tasks.

Three examples for different types of serrations.

Chris Reeve produced this dagger with a hollow handle and pronounced fuller in a small edition. According to Reeve, the production effort was enormous.
Photo Thomas Philippi

2.4 The Blade Steel

The most difficult question for sure is which steel is the best choice for an SD knife. Here, too, opinions differ widely. For the most part, this is due to personal preference for a special steel type and less because of insight based on scientific findings. At this point, knife books usually consult impressive steel tables listing the percentage of alloying elements in the steel. But what kind of insight is the user supposed to gain from these numbers? Generally, the currently used steel types are at such a high level that, with respect to pure SD use, there is almost no difference whether you stab or cut with a superior steel or a down-market, lower priced material.

To protect the blade tip against fracture, knife manufacturers have invented a wide range of different blade geometries. Here is the blunted tip of a Spec Recon II model by knifemaker James Piorek.

With his "Close-Quarter Combat" (CQC) series, Ernest Emerson leveraged the breakthrough of chisel-ground blades in the early 1990s.
Photo dp

Microtech uses blade fullers, especially for their OTF models.
Photo Microtech Knives

To protect blades against corrosion, TOPS Knives provides their non-stainless knives from 1095 carbon steel with a black coating of epoxy resin, as seen here with the SAW models.
Photo dp

For his knife models, James Piorek prefers A-2 steel which, as he states, can be hardened to a perfect degree and thus has great edge retention.
Photo dp

Ultimately, it depends on whether you want to use your knife for pure self-defense only—in a situation which may never occur at all—or whether you want to use it for daily chores. If you only carry the knife for defensive situations, it won't lose sharpness and will do its job when you are in extreme danger. But if you use the knife every day on materials of different hardness, you will quickly realize that it will lose its edge and it has to be re-sharpened constantly. This can become annoying in the long run. A blunt knife is not recommended in an SD situation. Thus, you ought to demand high quality steel and its ability to hold an edge.

Steels are divided into unalloyed, with a maximum carbon content of 1.7 percent; and alloyed steels which, besides carbon, can also contain alloying elements such as chromium, molybdenum, vanadium, cobalt, and others. Each of these elements influences the steel in a different way; for example: carbon and chromium. Carbon is the most important component of steel. If its percentage is raised, the achievable hardness and creation of carbides are raised as well. The more carbides within the steel, the higher the edge retention. The chromium content provides necessary corrosion resistance. From a chromium content of 13.5 percent onwards steel can be called "stainless," even though it can still rust under unfavorable conditions.

The decisive factor for edge retention is blade hardness, which is measured in units of Rockwell C (HRC). Each steel has to undergo an optimal heat treatment (hardening, quenching, annealing, and partially even freezing) to extract its full potential. The best steel is of no use if it was processed the wrong way, and each steel has a certain range of hardness within which it can be used for knife blades. Thus, it is not effective to harden a blade with low carbon content of 0.5 percent to a Rockwell hardness of 60 (which is possible), because then the steel will be too brittle and break, even under slight lateral loads.

Among the most well known unalloyed steels are A2, 1095, and O1. These are often called tool steels, even though they are actually spring steels. Because of their very small to nonexistent chromium content, they belong to the non-stainless steels. Knifemakers such as James Piorek, Wally Hayes, and Brent Beshara swear by these steels, because they can be selectively hardened easily and have a fine-grained material structure which, in turn, positively influences the blade's sharpness. The purpose of selective hardening is to get a different hardness in different areas of the blade. For example, a high hardness in the area of the blade edge provides good edge retention, while a softer back provides the knife with necessary flexibility.

When buying a non-stainless steel knife, you have to be aware that the blade may become tarnished and rusty if you do not tend to it regularly. After using it, you ought to clean the blade and oil it lightly. Bothersome corrosion stains can usually be removed with metal polish if the blade's surface is sufficiently smooth.

Blades satin-polished by sandblasting are not recommended; because of their rough surface, their contact area for corrosion is much larger. Besides, these blades can only be brought back to their original state by sandblasting them once more. Knife manufacturers with industrial production, such as TOPS Knives, use the edge retention of unalloyed steels, but protect their surfaces with extremely durable and corrosion-resistant layers of powder epoxy. The only remaining point of attack for corrosion is the blade edge itself. TOPS Knives focuses on 1095 steel, which is relatively low cost.

With respect to alloyed steels, stainless steels such as 440C, ATS-34, 154-CM, D2, VG-10, AUS-8, and BG-42 are one step beyond. High-quality steel types can be found in mid-priced models. Another step up are the powder-metallurgical steels; they achieve a carbon content of more than two percent by means of a special production process and are quite expensive. Their processing is very laborious, but the edge retention of PM steels is much higher, compared to "normal" steel types. While at first CPM-S60V (formerly called CPM-440V) was used almost exclusively, nowadays CPM-S30V is predominantly used for premium class SD knives.

Steel made of three layers used by Cold Steel (San Mai 111) or Fällkniven (laminated VG-10) are very effective, too. Here, a hard core steel, such as AUS-8 or VG-10—with a Rockwell hardness of 58 HRC—is embedded between two softer layers of 420J2. The result is an elastic blade with a hard edge. Knife blades from alternative materials, such as titanium, ceramics, or plastics, belong to the realm of special tactical use and should not be considered for SD use because of their deficient edge retention and higher likeliness to break.

Basically, the surface quality of a blade used for self-defense can be chosen freely. Because SD knives are only used in emergencies, reflections—which are unwanted for combat and tactical knives—play no role. Of course, you can also argue psychologically that a flashing blade signals the aggressor that he is not facing a defenseless victim. W. E. Fairbairn stated in his book *Get Tough!* (published in 1942) that a suddenly flashing blade can strike fear into your opponent, causing him to lose confidence. On the other hand, an SD knife with a dull or dark coated blade may have the tactical advantage that it is not obvious to the attacker when drawn, and thus the element of surprise is with the defender.

Coatings always make sense with blade steels of low corrosion resistance. Among the corrosion-reducing coatings are Teflon, epoxy powder, and Kalgard.

For military operations a dark, non-reflecting blade is a must, as shown here with the Böker KSK combat knife carried by the special forces of the German *Bundeswehr*. In contrast, blades used in self-defense can be shiny, because a flashing blade may provide a psychological advantage.

Knifemaker R. J. Martin uses stainless CPM-S30V steel for his Manta-Ray model.
Photo R. J. Martin, Point Seven Photos

Canadian master smith Wally Hayes demonstrates the different degrees in blade hardness with his Tactical Wakazashi Tsunami. The wave-shaped hardening line in Japanese is called a *hamon*.

Microtech resorted to titanium for the development of their Marfione Custom Assailant Card Knife. Although the name of the credit-card-sized knife hints at another usage, it is good enough for use in an SD situation.

THE KARAMBIT: A TIGER CLAW FROM SOUTHEAST ASIA

by Dieter Knüttel

The karambit is a unique knife originating in Southeast Asia. You can find different versions of the karambit in Indonesia, the Philippines, and in Malaysia. Clues exist that the karambit was already in use there as early as the eleventh century. Its name can vary; sometimes it is called *karambit*, *kerambit* or, more rarely, *korambit*. The speciality of this knife type is the combination of the curved blade—usually ground on both sides (the inner edge as primary and the outer as the secondary)—with a handle having a hole at its end. One version is the Philippine *sanggot*, which has the same blade shape, but instead of the hole, there is a loop fixed to the handle butt that provides the same function. Usually, the index finger is put through this hole so that the knife is held in a reverse grip, meaning the blade pokes out on the side of the little finger.

The blade shape per se is not unique; similar blades can be found with saddle knives or gardeners, who love to use knives with curved blades for cutting back flowers and bushes. But the blade shape of the karambit reminds one of the shape of tiger claws or the venomous teeth of snakes. The size of karambits varies greatly, from very small and handy to knives with an overall length of almost sixteen inches (40 centimeters). These look like a mixture of sickle and kama. While sickles have a strongly curved blade, the kama's blade is almost at a right angle with its haft.

Just the opposite for the karambit: for the large versions, the blade almost protrudes as an extension from the handle and then continues as a more or less curved blade shape, which in general is also valid for smaller karambits. In former times, the karambit fulfilled different functions. It was used as a tool for harvesting, but also as a weapon on the battlefield. If the karambit is used for harvesting, then the little finger is put through the hole and the knife is held in the normal forward position. This way, your grip is very secure and you can cut forcefully. During times of war, the blades were often covered with poison, so that a small cut was sufficient to inflict a deadly wound upon your opponent. The knowledge about effective poisons came from nature, from poisonous frogs, spiders, and snakes.

The smaller karambits, which today can be found in martial arts and self-defense, are knives for close combat and are not suited for Hollywood-style knife fights. As mentioned before, the blade is similar to the shape of a tiger claw. This shape is especially well suited to penetrate deeply into the flesh of prey animals and to hold them down. The karambit blade, which is ground on both sides, additionally supports this effect.

Amazingly, the karambit is especially well suited for stabbing techniques performed in the before-mentioned reverse grip. This turns the karambit into an especially dangerous weapon if you just box with it. Aim a bit off the target with the side of your little finger. This way, the blade can penetrate the body of the attacker using the enormous impact power created by the boxing technique.

Even smallest moves of the wrist lead to large changes in direction of the blade and can be used in a variety of ways. For example, you can control the arms or hands of an attacker and push them away while cutting at the same time. A quick succession of cuts in many different directions can easily be done with a karambit. The blade shape offers another advantage: if the blade is in contact with an arm which is then drawn back, the karambit not only simply cuts, but "bites" deeply and causes a violent injury. The more the blade is curved, the stronger this effect.

The handle with the hole has some advantages, too. Your grip is extremely firm; the knife can't slip out of your hand, not even when you have contact with sweat or blood. Even if you open your hand, the knife doesn't fall, but hangs on your index finger. If you meet strong resistance when stabbing, slipping of your hand into the edge is prevented because your index finger is attached to the handle hole. Besides, because of the hole in the handle, it is practically impossible to twist the knife from

Karambits of different manufacturers (left to right): Spyderco, Emerson, and Cold Steel.
Photo ACMA Reus

Helmut Lehner (Feinste Stahlwaren) from Munich, Germany, in accordance with customers' wishes, makes leather holsters to be fixed horizontally at the belt. In combination with the wave hook on the Emerson Karambit, drawing the knife at lightning speed is no longer impossible.

Messer König of Vienna designed the "Scimibit" (a word created from scimitar and karambit), a practice-oriented knife that is equally well-suited as an SD-knife and for everyday tasks.
Photo Messer König

Depending on the grip, either the forefinger or little finger is put through the karambit's ring (shown here is Strider Tarani).

somebody's hand. It is also very difficult to block an attack made at close quarters with the karambit, because almost every block can be dodged with a short movement of the wrist, while at the same time cutting the opponent.

Another advantage of the handle hole is that the blade can be flung forward. Because most karambits are ground on both sides, in this case the outer, secondary edge comes into play. In combat, this can pose a surprising increase of your range. Spectacular whirling techniques, during which the knife is swung around your index finger several times, are nevertheless pure show techniques and are of no use during combat.

The disadvantage of this weapon is its somewhat shorter range caused by the reverse grip and the curved blade. This also makes it difficult to carry the knife concealed. If you don't have a special sheath for the karambit, it is also difficult to draw—at least compared to straight knives, which can easily be carried in one's trouser pocket. Some of these can already be opened during drawing from the pocket by means of Ernest Emerson's patented wave mechanism. However, these knives are not ground on both sides.

The question remains how well these knives are suited as EDCs. The blade is very well suited for cutting strings and linen, for opening and cutting apart boxes, for gutting fish or rabbits, and for fishermen and hunters. But it is not suited for making sandwiches. The karambit has its advantages as a weapon in self-defense, but its aggressive appearance makes its use as an unobtrusive EDC almost impossible.

Dieter Knüttel holds a diploma as a sports teacher, is coach of the national Modern Arnis team, and is a representative for Modern Arnis in Europe. In 1996, he was awarded the title Datu (master), and in 2003 was awarded the 7th Dan. He is the first non-Filipino to receive this degree in Modern Arnis. In 2005, he was named "Senior Master of Modern Arnis." Besides his intensive work as a teacher, Dieter Knüttel distributes DVDs on martial arts via the Internet at www.abanico.de.

Karambit technique: The attacker (Ingo Hutschenreuter, 3rd Dan Modern Arnis) aims straight at the neck. The defender (Datu Dieter Knüttel, 7th Dan) keeps his guard close to the body with the karambit in his right hand.

The attack is countered from left to right and the karambit cuts the forearm of the attacker from below. At the same time, the left hand exerts counter pressure.

After the cut, the defender pulls his hand back in order to...

... stab the neck of the attacker. The attacker blocks this stab with his left hand.

Subsequently, the defender pulls back his knife hand a bit and prepares a trapping technique with his left hand. The left forearm still secures the knife hand of the attacker.

The left hand of the defender controls the left hand of the attacker; the left forearm controls the right knife arm. The left elbow presses against the thorax of the attacker. The defender now pulls his own knife hand back to his chest to loosen his grip.

The left elbow is now heavily pressed against the attacker's ribcage; this way both arms are controlled. The karambit is used for the strike against the attacker's neck.

Photos Dieter Knüttel

Whether a folder or a knife with a fixed blade is preferred for use in self-defense depends on a variety of factors; both systems have their advantages and disadvantages. From left: Spyderco's Civilian and Kumo.

CHAPTER 3

FIXED BLADE OR FOLDER?

Prior to buying an SD knife, you face the basic question whether it ought to be a fixed blade or a knife with a foldable blade (folding knife or folder). Both types are described to make the choice easier, and their advantages and disadvantages are shown in detail.

3.1 SD knives with Fixed Blade

Knives with fixed blades are usually made in such a way that the tang protrudes into the handle either visibly or not. Here, the distinction is made between full tang and hidden tang, which can be further divided into push tang and rat-tail tangs. Full tangs are the largest constructions, because the tang visibly runs through the entire handle. With this construction type the handle scales are either glued, riveted, or screwed onto the tang. The full tang can also comprise the entire handle, as is typical for skeletonized constructions.

The disadvantage of a full tang is the resulting high weight of the knife. By means of a tang that is tapered conically towards the handle end (tapered tang) or a number of drill holes, weight can be reduced and the balance is enhanced without reducing the knife's stability. A plastic handle can also be injection-molded directly onto the tang (encapsulated tang). A full tang can project a bit at the handle end in order to use it as an additional tool for striking. Good examples of this can be found among the knife models of Fällkniven.

More massive (and heavier, too) are integral constructions, in which blade, tang, and guard are made from a single piece of steel. However, this construction type can hardly be found among SD knives.

The cut down or push tang only runs halfway inside the handle and is kept in place by means of transverse pins, screws, or glue. If the finish is done well, no objections can be raised to this type of construction. Gerber constructed their Mark I and Mark II models this way for more than thirty years. The tang was simply held inside the aluminum handle by means of press fit and epoxy glue.

With rat-tail tangs, the blade continues into a short, massive tang within the handle and then tapers down to a rod that ends in a screw thread. This way, the entire handle construction is kept under tension. A good example of this construction type is the Fairbairn-Sykes combat dagger. Typically, the round rat-tail tang is used for knives with rounded handle shapes, such as the Kershaw Trooper, or various models of the company Randall. The classic Scandinavian

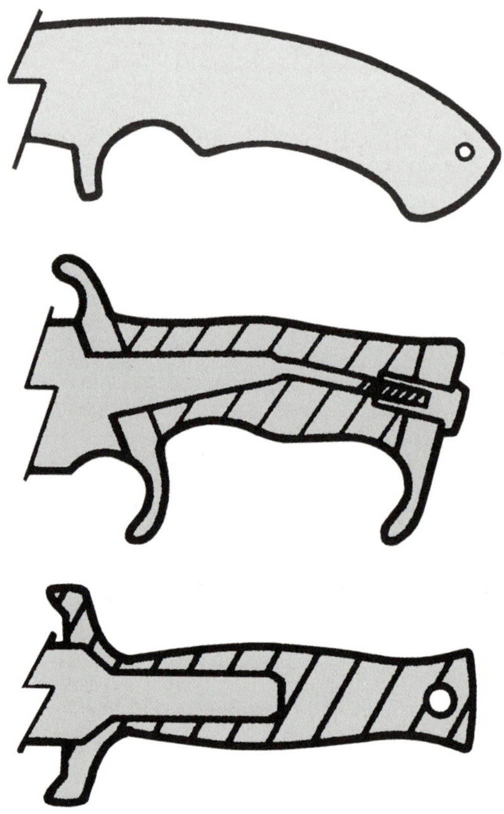

Graphic depiction of the different construction types. From top: full tang, rat-tail tang, and push tang.
Graphic: United Cutlery

Besides its stability, the ability to be quickly ready for action is an advantage of SD knives with a fixed blade. With modern kydex sheaths, a simple pull at the handle is sufficient to ready the knife. Shown here is the A-F Boot Custom model by Bill Harsey.

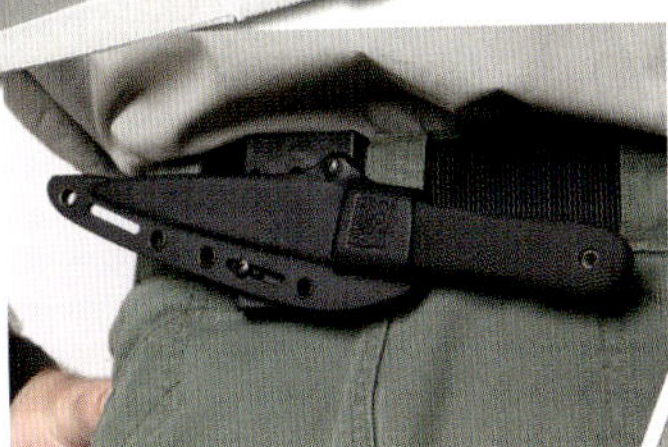

The biggest disadvantage of an SD-knife with a fixed blade is its size. It has to be attached to the body in such a way to guarantee quick access. This way of carrying the SOG Pentagon can become very unpleasant during long car trips. In addition, it always needs to be covered by concealing clothing.

Knife photo Herbertz, SOG Knives

The model ST-01 of Crusader Forge is produced as a massive full-tang construction and is thus quite heavy. The kydex sheath with its digital desert camouflage pattern is interesting, too.

Photo dp

The Austrian knifemaker Harald Stinner proves with this prototype that SD knives can also be opened sideways.

The company Benchmade produces a convincing series of folders for the weapons manufacturer Heckler & Koch. They can be easily opened with either hand and are provided with an enormously secure lock (Axis Lock). The photo depicts the Snody-Design model 14200.

Photo ACMA Reus, Benchmade Knives

In the 1970s, folders were regarded as not suitable for SD use. With respect to these modern models with liner lock, the knife combat experts of that time have to thoroughly revise their former assessment. A-F Custom Combat Folder by Bill Harsey (top), Tactical Custom Folder (anonymous maker).

Photo dp

models of this type make do without the screw thread and instead have a rivet without flange at the handle butt.

3.1.1 Advantages of Fixed Blade SD knives

The decisive advantage of a fixed blade lies in its high stability; it has a significantly higher sturdiness than any knife construction with a foldable blade. Another advantage is that fixed blades are ready for action quickly. Knives with fixed blades are carried in a sheath on the body and are immediately combat-ready after drawing. Depending on the sheath system, either a locking device has to be unlocked or—as with modern kydex sheaths—only the handle has to be pulled. For these, snap fasteners or velcro strips don't exist. The simpler the motion sequence during drawing, the quicker the defense. This is even more important when considering the high stress in a self-defense situation.

Another advantage of fixed blades is the choice of blade shape. Because the knife is carried in a sheath, daggers that are sharpened on both sides or other knives with a sharp edge on the back can also be chosen.

3.1.2 Disadvantages of Fixed Blade SD knives

Compared to knives with foldable blades, a fixed blade has to be stowed on the body or in one's clothing with its entire length, including the sheath. For an SD knife with an ideal blade length between three and five inches (eight and thirteen centimeters), this adds up to an overall length of between eight to ten inches (twenty and twenty-five centimeters). This means the knife can quickly become a disruptive factor in everyday life. Attachment may also pose a problem; for example, on clothes usually worn without a belt, such as sportswear. There are solutions available with trouser clips, but they are not very practical in combination with sports wear.

Another disadvantage: the person carrying a knife with a fixed blade automatically attracts the attention of surrounding people, unless the carrying system allows concealed carry. It doesn't take long to become fed up with the question why you have to lug such a "whacker" around. This problem is solved immediately when wearing a sheath system that can be carried concealed. If you can't make do without an everyday knife, you ought to purchase an additional small utility knife for this purpose.

3.2 SD Knives with Foldable Blade

Blades of folders can typically be opened sideways or frontally. With respect to knives that open out-of-the-front (short: OTF), you should not talk about unfolding, but pushing. Nevertheless, they belong to the group of folders. Classical folders are constructed in such a way that the blade rotates around the blade axis. In order to safely use such a knife, the blade has to have a sufficiently stable lock. In the past, missing or unreliable locks excluded folders from use in self-defense, as seen in many contemporary publications. In his compendium The Complete Book of Knife Fighting, knife expert William L. Cassidy wrote that a serious knife combatant should leave folding knives in his trouser pockets and only use them in case no other edged weapon is at hand. The German author H.-J. Fiedler described a simliar view in his book *Messerkampf*, published five years later.

Today, the authors would surely have to reconsider their earlier assessment, because much has changed with respect to locking mechanisms during the past twenty-five years. They are available in a multitude of varieties, from very simple to highly complicated. The same goes for the wide spectrum of names created by marketing strategists: back locks, ball-bearing locks, compression locks, liner locks, frame locks, axis locks, arc-actuator locks, ultra locks, deadbolt locks, E-locks, plunge locks, front locks, and many more. Each year new systems are added to this list.

But if you analyze the international knife market, you quickly realize that in fact only two types of locking mechanisms are widespread: the back lock (often called lockback in knife literature) and the liner lock. The back lock system—sometimes also called the backspring locking mechanism—belongs to the oldest locking mechanisms, and became especially well known on Buck's 110 folder model. With this system, a lug on a spring-loaded lever (also called a hammer) rests in a notch in the blade when the folder is open. In order to close the folder, the hammer is pressed down at its rear end, which in turn lifts the lug. The blade can then be closed. If done correctly, this locking mechanism is most reliable.

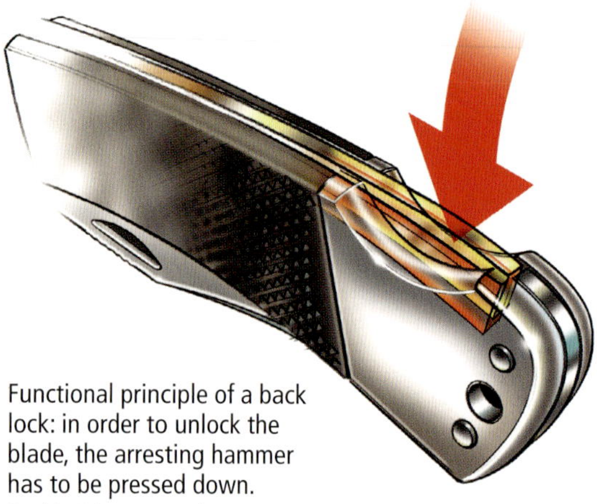

Functional principle of a back lock: in order to unlock the blade, the arresting hammer has to be pressed down.
Graphic: Kai Europe, Kershaw Knives

In any case, you have to take care that the restraint doesn't unlock inadvertently when gripping the knife firmly. In order to prevent this, the spring has to be strong enough and the position of the recess in the handle (for pressing the hammer) has to be chosen conveniently. Spyderco tries to minimize the risk of inadvertent closing by adding an additional recess to the hammer. Among experts this is called a Boye dent because of its inventor, David Boye. In contrast, Extrema Ratio secures its back lock system with a slider that arrests the hammer when the folder is open.

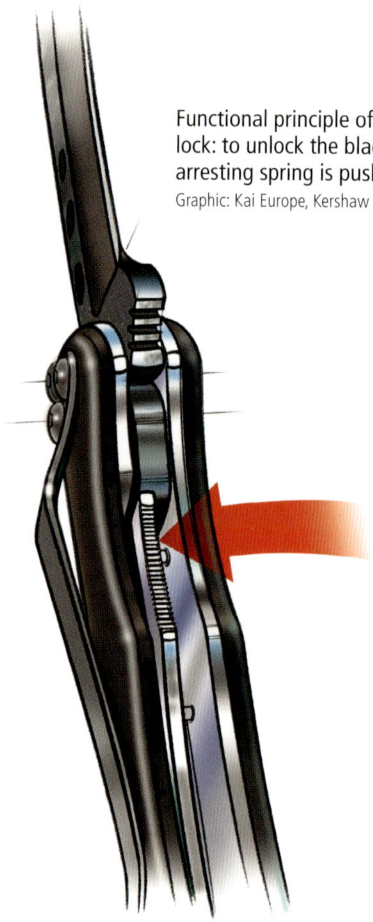

Functional principle of a liner lock: to unlock the blade, the arresting spring is pushed aside.
Graphic: Kai Europe, Kershaw Knives

The liner lock mechanism has also been well known in the knife industry for quite a few decades. But it was knifemaker Michael Walker who perfected this design in the 1980s and helped the liner lock find its resounding success. A large audience first saw the liner lock—which can be used with one hand—on the big screen in Sylvester Stallone's *Cobra*, produced in 1986. The knife can only be seen briefly in the opening scene in a supermarket, where police officer Marion Cobretti uses the Walker model as a throwing knife against a person running amok.

Sylvester Stallone entrusted knifemaker Michael Walker with producing a folder that could be opened with one hand for the movie *Cobra*.
Photo Thomas Ruhl, Warner Studios

The Killabanane model proves that folders used in self-defense can have large blades. This model by German knifemaker Jürgen Schanz has a blade length of 4.7 inches (twelve centimeters).
Photo dp

Established test series for checking a liner lock: 1. The liner must not unlock when the handle is gripped extremely tightly (white-knuckle test); 2. The blade should not have too much lateral play; and 3. When hitting the spine, the blade must not fold (spinewhack test).

Columbia River Knife & Tool provides many of their models with an additional LAWKS safety; the photo shows the manual version. In addtion, the new Auto-LAWKS version is marked with a red dot.
Photo CRKT

The big disadvantage of a folder that has to be opened with both hands: since both hands are needed to open the knife, you are not able to block attacks at the same time.

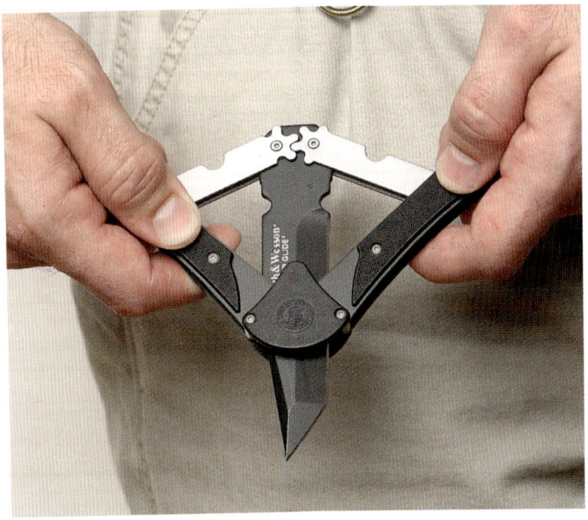

A technically sophisticated folder by Smith & Wesson: unfortunately, it is absolutely unsuitable for SD use because of its opening technique, which needs both hands.

Examples of opening aids for use with one hand: disc (Terzuola ATCF), oval hole plus wave-hook (Emerson Karambit), and a knurled thumb stud (Böker Turbine).

Beginning in the 1990s, the industrial manufacturers became interested in this mechanism as well and used it increasingly. Today, almost no manufacturer exists who does not use this locking mechanism on at least one model. Compared to the back lock, the liner lock can be opened and closed with one hand. When the folder is opened, a liner (retaining spring) moves against the blade and blocks it. To unlock the knife, the liner is simply pushed aside with the thumb and the blade is folded back. Here, the advantage of a liner lock becomes obvious, because with back locks usually both hands are needed to fold the blade back. The pressure of the retaining spring with the liner lock also prevents the knife from opening inadvertently. For this purpose, a small steel ball (detent ball) is impressed in the liner that fits in a recess on the blade and keeps it in place.

The liner lock is seen as challenging with respect to production and is cause for recurring criticism among many manufacturers and knifemakers. When you purchase a knife, you have to assure the locking mechanism really works reliably. Two test methods have become established for doing so: the spinewhack test and the white-knuckle test. For the first test, you hit the back of an opened blade against the edge of a table in order to see whether the blade snaps shut; if it does, it fails the test. For the second test, you hold the handle of the opened knife in your fist and press it hard until the knuckles of your hand turn white. If the retaining spring gives way during the process, the lock didn't pass this test, either. Time and again, both tests are discussed controversially within the knife world. The spinewhack test raises the question whether a blade will ever undergo stress like this.

The advantages of a folder that can be opened single-handedly are seen in this demonstration; while the left hand is blocking, the other hand draws and opens the weapon.

Ernest Emerson developed the wave-hook, with which the knife opens while being pulled from the trouser pocket. Sypderco uses this system under license for their Endura model.

A very convincing test recommendation for liner locks is given by the knifemaker A. T. Barr on the website of A. G. Russell (www.agrussell.com). At first, he points out that an expensive knife does not necessarily mean it has a better liner lock mechanism. Instead, handmade knives quite often fare worse compared to industrially produced models. His recommendation is:

- Initially check whether the blade is held well in its closed position by the liner's detent ball. Open the knife in a normal way, then close it very slowly. The detent ball ought to let the blade snap shut at the last moment.
- For the next test, the blade should be opened slowly, until the lock arrests the blade. Under no circumstances should the blade be flipped open. Then, two further things should be tested: apply pressure on the blade back with the palm of your hand and subsequently whack it against the edge of a table with not too much force. The blade should not snap shut in either case.
- Next, flip the blade open with verve. If the knife can only be closed by applying substantial force afterwards because the liner got jammed, do not buy the knife!
- Last but not least, open the blade slowly and check for lateral or vertical play. Sometimes slightly tightening the screw of the blade axis helps, but quite often it doesn't.

During all tests, you absolutely have to take care that your fingers are never positioned within the knife blade's dangerous radius of movement!

Some knife manufacturers provide their liner lock models with further safeguards, such as among the knives of CRKT and Gerber. CRKT additionally provides most models with its so-called AutoLAWKS mechanism. This mechanism automatically blocks the liner after opening the folder; however, you have to get used to closing the knife in a special way. Gerber counts on an additional, manual safeguard with respect to large and medium-sized versions of the Applegate-Fairbairn folder. Both types of safeguard work absolutely reliably and offer additional safety to the user, but the question arises whether these duplicate locking mechanisms are indeed necessary. If the liner lock mechanism is done well, it should be sufficient. If you take into account that you will be under extreme pressure in a real combat situation, additionally locking and unlocking a folder may become a problem.

Another possibility to prevent a folder from inadvertently closing is provided by the handle design itself. During the early years of liner lock technology, generous recesses in the handle existed in order to give the thumb access to the liner. Meanwhile, the standard is to not let the liner poke out from the handle this much. The advantage: the handle can be pressed together tightly without unlocking the blade. The disadvantage: unlocking the blade becomes more difficult, because the thumb does not have free access to pressing the retaining spring.

The most important disadvantage of a liner lock is that it can not easily be used with both hands, because the retaining spring can only be pressed from one side. Usually, the knives are made for right-handed persons; only in rare cases does a company offer a version for left-handers.

Besides the back lock and liner lock, a number of other locking mechanisms exist that work equally reliably and, in addition, have the advantage use for right-handed as well as left-handed persons. Good examples of this are Benchmade's axis lock, the arc-actuator lock of SOG, and Spyderco's ball bearing lock. Here, a spring pushes a bolt or ball into a recess of the blade and arrests it in the open position. Although the basic principle is more or less the same, nevertheless, manufacturers manage to circumvent existing patents and create new designs.

Besides the blade's locking mechanism, quick and controlled opening of the blade is of decisive importance. It is mandatory that the blade can be opened single-handedly. Folders that need two hands for opening are not suited for use as SD knives; opening the knife with two hands takes too much time. Besides that, one hand should always be free for blocking movements while the other grabs the knife.

Opening aids for knives that can be opened single-handedly are available in a multitude of shapes. They range from round or oval holes in the blade and thumb-studs to round discs and small plates. No recommendation can be given as to which opening aid is the best. Here, simply one's own dexterity is decisive. It is optimal if the opening mechanism can be triggered from both sides. If you are forced for some reason not to use your usual, dominant knife hand—maybe because it is injured or is blocking an attack—you ought to be able to open the knife with your other hand. Today, most tactical knives are already designed for ambidextrous use.

Besides opening aids that can be triggered with the thumb, so-called flippers with which you can "flip" open a knife have grown in importance. Here, the flipper—a protrusion of the blade that acts as a guard when the blade is in the open position—pokes out at the blade's back when the folder is closed. A prerequisite for this is a knife with an open handle back. The index finger hooks on the flipper and snaps it open forcefully. Usually this is supported by a short flick of the wrist.

Alternative opening aids are not having an easy time in the knife industry. The blade of the CUDA, produced by Camillus, which could be opened manually by means of a slider, failed to win knife buyers' favor. The opposite is true for the Wave technology of Emerson Knives. By means of a hook integrated into the knife's back, the blade can be opened while it is being drawn from one's trouser pocket. Spyderco licensed the patented Wave technology for their Delica and Endura models.

Apart from manual opening techniques, there also exists the spring-assisted opening technique of switchblades. One of the oldest switchblade mechanisms works by means of a leaf spring or bar spring in the handle. It is put under tension inside the handle scale and arrested there. When the spring is unlocked, the blade is flipped open forcefully. In recent years, this technology has been used for so-called double action knives. You can choose whether you want to open the knife manually or automatically. Convincing double action models are, among others, delivered by knifemaker Butch Vallotton and Microtech, Lone Wolf, and Böker.

Since the early 1990s, switchblades working on the principle of the late knifemaker Ron Miller have become much more popular. A coil spring is wrapped around the blade axis. Each time the blade is closed, it is rotated through 180°, thus winding the spring. Classic pioneers of this type are Benchmade, Microtech, Masters of Defense, Protech, and Böker.

For the third type of switchblade, the blade is pushed from the handle and out the front by means of a strong spring. These knives are called *OTF*. The models in Microtech's HALO series are examples of this technology.

Switchblades are prohibited in many countries and states, or you need a special permit for carrying.

In the mid-1990s, Hawaiian-based knifemaker Ken Onion achieved the hat trick of constructing a type of automatic knife that is not restricted in almost all countries. The blade of his Speedsafe system at first is opened like a conventional liner lock folder, but after a short distance a spring takes over and helps to flip the knife open. Companies such as CRKT, Camillus, and United Cutlery adapted this principle and developed systems of their own. Since no button or lever is pushed but the blade itself is forced to open, these knives are seen as normal folders in most countries, and thus the restrictions for switchblades do not apply.

3.2.1 Advantages of SD-Folders

The advantages are clearly in the compact size, which allows carrying a folder concealed and comfortably every day. SD folders can easily be put into a trouser pocket or the inside of your trouser waistband by means of a clip in the morning. Knives with foldable blades are also

Double-action knives can either be opened manually, like a conventional single-handed knife, or automatically by means of a concealed button and the force of a spring. Here is a prototype by American knifemaker Butch Vallotton (left) and the Action^2 of Boker Plus.
Photo dp

A tactical switchblade (Böker T4) according to the technical principle of Ron Miller. It has been available on the market in many variations since the early 1990s.

An OTF switchblade (Microtech Scarab) with the blade popping out the front: the interesting feature of this model is that everything can be done with only one hand. To close the knife, you only have to pull the slider and the blade shoots back into the handle with the same spring force as when it opens.

Folders for use in SD should not exceed a certain length, because otherwise, you'll have the same problem as with fixed blades. The Lone Wolf Harsey Tactical Folder is so large and heavy that it is difficult to carry this model concealed.

Kershaw's spring-assisted Spec Bump is activated by means of the guard projecting from the handle's back ("Carson Flipper"). If you pull the flipper, the blade snaps open by means of spring force. A kind of switchblade that is amazingly legal in most countries.

Folders with dagger blades sharpened on both sides are the exception in the knife industry. The A-F Combat Folder series is representative of a successful conversion.
Photo Herbertz, Gerber Knives

seen less as a threat than models with fixed blades. Folders in general fit with every type of clothing, regardless of whether you are wearing them on the job or during your spare time. If necessary, a folder can also be put aside quickly. Folders can also be used in their closed state for certain nonlethal tactics, such as striking with the pommel, and for even less dangerous methods. Nevertheless, the blade can be opened instantaneously with the thumb when needed. Because no sheath is needed, you save additional weight.

3.2.2 Disadvantages of SD-Folders

Disadvantages are possible problems with stability and safe handling under stress. In case the blade hits a hard target and the lock gives way, the folder's snapping shut may result in the immediate loss of your ability to fight (and of some fingers, as well). Faulty handling also can't be eliminated completely in an extreme situation. Handling folders with gloves can pose another problem; quite often, the opening mechanism can't be grabbed accurately with a gloved hand.

An argument mentioned quite often in the past is the delay until folders are ready for action. This was surely true for models that had to be opened with both hands. But with modern, single-hand technology, this disadvantage no longer exists. Nevertheless, folders still need a good deal more care compared to knives with fixed blades. In addition, the blade length for folders is restricted by the handle length. The use of daggers is restricted to a few models, because the blades have to be stowed safe and secure inside the handle. Examples with a good solution for this task are the Applegate-Fairbairn folder and most OTF constructions.

Each concept has its advantages and disadvantages. Fixed blades are simply more stable and easier to handle, but most times they are quite uncomfortable to carry for everyday use because of their size. Folders are less obvious and more comfortable to carry, which means they are the ideal everyday companion. With a good locking mechanism, the danger of the blade suddenly snapping shut is very low, but not completely excluded. Both systems are qualified for the realm of self-defense with knives.

The best solution is to own a convincing model from both worlds. In warm weather, when you are wearing light and comfortable clothing, the use of a folder is recommended. During the cold season, when wearing a sheathed knife is less obvious, switching to a fixed blade knife is advisable. Some people even carry both knife types all the time. In this case, the folder is mostly seen as a last-ditch weapon.

Today, modern materials and production technologies offer an astonishingly large variety of carrying possibilities for SD use.

CHAPTER 4

CARRYING SYSTEMS FOR SD KNIVES

As with all weapons, carrying an SD knife requires some thinking as to how to best carry it and how it can be put into action quickly when you have to defend yourself. Luckily, not only the knives, but also their carrying systems have undergone further development within the last two decades. This is true for fixed blade models as well as folders. Safe carry and quick access have increasingly come into focus for the designers.

While in the past a folder had to either be carried in the trouser pocket or in a belt sheath, today, clips offer a large number of possibilities. The clip not only speeds up access, but enables the knife to be fixed in a variety of different positions, such as trouser pocket, waistband, boot leg, and other places. For knives with fixed blades, modern materials such as kydex make additional locks that have to be opened prior to drawing the knife superfluous. A simple yank and your weapon is ready for action. Adapters that can be screwed on, loops, chains, velcro connections, and similar methods provide the best conditions for carrying a knife on your body in a readily available and anatomically favorable way.

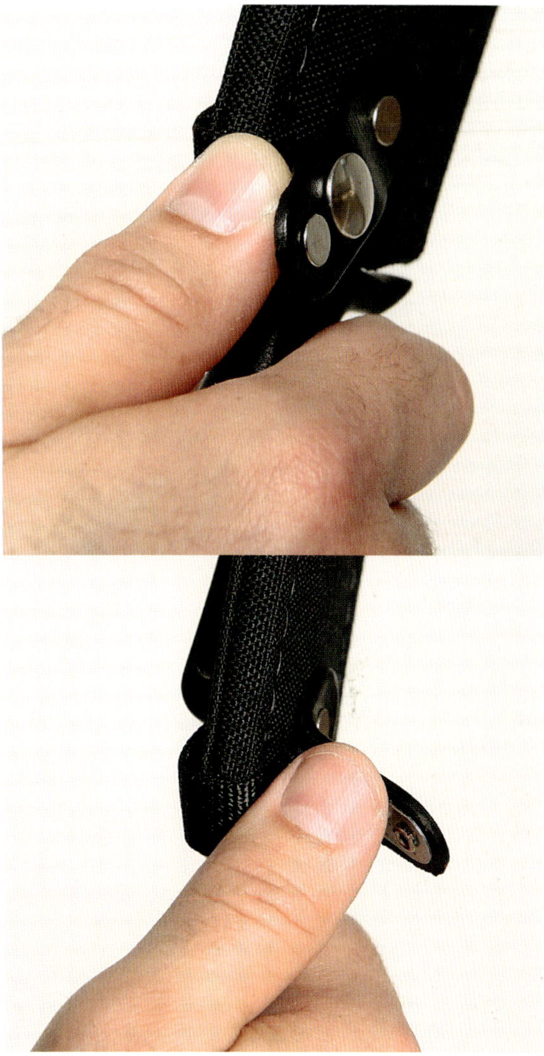

For decades, the "thumb break" lock determined the look of quick-draw sheaths from leather or cordura. Grabbing and opening with the thumb is done with very little time loss. With modern kydex sheaths, the additional step for opening is dispensed with.

4.1 Carrying Systems for Fixed Blades

What should the properties of a sheath for a fixed blade SD knife be? US knife expert and SD trainer Michael Janich formulated the requirements in his book *Street Steel* this way:

- Any quality sheath should protect you from the sharp edges and point of your blade.

- A good sheath must also retain the knife so it doesn't come out until you want it to.
- The sheath should expose enough of the handle to allow you to grip the knife firmly before you draw the knife.
- The sheath should release the knife smoothly and easily.
- The sheath must have adequate possibilities for attaching it so you are able to draw the knife at an optimal angle.

In addition, the ability to use the knife with both hands has to be mentioned as well. If the sheath does not fulfill these requirements, it is not suited for SD use. Today, four established materials are used for knife sheaths: leather, cordura, kydex, and injection-molded plastics.

Leather

Leather is a natural material that has been used in knifemaking for generations. Leather

Four common sheath materials used in the knife industry for many years (from top): cordura (Spec Ops), injection-molded plastics (Mission Knives), kydex (Mission Knives), and leather (Kleinhuber).

has good looks, a pleasant feel, and is versatile in its processing. The early carrying systems for concealed carry within the SOE and OSS in World War II were almost exclusively made of leather.

The following criteria should be taken into account when choosing a high-quality sheath: the leather ought to be as firm as possible and of appropriate thickness. If it is too soft, injuries can be caused when putting away a knife. An additional leather layer of about the blade's thickness should be between the frontside and backside of the sheath. This layer prevents the blade edge from cutting through the seams. The yarn for sewing the sheath has to be impregnated and possess high tensile strength, preventing it from taking in moisture and making the sheath resilient. In addition, the knife should rest in the sheath with as little play as possible and the securing flap—if present—should fit tightly around the pommel or handle.

The big tactical advantage of a leather sheath is it allows you to silently draw the knife. Besides that, you can manage repairs yourself with either needle and thread or rivets without too much difficulty. Leather's disadvantage is its restricted tolerance to moisture and temperature changes. If the leather sheath gets wet, it easily loses its shape and thus its tight fit. A mere quiver-like sheath, as used with boot knives in the early 1970s—without any securing flap or strap—can hardly hold a knife securely. Particles of dirt or sand inside the sheath—which can lead to ugly scratches on the blade—can't be removed easily either. Rinsing with water poses no problem for plastic sheaths, but is problematic for leather. Some knifemakers swear by blades of non-stainless carbon steel, but when stored in the sheath over a long time period, the knife suffers from corrosion due to the leather's tanning agents and existing moisture.

Cordura

Besides leather, a synthetic fabric called cordura has been increasingly used since the 1980s. It is distinguishable due to its special resistance to wear. Cordura is produced by the chemical company DuPont. Because of its high tear resistance and melting temperature, this nylon fabric is designed for extreme loads. Even ultraviolet radiation leads to only a little bleaching. Today, cordura can still be found in weatherproof clothing and backpacks.

Sheaths of cordura can be sewn in a similar way to leather, but a stabilizing material (leather or plastics) has to be used as a foundation; cordura alone is not stable enough to protect a blade. Plastics are better suited, because they don't have leather's disadvantages. Plastics offer reliable protection against penetration of the blade edge, while at the same time keeping their shape. In order to keep the blade well ventilated and to prevent moisture from collecting, most cordura sheaths have a small hole in the area of the blade tip. When purchasing a knife with a cordura sheath, you should take care that the corners have a tuck and, if possible, are sewn double. This way, the disintegration of the fabric at these highly stressed spots is prevented.

Kydex

Kydex has revolutionized sheathmaking like no other material. Using kydex, it is possible to pull a knife from a sheath without the time-consuming effort of unlocking a safety latch. The chemical foundation of this thermoplastic is acrylic polyvinyl chloride (PVC). Because of its high resistance to breakage and impact strength, as well as its flame-retardant properties, kydex is used in aircraft construction and the electrical industry. Kydex can be shaped easily under heat and pressure.

Details, such as blades, pommels, and handles, can be contoured with top quality and shaped to an accurate fit. The sheath orifice can be formed in such a way that the guard rests in a recess and fixes the blade within the sheath. Due to the springy properties of the kydex, the guard is released during pulling. Using the type of deformation, the tensile strength can be adjusted. Kydex is available in different colors and with printed camouflage patterns.

Among the advantages of kydex are its safe storage of the knife and protection of the user from his own blade. You can remove dirt from a kydex sheath by simply rinsing it. You don't have to fear deformation as can occur with leather sheaths, or cordura sheaths lined with leather. Most kydex sheaths are glued at the sides and are additionally fastened with rivets. The rivets can also be used to add an adapter for carrying (e.g., Tek-Lok). This way, the angle for drawing the knife can be chosen freely.

A disadvantage of kydex sheaths is the noise they create when you pull the knife. If you want a concealed draw of the knife from its sheath prior to combat to have it ready for action, the kydex sheath may create unwanted noise because of the springy behavior of the plastics. Besides that, kydex sheaths in the long run quite often cause shabby-looking scratches on the blade and guard. But this is the price you will pay for being able to draw the knife tactically fast. After all, SD knives are no collector's item, are but meant for hard use.

Injection-Molded Plastics

Prior to kydex, other thermoplastics, such as polyamide and acrylonitride-butadien styrene rubber (better known as ABS), were already in use by the knife industry. But these materials are processed by means of injection molding, which is only suitable for large serial production, because expensive dies have to be created. In order to guarantee an accurate fit without play, a precise adjustment between knife and sheath has to be made, because otherwise, either the knife rattles in the sheath or it is too tight. There is no chance for a simple readjustment later as can be done with kydex. The advantages of this sheath type are its toughness, the protection against the blade's edge, and its ease of cleaning. Generally, the disadvantages are the same as kydex sheaths. While in earlier days very elaborate plastic sheaths were produced as a single piece, it has become increasingly common in recent years to injection-mold the front and back part separately and to rivet them together.

All four sheath materials have their stable place in the knife industry and each of them has its own advantages and disadvantages. Leather still has the most attractive charisma, but with modern SD knives, the choice should tend towards plastics. In order to combine leather and kydex, the knives of Montana-based knifemaker James Piorek are a good choice; he offers kydex sheaths covered with leather. However, they are not cheap and the waiting list is several years.

Neck knives, such as the "Hornet" by Wally Hayes, can be carried comfortably because of their size, but are hard to reach underneath the shirt. In a serious situation, ripping open the shirt is the only solution.
Knife photo Marc Götzmann

4.1.2 Eight Carrying Positions

Today, concealed carry of knives with fixed blades is simplified by a multitude of carrying systems. These either belong to the knife or can be bought as extras. Talented sheath makers can fulfill any unusual wish a customer may have. Usually, the sheath maker needs the knife for this, in order to fit it to the sheath without play. If possible, leather sheaths should not be black, because they can be seen underneath light-colored shirts or T-shirts all too easily. Kydex or cordura carrying systems, in theory, can also be offered in lighter colors, but the market is apparently fixated on black. To give you an idea about the variety of positions in which fixed blade SD knives can be carried, the following passages describe eight different positions, together with their advantages and disadvantages.

Neck Carry

The sheath is simply put around the neck with a ribbon, string, or chain. Since the knife handle is facing downwards, the knife can be drawn from the sheath by simply pulling it and is immediately ready for action. The big advantage of these so-called neck knives is in their comfortable carrying, regardless of whether sitting in a car or during jogging. The sheaths of neck knives are usually kydex. The string or chain visible around the neck is readily interpreted as a necklace and does not give any hint of one being armed. The T-shirt should not sit too tightly, because otherwise, the knife's contours can be seen on the chest. Besides that, the T-shirt ought to have a loose fit on top of the trousers.

But this way of carrying also has disadvantages: if the knife should be ready for quick action, then tightly buttoned shirts are

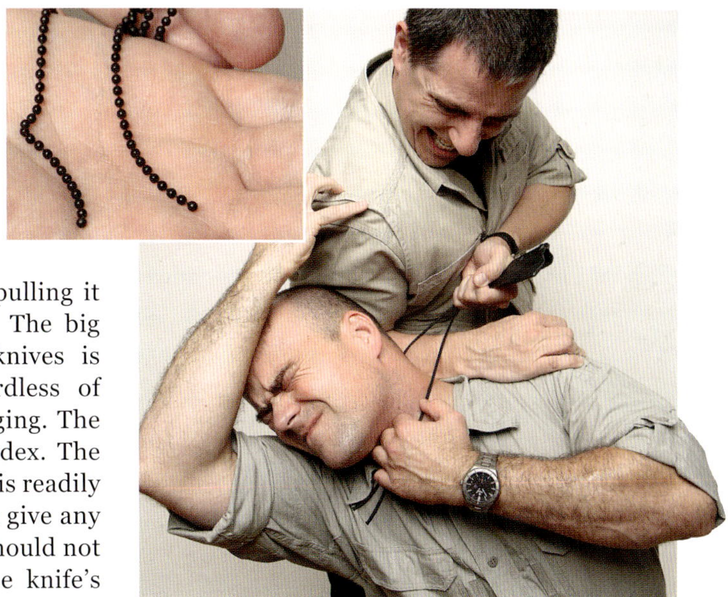
If the cord of the neck-knife sheath is made from a tear-resistant material such as paracord 550, it may turn out fatal for the person wearing it. Many companies thus provide their neck knives with metal bead necklaces that tear under a certain amount of load. Thus, the danger of being strangled is practically eliminated.

already out of the question. It also doesn't work to wear the knife on top of the shirt and cover it with a tie. Best suited are T-shirts or pullovers that give easy access to the knife from below. However, this is difficult if you are already fighting on the ground and the knife is located somewhere at the side of your body.

Many dealers of neck knives are apparently not aware that a nylon cord for carrying a knife holds serious danger. The often used nylon parachute cord 550 (paracord) has a tensile strength of 550 lb. (almost 200 kg) and, in the worst case, can be used against the wearer himself; if the attacker manages to grab the cord, he can strangle you. Because of this, makers like Bud Nealy, Böker, Spyderco, and Blackhawk prefer chains that rupture under a certain load. The limit is defined differently by each manufacturer.

Belt Carry

This is the classic way to carry a fixed blade knife and is probably the most obvious. If you don't wear a jacket, coat, pullover, or long shirt that completely hides the sheath, the weapon is visible. Because the sheath has to ride relatively high on the belt, two severe disadvantages result: on the one hand, the handle presses unpleasantly against your torso; on the other, the drawing angle is extremely unfavorable. The knife can best be drawn in the so-called ice pick grip, but basically, nothing can be said against belt carry if the sheath system allows a change of the drawing angle. For example, leather pancake sheaths (so-called because of their shape) can be provided with differently aligned belt slots and the knife can be carried at the belt with a transverse drawing angle.

Even more possibilities exist for kydex sheaths. The company TOPS, for example, provides its kydex sheaths with a rotatable metal clip, allowing individual adjustment of the drawing angle. The same effect can also be achieved with a Tek-Lok adapter that is available in two sizes. The idea for this stems from the inventive knifemaker Bob Terzuola who, together with the company Blade Tech, brought it to production. The Tek-Lok is attached to the kydex sheath by means of two screws and—with the big model—can be adjusted to various angles with the help of seven holes and two slits (the small model provides nine holes). A prerequisite for this is holes 3/16 of an inch (five millimeters) in diameter on the sheath that are the same distance apart as the drill holes on the Tek-Lok.

Besides the possibilities for adjusting the angle, the adapter is also distinguished by its easy attachment to the belt: just press both plastic flanks together and its upper part opens. This way, the Tek-Lok and the attached sheath can be fastened to the belt and removed again at any time. This is especially practical in case the knife should be put away in the car or office without awkwardly having to open one's belt first.

Classic sheaths with a belt clip ought to be checked prior to purchase whether the clip really keeps its position on the belt when the knife is drawn. Unfortunately, relatively old metal clips quite often do not have the required spring force. Modern plastic clips usually have a protruding edge that actually hooks the clip to the belt. Good examples of this are made by the company Blade Tech, which produces kydex sheaths with belt and boot clips for various knife companies, including the company that offers the boot knife version of the A-F combat knife. If you have any doubts as to whether the sheath really remains at its proper place when drawing the knife, you can additionally attach the sheath to the belt by means of a short safety line. If the clip gives way, the string will hold back the sheath.

Whoever wants to attach and detach the sheath in an even easier manner can use a so-called paddle adapter, similar to those used with firearm holsters. The paddle adapter is simply attached to the inside of the waistband. Together, two lugs on the adapter fix it to the belt from the outside, preventing the adapter from coming loose when drawing the knife. Masters of Defense offers a paddle adapter in series with some of their models. In addition, this type of adapter is available as an add-on for weapon holsters from Blackhawk.

Solidly made pancake leather belt sheath of the US company TOPS Knives. The drawing angle for this way of carry is rather unfavorable.

TOPS Knives provides kydex sheaths for their SAW model with a rotatable metal clip that allows a multitude of drawing angles.

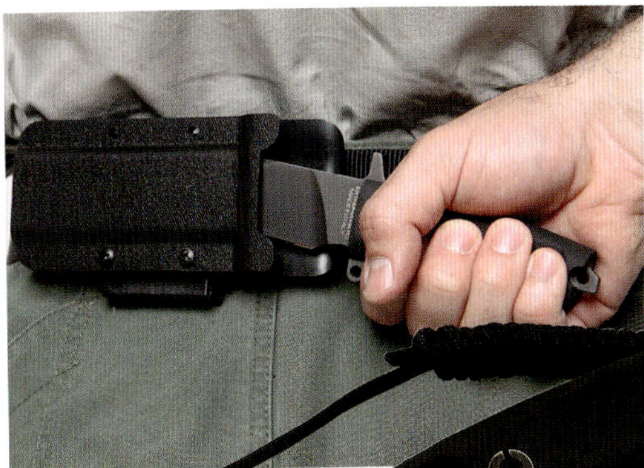

Horizontal carry at the belt makes sense only if the knife is suitably compact; otherwise, the knife will protrude at the sides. The biggest disadvantage is that the knife can only be reached with one hand. Shown is the Shrapnel model of Italian manufacturer Extrema Ratio.

Knife photo: dp

Paddle adapters are known from the assortment of holsters for firearms. Blackhawk's paddle adapter can be screwed to kydex sheaths with no trouble and can be purchased separately. Here it is fitting for the Blackhawk Crucible Fixed model.

The Tek-Lok downright revolutionized the carry possibilities of kydex sheaths. Among the members of special forces, carrying the sheath on the thigh by means of Tek-Lok is especially favored.

Photo dp, Frank Soens

Classic way of carry on the inside of one's waistband with the Gerber Mark I.

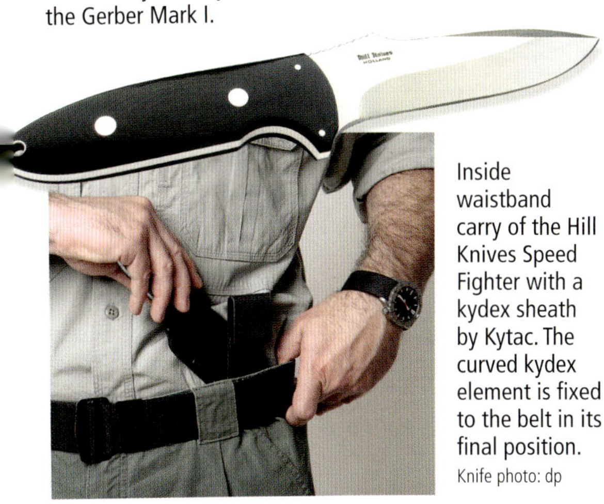

Inside waistband carry of the Hill Knives Speed Fighter with a kydex sheath by Kytac. The curved kydex element is fixed to the belt in its final position.
Knife photo: dp

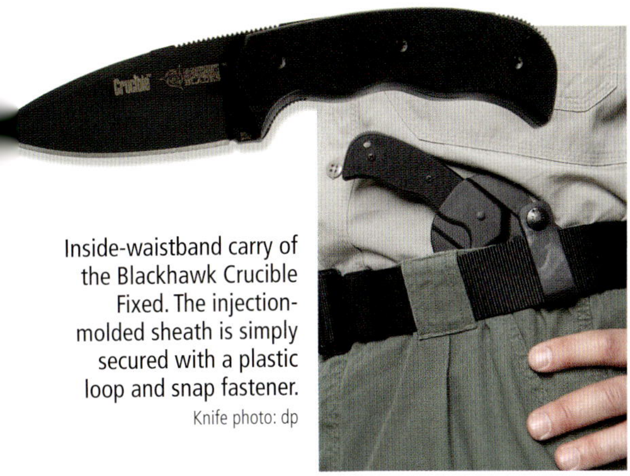

Inside-waistband carry of the Blackhawk Crucible Fixed. The injection-molded sheath is simply secured with a plastic loop and snap fastener.
Knife photo: dp

The advantage of belt carry is the very exact positioning of the knife. If the sheath is fixed securely to the belt and the drawing angle is optimal, this carrying system is one of the most effective. A disadvantage is that belt carry is not always suitable for daily use. If you predominantly wear casual clothes that end below the belt line, such as pullovers, T-shirts, or shirts that are not tucked inside one's trousers, then belt carry is ideal. But if this is not the case, the knife becomes visible to others. If the people in your environment accept belt carry then there is nothing against it, but the knife should be out of view of potential attackers. In addition, you should be aware that the knife can't be reached with both hands when carried at certain positions. If you carry the knife horizontally on your back, the probability is very high that you can only draw it from one side.

Inside Pants Carry

Knife sheaths are less obvious when carried on the inside of the waistband; the handle and a small part of the sheath orifice poke out of the trousers, while the rest vanishes behind the waistband. In the ideal case, the knife is pulled diagonally in a crossdraw. All types of sheaths with a belt clip can be carried on the inside of the waistband because there is no difference whether the sheath is attached to the belt from the outside or it is attached to the waistband's inside. A securing string also provides a precious advantage, in case you draw the knife along with the sheath in the heat of battle. Knifemaker James Piorek even created a whole system out of this securing string which he calls static cord. Sheaths of this type are simply put inside the waistband, and in times of need are just drawn together with the sheath. The advantage: the sheath keeps the blade back until it has left direct proximity of the body. When the end of the cord is reached, the sheath releases the knife automatically and the knife is ready for action.

A rather classic way to attach to the waistband is the belt loop, which keeps the sheath in place. The loop can either be nylon or a soft, flexible kind of plastic like that used by the company Blackhawk for some of its sheath models. In the ideal case, the belt loop can be opened and closed with a snap fastener, because otherwise, the belt has to be pulled through the loop each time you want to attach or detach the sheath. It is easier with a small kydex retaining clip or injection-molded plastics. Here, the sheath is pushed into the waistband as usual and is fixed to the belt by means of a screwed-on retaining clip.

The disadvantage of inside pants carry is that the sheath and the blade are always exposed to hot and humid body climate, and blades of non-stainless steel can corrode rather quickly. In addition, depending on the blade length, this type of carry is not really comfortable, especially when sitting.

Shoulder Harness Carry

Shoulder harnesses are the most effective carry option for knives with fixed blades; even large-size combat knives can be carried comfortably this way. The sheath is attached to the harness with the knife handle facing downwards in a similar manner to a pistol holster. In some cases, the carrying system can also hold either a pistol or a knife by with an adapter, such as those offered by the company Blackhawk. The sheath is usually either located next to the ribs or in front of the chest, depending on the carrying system.

The downwards draw direction provides the quickest and safest access. The biggest advantage: the knife can be drawn with either the right or left hand. In addition, this carrying method is well suited for the car, because the knife can still be accessed easily and is not in the way.

Once again, the disadvantage is the restricted ability for concealed carry. If you wear a coat or jacket, there surely is no better carrying system, but when you remove them, it will become difficult to explain to bystanders why you are armed in such a way. If you are wearing casual clothes, such as a pullover or an open shirt, the shoulder harness can be recommended without any restrictions. Similar

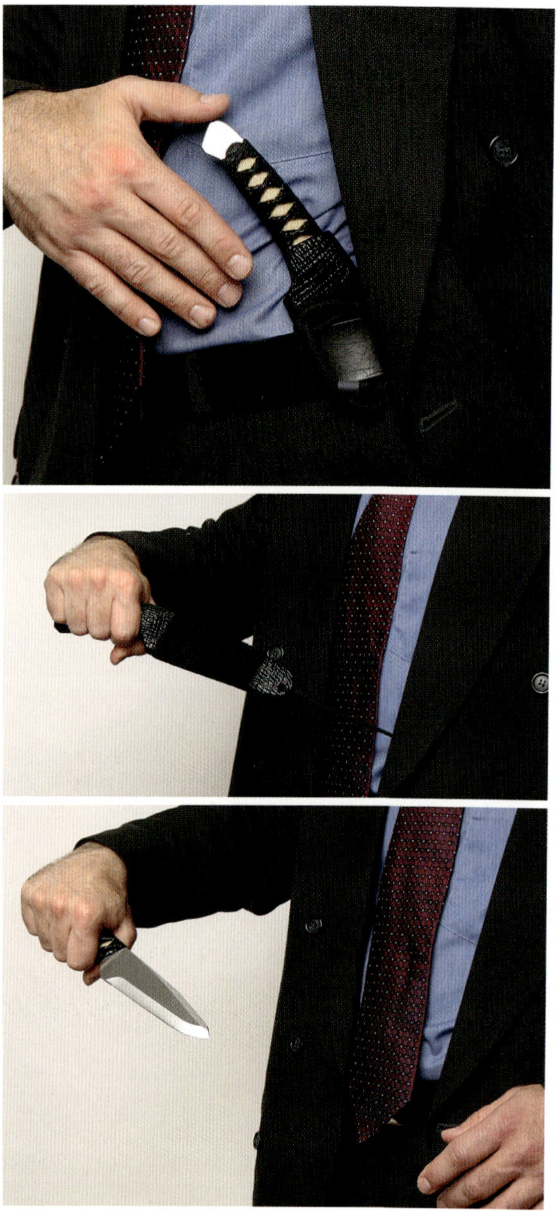

James Piorek's Spec Recon II model is simply put on the inside of the waistband with its sheath. When drawing the knife, the sheath stays attached to the knife until the securing cord (Static Cord) is taut. Only then is the knife released. The big advantage: the knife can be drawn without danger of cutting oneself in the hectic rush of events.

Luxury-class shoulder harness: James Piorek's Execulite shoulder harness of kydex with ray skin cover. The very elaborately designed three-point strap system reliably prevents the sheath from shifting.

Optional shoulder harness system by Tactical Tools. Almost all kydex sheaths can be retrofitted with this system. This sheath by Kytac contains the A-F Urban Fighter of knifemaker Bill Harsey.

The shoulder harness system by Blackhawk is actually made for firearm holsters, but can also be used for knife sheaths. That it can even allow concealed carry of really large combat knives is proven here by the Gil Hibben sub-hilt fighter with Kytac sheath.

Whoever wants to carry his knife in a shoulder harness system of leather can have this done by a skilled saddler. Here it was done for the sub-hilt fighter of Peter Herbst. The very accurate work was done by Siegfried Raschke.

Whoever searches for a complete system (kydex sheath plus shoulder straps) will find it with the American company Survival Sheath System. Here is the version for a Cold Steel tanto.

Knife Photo Marc Götzmann

Helmut Lehner from Munich ("Feinste Stahlwaren") offers a leather carry system suitable for a wide variety of common leather sheaths. The sheaths are simply threaded in.

to pistol holsters, you ought to critically check in front of the mirror whether the sheath or handle creates conspicuous bulges in one's clothing.

You should be able to carry the entire system comfortably. Here, too, great differences in quality exist. While in the past the sheaths were made of leather and the knives were secured by means of snap fasteners or velcro, most of the modern models are made of kydex. The carrying system itself can be made of leather or nylon. Here, subjective feel should be the decisive factor.

Shoulder harnesses are available in simple and more sophisticated versions that are reflected in their pricing. The simplest version is a nylon belt running straight down your chest and diagonally across your back. Both ends are fixed to the belt. In this case, the sheath is positioned vertically on the chest belt, with the knife handle facing downward. This system, which is not unlike suspenders, is not very comfortable to wear—all the more so if no flexible insert is sewn into the belt band. Some companies offer this type of belt with an adapter for their boot knife sheaths, but this is not really a practicable solution for everyday use.

A modification of this carrying system is a loop for the arm on the end of the belt instead of the diagonal back belt. Examples of this system are offered by United Cutlery, Magnum, and Junglee, but also by renowned manufacturers such as Kershaw. Gerber was among the first to offer such a carrying system.

Top-class shoulder harness carrying systems are offered by knifemaker James Piorek. Almost no other person has thought so much about the perfect way of carrying and drawing knives. His kydex sheaths are covered with leather, and thus

The Rigid combat dagger of United Cutlery is delivered together with a shoulder harness system. It is a simple one, but nevertheless halfway comfortable to carry.
Knife Photo United Cutlery

appear less clinical. He also has a separately developed solution for each carrying position. For example, the "Execulite" shoulder harness system is not just convincing because it follows the direction of drawing to some extent in order to guide the knife away from the jacket area free of dangers, but also guarantees by being fixed at three places that it always sits at the correct spot on the torso. The same goes for his Spinal Back-Up 3 shoulder carrying system, which does not keep the sheath in the area of the chest or the side of the ribs, but on the back. Here, too, the system is convincing because of the adjustable base plate, which always provides optimal access to the knife. The disadvantage of these highly specialized sheath carrying systems is their long delivery time; customers have to wait about three to five years. But after that time they'll receive an uncompromisingly good SD knife system.

If you want to provide your knife with a shoulder harness system, you have to rely on the available accessories market. Some manufacturers of kydex sheaths have specialized in this. For example, Tactical Tools produces a carrying system similar to the Piorek Execulite, but Tactical Tools uses a very well thought out two point attachment system. The system can be used for an already existing kydex sheath. If the necessary drill holes are not there, they can easily be added with a conventional drill. If you want to, you can even attach two knives to this system or relocate the sheath from left to right. Even larger knives can be carried comfortably with this system.

A wide range of shoulder harness systems is offered by Survival Sheath System. Here, the kydex sheath is already part of the system and is delivered fitted to the knife. Besides the classical carrying positions, there are also solutions available for carrying the knife concealed on one's back. Because of the sheath's centered alignment, the knife can be drawn from both sides. But since the knife rests directly on the

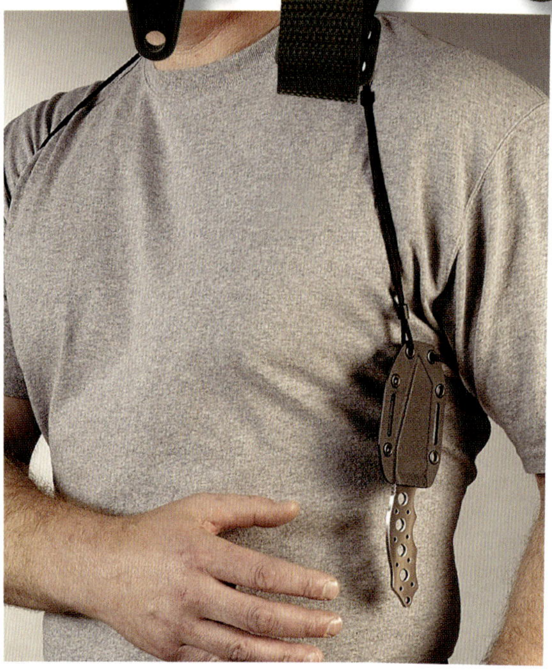

Top: Kershaw, for its re-launch of the earlier combat knife design of Anton Wingen (now the Kershaw Military Boot Knife), also relied on the simple shoulder harness system used by United Cutlery. Bottom: The Merc harness system of CRKT.

Photos: Kai Europe, Kershaw Knives, CRKT

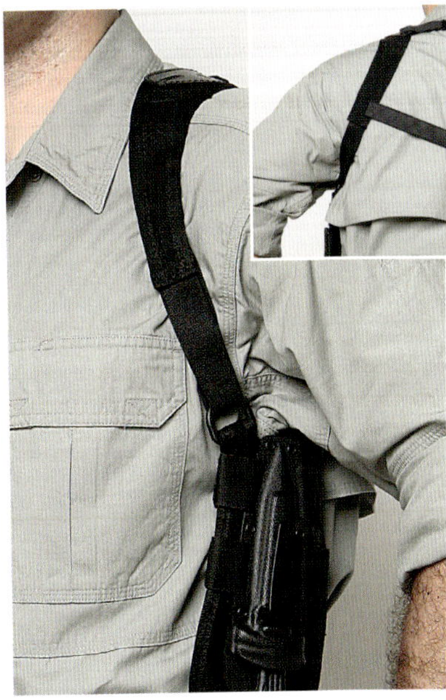

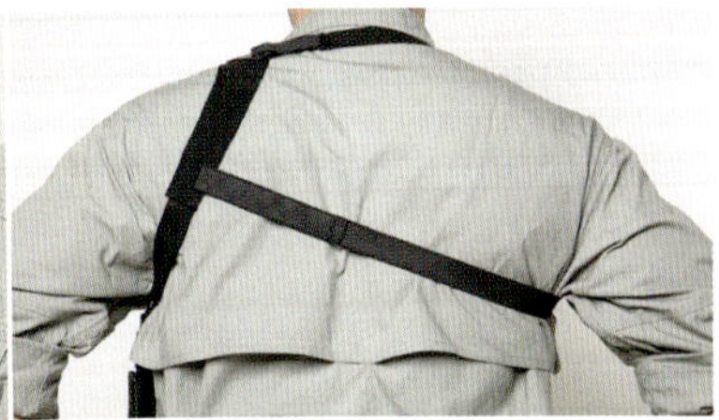

Nowar of Wiehl, Germany, offers this cordura carrying system fitting to the kydex sheaths of the Böker A-F Combat and A-F Boot models. Within limitations, it is also suited for other models.
Knife photo Böker

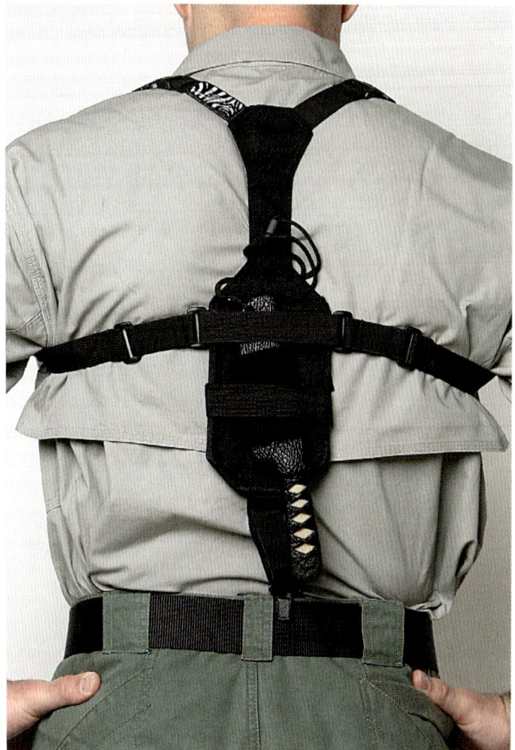

Another, extremely well thought out carrying system of knifemaker James Piorek: with the Spinal Back-Up 3, the knife can be attached to the back in an optimal way. The drawing angle can be adjusted by means of the hook and loop fastener.

The company Survival Sheath System offers back-carry systems for a number of serial knives. The drawing angle can't be adjusted for this system, but the knife can be easily reached nevertheless, as with the Böker KSK combat knife shown here.
Knife photo Böker Baumwerk

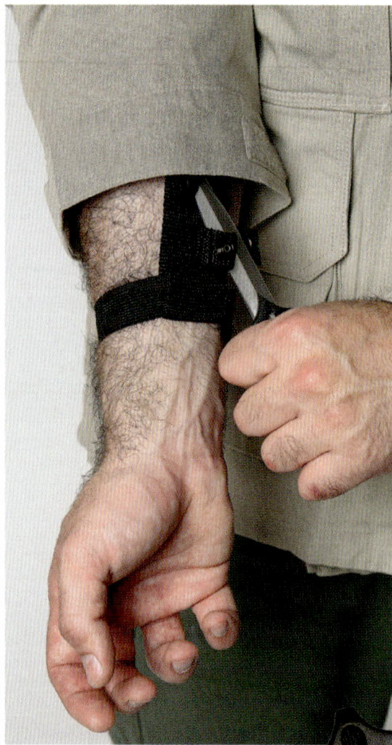

With sleeve carry, drawing the knife poses a problem if the knife in the sheath is secured by means of a conventional snap fastener that has to be opened first in case of an emergency. Here is United Cutlery's Special Agent Stinger model.
Knife photo United Cutlery

Inside chest pockets of vests, jackets, or coats also offer the possibility of attaching the sheath with the handle facing downward. For this purpose, Bud Nealy's MCS system is provided with a special adapter with a large area to prevent damaging the inside pocket when drawing the knife and ensuring the straight position of the sheath.

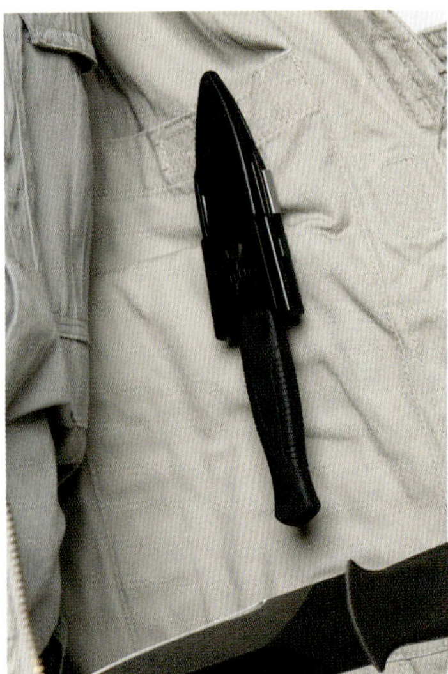

The Gerber Guardian Back-Up with exchangeable sheath clip is convincing in this position, too. In addition, the resistance to pull can be regulated.
Knife photo Herbertz, Gerber Knives

The CRKT Sting is provided with a quick-drawing sheath of cordura with a plastic inlay. The bands, which are close together, make a permanent attachment to the forearm quite difficult.

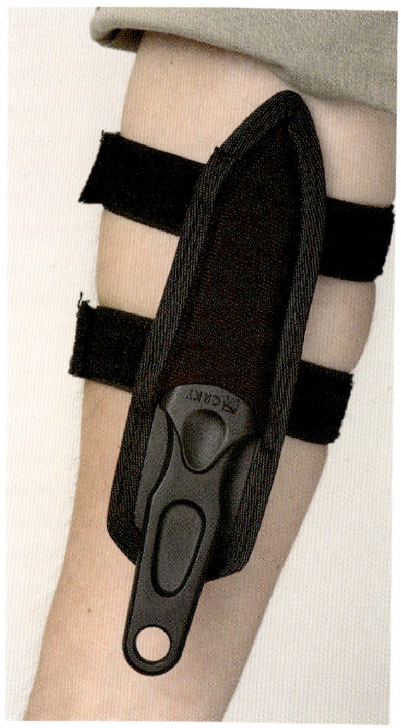

spine, it is annoying when sitting. Blindly putting the knife back also needs some time getting used to.

Among the German producers of shoulder harness systems are NOWAR, based in Wiehl, and the knife specialist Helmut Lehner ("Feinste Stahlwaren") in Munich. Both offer carrying systems suited for leather as well as kydex belt sheaths. While the NOWAR system is available in a leather/nylon version and one completely made of nylon, Lehner, as a trained saddler, focuses on leather, which he often embellishes with artful embossing. No special alterations are necessary with with the products from either of these companies.

Breast Pocket Carry

Carrying a knife in the breast pocket on the inside of your jacket, sports coat, or coat has the advantage that your environment doesn't necessarily realize you are armed with a weapon. This solution only makes sense when the knife can be carried in the sheath with the handle facing downward. If the handle faces upward, you'll draw the knife at an angle that is dangerously close to your face. Besides that, unlocking the safety latch is very cumbersome. The danger also exists that, for a boot sheath with clip, you'll suddenly hold the entire knife—including the sheath—in your hand. This means the clip has to be securely fixed on the rim of your breast pocket. But usually the fabric of inside breast pockets is rather thin and only has a limited toughness. Knives that are too heavy should not be hung inside jackets anyway. If the resistance against pulling is too strong, you risk tearing the pocket.

A very practicable solution is offered by the Gerber Guardian Back-Up. The sheath clip can be turned 180° and the pulling strength of the sheath itself can be adjusted. Knifemaker Bud Nealy takes carrying his MCS system in the inside breast pocket into account, too, and for this purpose offers an especially broad kydex assembly.

Although the knife can be carried comfortably this way, you do not have direct access to your weapon after taking off your jacket. Mindlessly hanging up your jacket at collectively used coat racks should also be avoided for obvious reasons.

Sleeve Carry

A classic of agent movies is carrying the knife on your forearm; the knife seems to magically appear from the sleeve at the right moment. In reality, because of the forearm's anatomical shape, the probability is very high that the sheath, including the knife, would slip down to the wrist during an attempt to draw the knife. If the sheath is secured by a snap fastener, this has to be reached during drawing and the sleeves have to be quite wide. This way or that, it is very difficult to reach into the sleeve of a jacket or shirt. Knife size is also restricted by the length of the forearm. In addition, the carrying comfort is limited by the bands. A basic prerequisite is bands with flexible inserts to allow the forearm muscles to contract.

The biggest disadvantage of this carry system is if the drawing hand is injured during combat or gets restricted in any way, it is practically impossible to reach the knife. Furthermore, under stress this way of drawing the knife enhances the danger of cutting your forearm. Nevertheless, if compelling reasons exist for carrying a knife on the forearm, using an SD knife with a flat handle that looks less obvious is recommended. The sheath should be attached with medical tape to provide a secure fit on the forearm. This way of carry is definitely not suited for everyday use.

Boot Carry

Boot carry requires that you indeed have such shoes and that you wear them together with your everyday clothes. The boot shaft has to have a certain length and width in order to accommodate the sheath. If the sheath is too long or the boot shaft is too short, after a brief time, the sheath tip will unpleasantly rub against your ankle. As an alternative, the sheath could be clipped on the outside of the shaft, but this creates the danger of your trouser leg slipping upwards when sitting, thus clearing the view of your knife.

The leg of your trousers is already a problem with this type of carry. First, it has to be wide enough to be pulled upwards without difficulty. In addition, this type of carry has a tactical disadvantage, because both hands are needed to pull up the trouser leg and to draw the knife from the sheath. Thus, you have to first move out of the direct sphere of influence of the opponent in order to safely reach your knife.

A further alternative is wearing the knife on the outside of the boot shaft with the handle facing downward. Here, you have the small advantage that you can draw the knife single-handedly without pulling up your trouser leg first. To attach the sheath this way, you need a sheath system with an exchangeable clip or a clip that can be turned 180°. Once more, a good example is the Gerber Guardian Back-Up. Sheaths that are suitable for carrying inside breast pockets generally are also suitable for carrying at the boot. Bud Nealy's MCS systems are especially made for this type of carrying, regardless of whether it is his handmade version or the Solingen-produced version by Böker. For his own version, Nealy additionally secures the sheath against lateral movement with nylon cord.

Besides attaching it to the boot, there is also the possibility of attaching the knife on the lower leg itself. Similar to carrying it on the lower arm, the sheath can be attached to the lower leg with bands. The advantage: you can wear any type of shoe and don't have to rely on boots. Similar to the attachment to boots, there are two approaches available here: either the sheath is attached to the ankle in such a way that the knife handle is facing upward, or the sheath is placed on the calf with the handle facing downward. The advantages and disadvantages of both positions correspond to those of boot carry.

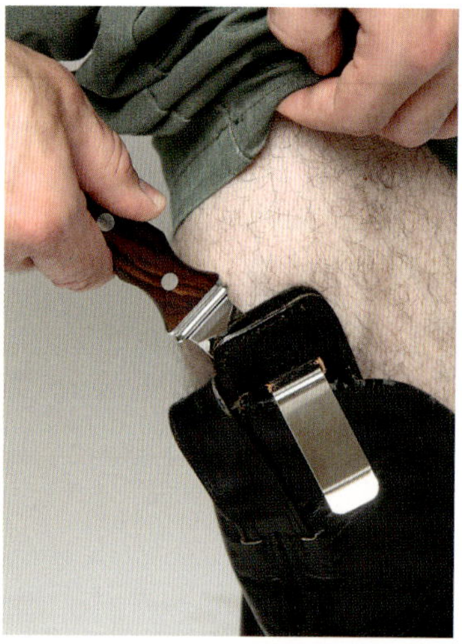

The biggest disadvantage of the classic boot carry with the knife handle facing upward is the fact that you need both hands to access your weapon: one hand to lift the trouser leg, the other for drawing the knife.

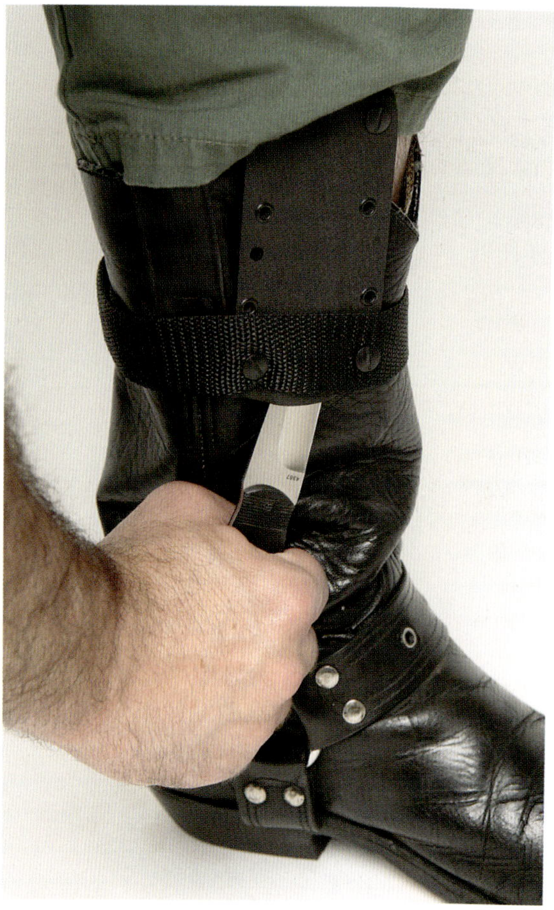

Bud Nealy's MCS system offers the possibility to pull the knife out of the sheath downward with one hand only.

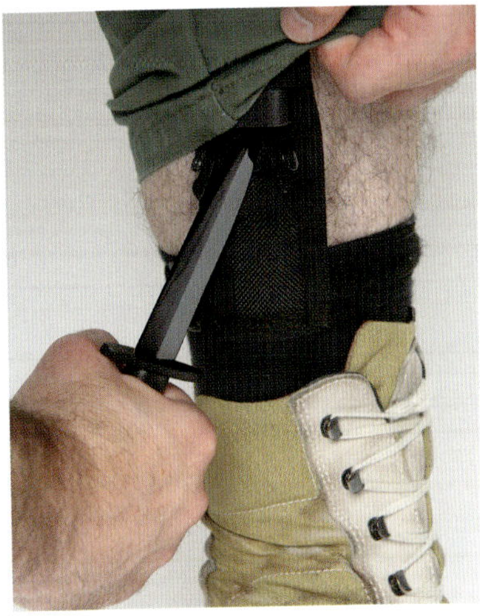

If you don't wear a boot with a long shaft, certain sheaths can also be attached with bands to the leg directly—in this case with the F-S Mini— even with the handle facing downward. But since the knife is held by a snap fastener loop, drawing it poses some problems.

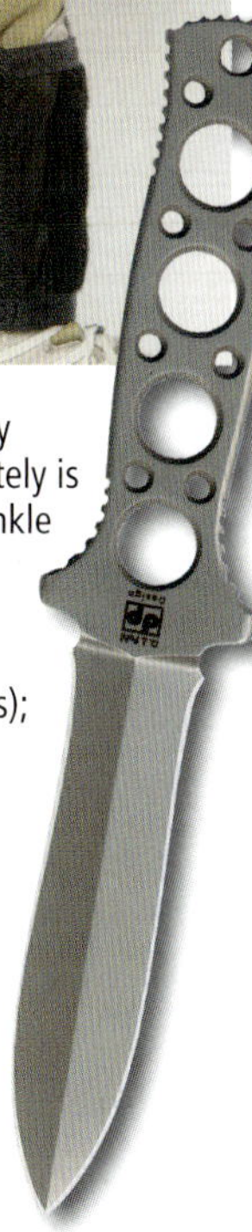

A classic of US company Eagle, which unfortunately is no longer produced. The ankle cuff sheath could contain different knives with a maximum blade length of four inches (10 centimeters); the photo shows a handmade skeletonized dagger by Peter Herbst.

Knife photo dp

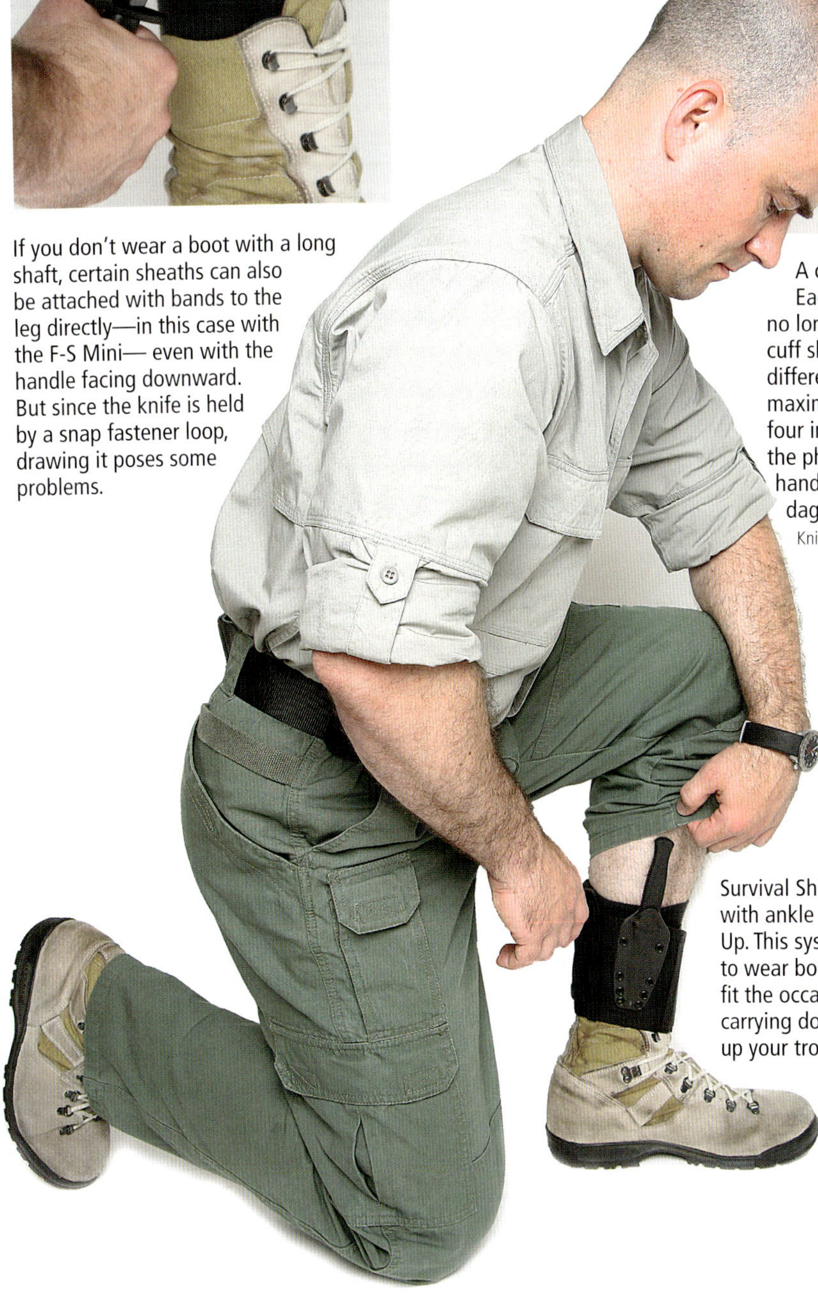

Survival Sheath System offers a kydex sheath with ankle cuff for the Gerber Guardian Back-Up. This system is well suited if you don't want to wear boots with high shaft or these don't fit the occasion. Unfortunately, this way of carrying doesn't spare you the effort of pulling up your trouser leg first.

4.2 Carrying Systems for Folders

The advantage of a folder compared to a fixed blade is in its compact size and the possibility of easily carrying the knife concealed. The following passages describe the possibilities of carry and which of these really make sense. As with fixed blades, not all carrying options are recommended for all situations.

Pocket Carry

Depending on their size, folders can be comfortably carried in the jacket or trouser pocket. With a jacket, this way of carry can be used as a tactical advantage in case one's hands are not only in the jacket pockets for warming, but can already hold the knife, ready for action. But a disadvantage is that the weapon is not ready at hand after you take off the jacket.

It is better to carry your SD knife in the trouser pocket. First rule for this way of carrying your knife: "Don't cram other things into the pocket together with your knife!" In a stressful situation, it would be very dangerous if you had to search for your knife among the other things in your trouser pocket.

Customary men's trousers usually have three or four pockets. The better choice is the back pockets which, at least for jeans, are sewn onto the outside. In order to draw and open the knife effectively, it already ought to be lying in the pocket in the best position for this purpose. Several tests are necessary to determine this position for yourself. This way of carrying also makes sense from a tactical point of view, because male citizens quite often carry their wallet in the back pocket of the trousers, so reaching towards it is not suspicious and the surprise will be all the greater if the attacker suddenly sees a knife moving in.

Whoever decides on this way of carrying ought to choose an SD knife with a handle as flat as possible. If a switchblade is chosen, you have to absolutely take care that it can't be inadvertently triggered when sitting down. An additional safety for the trigger, as is customary with modern switchblades, minimizes the risk, but the time necessary for deactivating this safety also increases the time you need for making the knife ready for action.

Belt Sheath or Holster Carry

Many folders are not suited for pocket carry because of their size and are better carried within a sheath or holster. Common materials are leather, cordura, and kydex. A sheath here is a closed bag that secures the knife completely with a latch. Depending on its design, the latch can be secured with a snap fastener, velcro tape, or a quick fastener (e.g., Fastex). In contrast, the holster is an open system, with the knife sitting in a pre-shaped sheath without any kind of latch. Sheaths are usually made of leather or nylon. Holsters were also made of leather, although since the 1990s kydex is also used.

The decision for either of these systems also informs others that you are carrying a knife. If you don't wear a long pullover all the time that reaches below the belt, you cannot even think of concealed carry. A disadvantage of sheaths is the time delay when drawing the folder. Before the weapon is ready for action, you first have to open the latch, draw the knife, and subsequently open it. Here, the advantage of the holster is obvious; you don't have to open any latch.

Sheaths and holsters can be carried vertically or horizontally. The vertical carry, with the opening facing upward, is the traditional way, but it also creates an unfavorable drawing angle that can be improved with diagonal or horizontal carry. In addition, horizontally carried sheaths provide better comfort when sitting. But horizontal carry increases the danger of loss. Thus, the tight fit of the latch, regardless if it's a snap fastener or velcro strip, has to be checked regularly. Whether you prefer snap fastener or velcro strip depends on practical and tactical reasons. Practically, for the snap fastener, you always have to assure whether both parts are indeed pressed together correctly. For velcro fasteners, simply pressing it on is good enough to secure the knife. Tactically, the snap fastener doesn't create loud noises, but a velcro fastener has a considerable noise "footprint" that may warn an attacker.

A special outside pocket on the thigh of these 5.11 Tactical Trousers can accommodate folders with a handle length of up to five inches (13 centimeters)—ideal for concealed carry of folders. A study of the 5.11 program is worth the effort in any case, because the rest of the functional clothes of this company provide a lot of well thought out carrying possibilities for knives.

This cordura pouch by Maxpedition, which is worn vertically, offers a wide variety of carry possibilities and can also be adjusted in size. Unfortunately, folder pouches clearly show people that you are armed.

Horizontal carry makes quick access even easier. In the ideal case, the knife ought to be located with the blade tip positioned inside the pouch so your thumb will be at the opening immediately and you can open the knife quickly. In the photo the voluminous, braided lace prevents this.

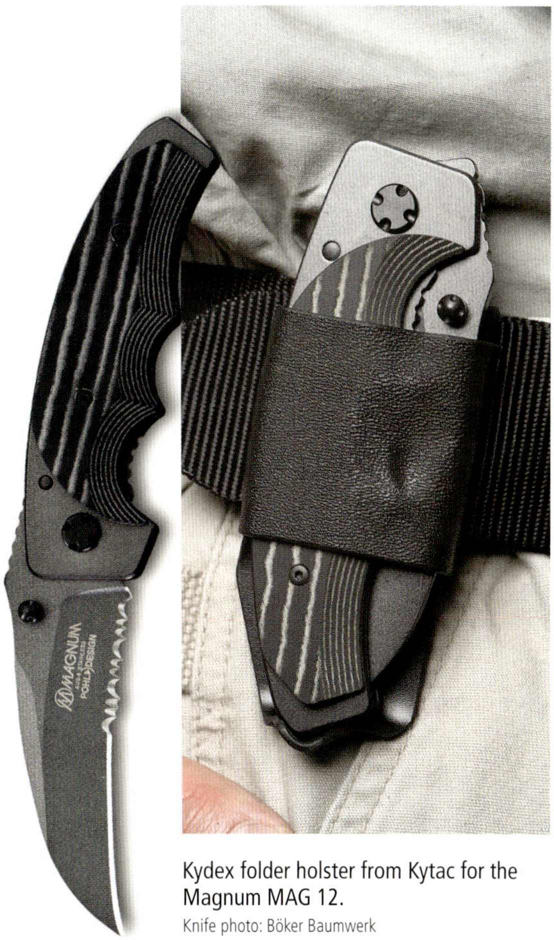

Kydex folder holster from Kytac for the Magnum MAG 12.
Knife photo: Böker Baumwerk

Tip-up means carrying the knife with the blade tip facing upward. Tip-down means the tip is facing downward. From left: Turbine (Böker) and Tactical Custom Folder (anonymous knifemaker/manufacturer).

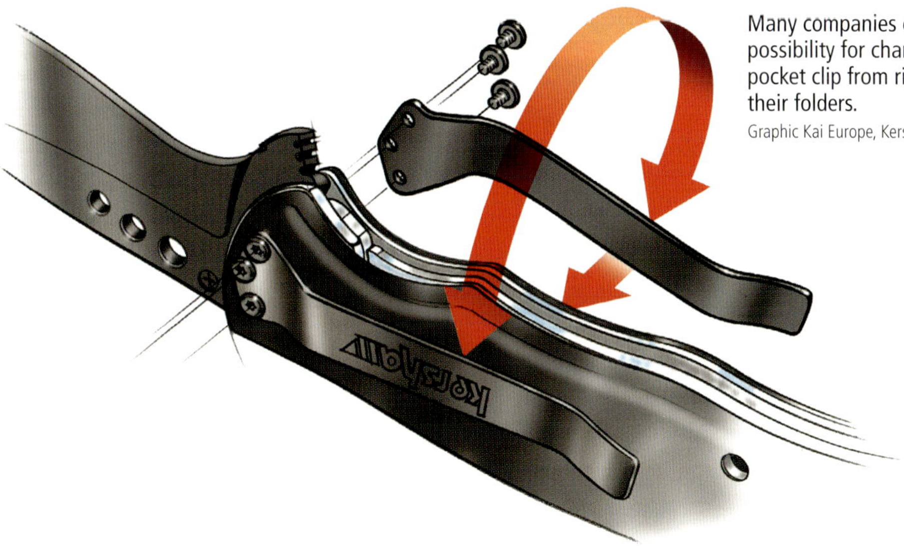

Many companies offer the possibility for changing the pocket clip from right to left on their folders.
Graphic Kai Europe, Kershaw Knives

How should you carry your SD folder in a sheath? This question is easy to answer: with vertical carry, in such a way that the blade tip is facing downward and the handle back is forward. If you reach for the knife, your index finger has already curved around the knife's upper part and the thumb rests against the flipper. Drawing and single-handedly opening the knife follows subsequently with a flowing movement. For horizontal carry, the following is valid: the blade tip faces backward and the handle back downward. Reaching for, drawing, and opening are analogous to the vertical carry. Of course, sophisticated sheaths are available that unfold the knife while drawing it. In this case, the knife is resting upside down within the sheath.

In contrast to sheaths, holsters have to be fitted to the knife in order to guarantee a fit free of play and to prevent loss. While leather over time loses its fitting accuracy due to use and moisture, kydex keeps its shape many years later. Since kydex is dimensionally stable, the knife doesn't have to sit as deeply in the holster as with leather and rests more comfortably in the hand while drawing it. But here the different tastes collide: while some point out the high quality aura of leather, functionality oriented users emphasize the ability for controlled drawing. If well made, both materials pass in use.

Clip-On Carry

Besides the single-handed opening technique and the safe locking of blades, the clip is one of the most important inventions regarding folders. It enables fixing the knife in certain positions. This doesn't have to necessarily be one's clothing, but can also be a backpack, safety belt, or something else.

In all, there are four positions for a clip at the knife handle. Either the clip is located at the lower or upper end of the handle (with "up" meaning the side where the blade axis is located). If the folder is a model also suited for left-handed users, these positions also exist laterally transposed. If the clip is at the bottom of the handle this is called tip-up. This means the blade tip points upward if the knife is clipped to the trousers in the closed position. Tip-down is the opposite case; here, the clip is attached to the handle's upper end and the blade tip points downward.

Which way of carrying is better, tip-up or tip-down? Opinions are divided. One side emphasizes that your thumb is already at the opening mechanism and you never run the risk of grasping an already opened knife, in case the folder is not closed completely. The other side sees the advantage of the tip-up carry in the handle is already resting in your hand properly when grabbing for it and that you can also use a lanyard as an aid for pulling out the knife. Both approaches are right. In the end, only individual taste and dexterity with drawing are decisive here.

It is optimal when the manufacturer has planned for both (or all four) attachment positions. Many companies have already implemented this concept. In addition, the clip should be attached as close as possible to the handle's end. This prevents the folder from sticking far out of the pocket.

Where should the folder with a clip be carried? Ideally, at a position where the visible part of the clip is the least obvious and the knife can easily be reached. The color of the clip also plays an important role as to how the knife is seen by others. Clips are usually either steel (shiny or dull), treated gray, or coated black. Depending on the kind of trousers you wear, the clip is more or less obvious. Many experts in SD recommend carrying the folder on the inside of the waistband. The big advantage of this is that the clip is almost completely covered by the belt. In general, this position is suited for all kinds of trousers, including sports trousers. But not every knife is suited for carry on the inside of the waistband. If the handle is too long or too bulky, its carry quickly becomes uncomfortable. Thus, you ought to choose a compact folder with a preferably flat handle.

Whoever wants to carry his folder with the blade open can do this quite comfortably with a shoulder harness system from Survival Sheath System.

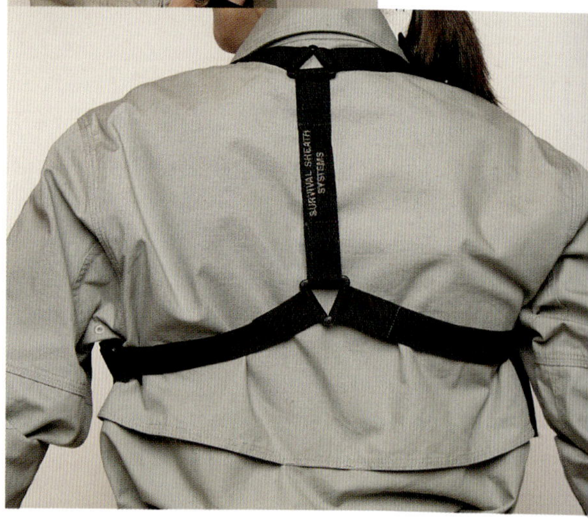

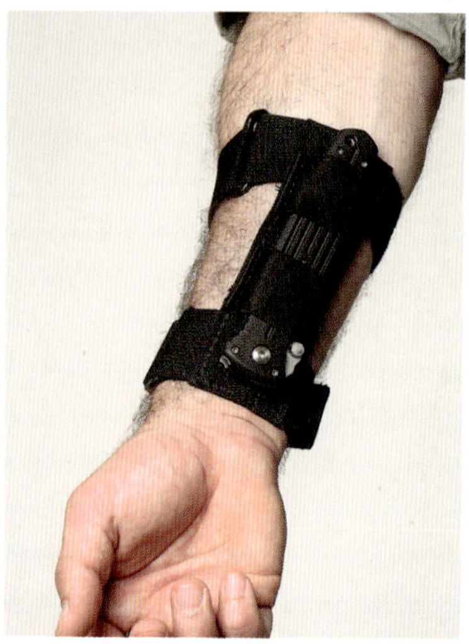

By means of the ammo clip/flashlight forearm carrying system by Blackhawk, a folder, too, can be carried concealed on the forearm without problems.

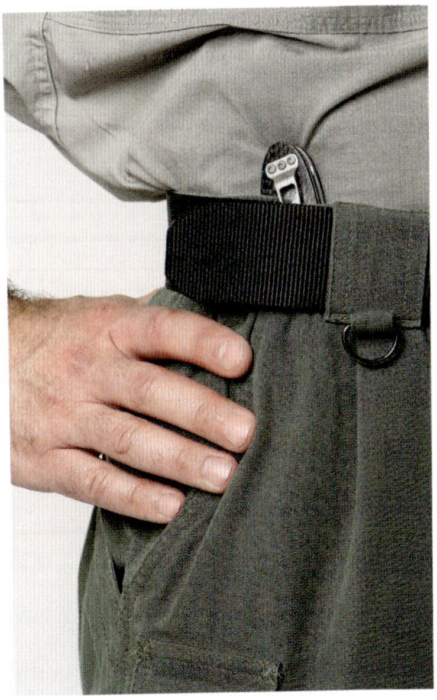

This way of carrying a folder reveals only a small part of its handle. In addition, the clip is hidden unobtrusively behind the belt. Recommended!

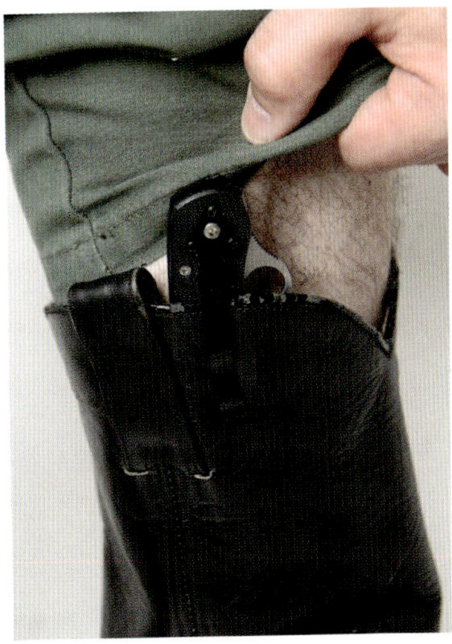

The clip also gives you the opportunity to carry the folder at the boot shaft. Disadvantage: To draw the knife, once again, you first have to lift the trouser leg.

For tip-up carry, braided or knotted cords and laces can be used as an aid for pulling. There are almost no limits with respect to shape and size. Disadvantage: you call attention to your knife.

Freestyle or full contact exercises should always be practiced with protective gear; all the more if the attacker uses a metal training knife. Here, the High Gear protective suit designed by SD-expert Tony Blauer.

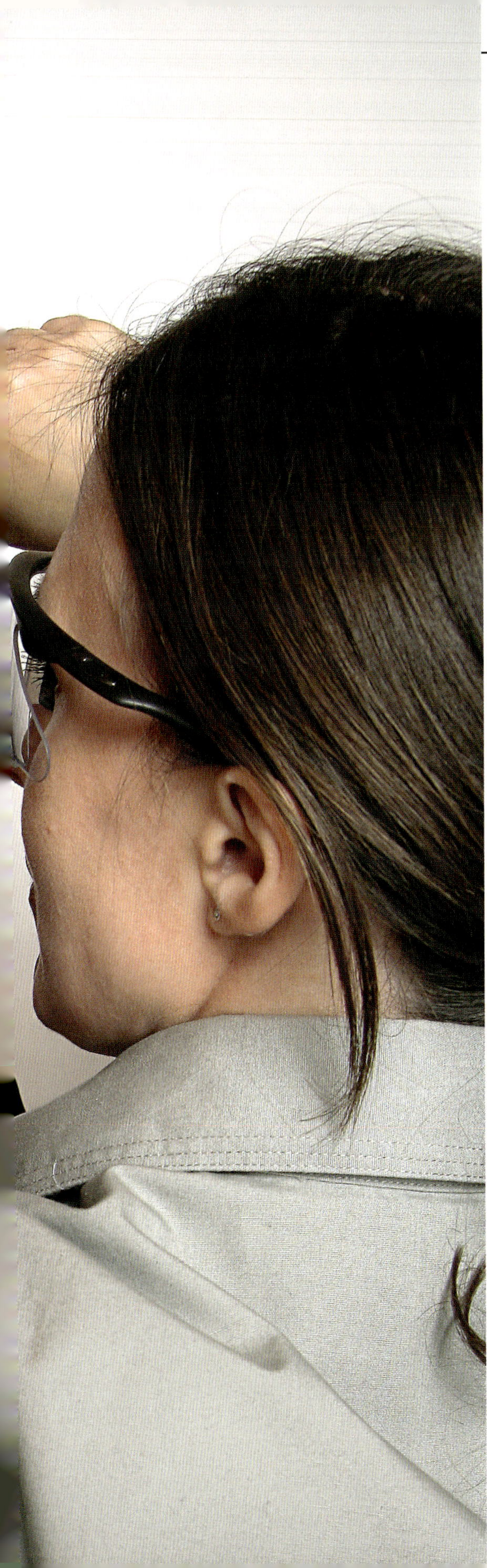

CHAPTER 5
TRAINING KNIVES

While in the past knife combat could only be practiced with training tools remotely resembling knives, or with rubber knives from the toy store, today, a multitude of highly specialized training knives are available. These substantially differ in finish and price. Basically, training knives can be divided into four main groups.

General Training Knives

These are classical examples made from plastics or metal and don't have any real similarity with existing knives regarding the shape of their handles or blades. In the scope of martial arts and SD training, they belong to everyday life.

Plastic Training Knives Made After Originals

These are training knives completely made of plastics that essentially resemble original knives with respect to blade length or handle design. Among the first providers of such knives was Al Mar, with its model AF-AMK RTK. Based on the legendary Applegate-Fairbairn combat knife, Al Mar created their corresponding model from flexible plastic. For marking the hits, the flat sides of the blade should be covered with chalk. After Al Mar stopped production, production of this special knife continued at Böker by Applegate's special wish. Besides this licensed model, other companies such as RAM (Black Training Knife), ASP (Red Training Knife), and Rings (Blue Gun Training Knives) also offer copies of the A-F training knife.

Other suppliers of plastic training knives made after original designs are Cold Steel's trainer models Recon Tanto, Peace Keeper I, R1 Military Classic, and Black Bear Classic, as well as Columbia River Knife & Tool's training versions of their Hissatsu and Ultima models.

During training, the Shock Knife punishes tactical mistakes without mercy. Instead of cuts, you receive unpleasant electric jolts.
Photo Shock Knife

Contemporary advertisement of Al Mar Knives from the early 1990s for the first Applegate-Fairbairn Rubber Training Knife (RTK). To mark hits, the edges are coated with chalk. At right: Shock Knife.

Even though the plastic material of these models is very flexible, a forceful strike against the eyes and face can lead to serious injury. The big advantage of these training knives is in their handling. which is the same as that of the originals. This means you don't have to make do with an unfamiliar handle, but can realistically train, even though the knives do not possess the same weight as the originals. These plastic training knives are affordable and recommendable. The CRKT model Hissatsu additionally comes with a fitting sheath, so that drawing the knife can be practiced without risk as well.

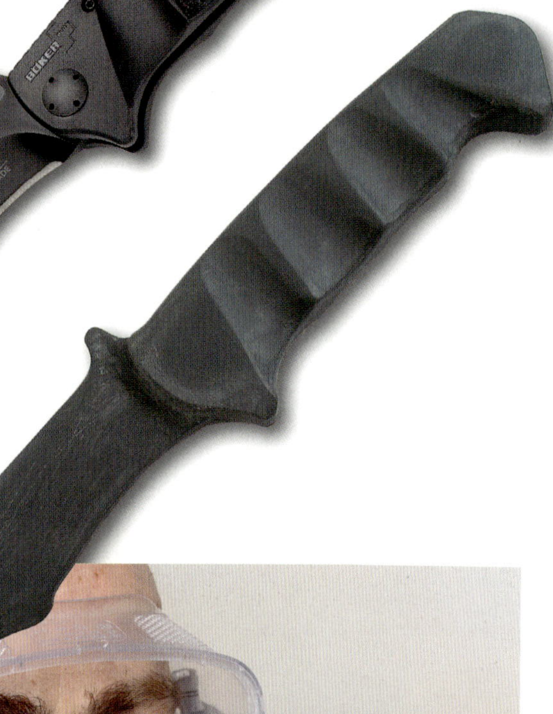

At www.plastictrainer.com Martin Müller offers individual handmade plastic training knives that correspond to the originals in almost all details. Here is an example of the Boker Plus RBB.
Photos Böker Baumwerk, dp

Original Knives with Dummy Blades

These models belong to the upper class of training knives. Here, the manufacturer only exchanges the sharp blade for a blunt dummy of cheap steel. The handling and weight of these knives are extremely realistic. To give the steel blade its proper balance, usually a number of holes are drilled through it. Because of the original clip and locking mechanism, folders can not only train in combat tactics, but also the controlled drawing, opening, and closing of the knife. Knives with fixed blades are also offered by some manufacturers, such as Spyderco, Extrema Ratio, and Benchmade.

To distinguish the training knife from the sharp knife visually, the handle usually has a signal color (red / orange). The disadvantage of these knives is quite often their high price, which frequently equals that of the original knife. Thus, the range of choice is moderate. During practice, even these models with rounded blade tips pose no small danger of injury. One's face is especially endangered. When training freestyle you need special protection for the face.

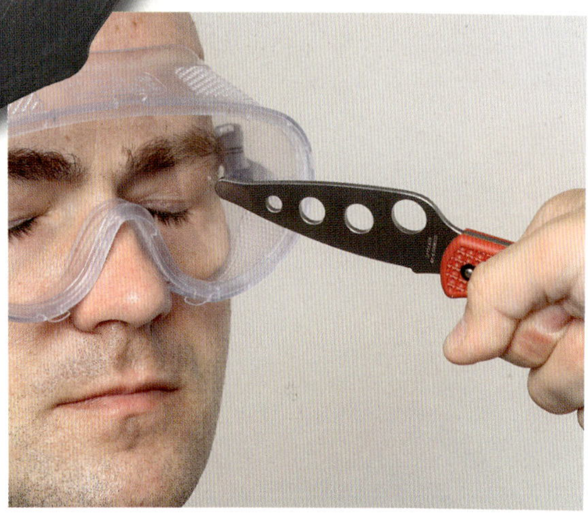

Protective goggles are a must among the basic equipment for knife combat training.

Metal training knives with rubber handles by the French special outfitter GK.

Special Training Knives

For these knives, it's not their accurate resemblance of originals that is important, but their special effects with hits. As an example, two different approaches are introduced here. The Nolie Blade (non-lying blade) is made of aluminum and has a felt edge that can be covered with common lipstick. If the blade hits the body, it leaves a colored hit mark behind. For the target person, it often comes as a shock when he realizes how many places on their body the blade has reached.

A shock of a different kind is provided by the Shock Knife. This is a taser shaped like a knife whose effect can be regulated. Every hit becomes perceptible. As convincing as the Shock Knife is during training, for many people, it nevertheless is out of reach because of its high price. The main customers are government agencies and academies for personal security.

Conclusion

Regardless which training knife you choose, safety during training always comes first. Proper eye protection is an absolute must. Tooth protection prevents unwanted dentist bills and a protective cup prevents you from painful hits in the genital area. With blade dummies of metal, or with the Shock Knife, protective masks covering the entire face are unconditionally recommended for freestyle combat.

With realistic training knives such as the Crucible Training Knife by Blackhawk, drawing and opening an SD knife can be trained under authentic conditions.
Photo Michael Janich

Training knives of different manufacturers and different types (left to right): Böker A-F Training Knife, Ring's Blue Gun Training Knife, and the color-marking training knife Nolie Blade.

Benico Del Toro plays former special forces member Aaron Hallam in the movie *The Hunted*.
Photo Paramount Pictures, Lakeshore Entertainment

CHAPTER 6
KNIFE COMBAT Á LA HOLLYWOOD

One of the most unusual movies ever showing fighting with knives was *Exposure* (original title: *A Grande Arte*), made in 1991. In this Brazilian-American co-production, character actor Peter Coyote plays the role of photo journalist Peter Mandrake, who is forced to fight with a knife during the course of events in the movie. Director Walter Salles Jr. provided his actors with impressive knives. Besides the knives of well known custom knifemakers, products of renowned companies such as Spyderco, Buck, Benchmade, and Al Mar can be seen as well.

Dave Harvey, manager of the company Nordic Knives in Solvang, California, was significantly involved in the choice of the knives. According to his tale, the movie director and his assistant came to Harvey's shop and explained to him that he was on a search for knives for his latest movie. At this time the movie still had the working title *High Art* and was planning for "Easy Rider" Dennis Hopper as the main actor.

The contact with Dave Harvey was implemented by knifemaker legend Bob Loveless. Loveless is the man who leveraged the so-called drop point knives to their breakthrough in the 1960s. Initially, the movie director wanted to have combat and boot knives from his workshop, but Loveless unmistakably made it clear that the delivery times were too long and the budget of the production company was too small for his knives. He recommended Nordic Knives which, as he said, had a great assortment of combat knives and could deliver immediately. Loveless especially recommended Model 14 of Randall Knives, Orlando, Florida. Probably this advice made a special impression on the movie director, because no other knife is highlighted in the movie as much as Randall's Model 14. The knife is also shown in the hand of main actor Peter Coyote in the movie's main advertising poster.

French character actor Tcheky Karyo, who became famous in movies such as *Nostradamus* and *Bad Guys*, plays the role of knife combat trainer Hermes in *Exposure*. He teaches knife fighting to Peter Mandrake. The knife combat techniques and training methods shown in *Exposure* are very realistic and allow the conclusion that the film crew either had a very experienced advisor, or they pored over all the relevant specialist literature.

The used handmade knives were not—like other movie knives—especially developed for this purpose. But this movie is so unusual that the knives and their makers have to be given a closer look. Randall's Model 14 combat knife is especially highlighted in the movie for good reason: it belongs to the most important developments in this area. Late knifemaker Bo Randall, who died in 1989, initially developed this model for the United States Marine Corps, but an official introduction was never made. The knife nevertheless became a legend in the holsters of American GIs during their tour in Vietnam.

Randall Knives, which has produced handmade knives since 1938, offers the Model 14 in two different steel alloys: O1 carbon steel and stainless steel. As a matter of principle, at Randall Knives all blades are forged, ground, and assembled manually. The handle of black micarta—besides the manually ground finger grooves, which promise an absolutely non-slip grip—has a 0.079 inch (two centimeter) deep slot ground for accommodating the tang, with a thickness of 0.236 inches (six millimeters). This system, patented by Randall in the 1960s, guarantees minimal danger of breaking near the handle area. After more than forty years, the Model 14 still lists as Randall Knives's most sold. It is delivered together with a leather sheath of superior quality. The downside: customers have to wait almost five years. But for this, they'll receive a handmade knife of top quality. Besides the Model 14, Models 2 and 18 can also be seen briefly in *Exposure*.

Knifemaker Joe Kious of Kerrville, Texas, is one of the most talented knifemakers worldwide. His knives are perfectly made down to the minutest detail. The Kious fighter that knife combat trainer Hermes wants to buy for a friend and which, in the words of the weapons dealer, is a good choice, belongs to the most beautiful knives of the movie. The double-edged blade of 440C steel has a mirror-polished hollow grind and a ridge masterly polished by hand. The handle is provided with a sub-hilt, providing an inseparable grip on the knife between the index and middle fingers. The handle scales are from carefully selected cocobolo wood.

Like Gary Randall and Joe Kious, knifemaker D'Alton Holder didn't know that one of his knives was taking part in a movie. Only when requests from knife collectors came in did he realize that the knife he had sold to Nordic

James Bowie belongs to the most famous knife combatants in history. Since the 1950s, his life has been the inspiration for many scripts of Hollywood productions. The most famous film adaptation was *The Iron Mistress*, made in 1953 with Alan Ladd playing James Bowie. The knife and knife combat scenes have influenced an entire generation of knifemakers, such as Gil Hibben. His reproduction of the original movie knife on the German movie poster is seen here.
Photo Weyer Studio

Tcheky Karyo and Peter Coyote (at right) in the movie *Exposure*. Although the film was no big success in the movie theaters, it convinces by means of a number of realistic knife combat scenes.

The weapons of both main actors: (left) Randall Model 14 of Peter Mandrake and at right, the Bowie of D'Alton Holder carried by Hermes.

Photo Caliber

Knives had become a movie prop. The knife of D'Alton Holder is the one seen most often in the movie besides the Randall Model 14. It is the personal weapon of knife expert Hermes. The design of D'Holder is a light Bowie knife with a mirror-polished blade of 440C and a Rockwell hardness of 58 HRC. The guard is made of nickel silver and was decorated with fileworks. For the handle, D'Holder used Arizona iron wood which he sort of found right in front of his door. The hunter-Bowie is rounded off by a handle end of steel with underlying red vulcanized fiber. D'Alton Holder was a board member of the American Knifemakers Guild for many years and is well known for his artistically embellished drop point hunters and leather sheaths.

The described knives are by no means limited special editions, such as the knives of the *Rambo* movies, but are from the knifemakers' standard programs. Nevertheless, they are handmade individual items that play an active role in one of the most unusual movies of this genre. Especially important: they are still available for enthusiastic collectors.

Twelve years later, another movie had knife combat as a topic. In *The Hunted*, actors Tommy Lee Jones and Benicio Del Toro had the chance to demonstrate their learned abilities in knife fighting on the big screen.

Benicio Del Toro plays the role of former special forces member Aaron Hallam, who suffers from Post Traumatic Stress Disorder due to events in Kosovo, where he bore witness to the brutal executions of Albanian civilians by Serbian soldiers. More and more he loses his sense of reality and murders two hunters with his survival knife. He thus causes a pursuit that is supported by his former close combat trainer, L.T. Bonham (Tommy Lee Jones).

Joe Kious's sub-hilt fighter can be seen during a short take in the movie *Exposure*, but was not used in any of the combat scenes. In the movie, knife combat teacher Hermes buys it for a friend.

Photo Caliber

The Al Mar Warrior can be seen in the opening combat scene of *Exposure*, but otherwise plays no important role in the movie. Today this rare Al Mar knife is a much sought after collector's item.
Photo dp

Tom Brown's Tracker Knife as a handmade version with wooden handle scales made by knifemaker Dave Beck.
Photo Tracker School

Benico Del Toro and Tommy Lee Jones in the final battle scene of *The Hunted*.
Photo Paramount Pictures, Lakeshore Entertainment

To act the military combat scenes and knife combat techniques as realistically as possible, Benico Del Toro had to undergo specialized training.
Photo Paramount Pictures, Lakeshore Entertainment

In flashbacks, the movie shows how Bonham trains Hallam in knife combat. This knowledge of knife combat was taught to the actors and their stunt doubles by Sayoc-Kali knife specialists Thomas Kier and Rafael Kayanan, who also transferred their expertise to the US Navy SEALs, among others. For the duration of the movie, they trained together for about two hours a day, five days a week. Director William Friedkin wanted the knife combat scenes in the movie to look as realistic as possible and drove the crew to top performance. Tommy Lee Jones later commented that he now knows more about knife fighting than he ever wanted to. But at the same time, he insinuated it was nevertheless fun to really understand the combat techniques shown in the movie. Del Toro said about his role that Aaron Hallam was a knife type through and through, somebody who even in Kosovo would prefer a knife fight over one with firearms.

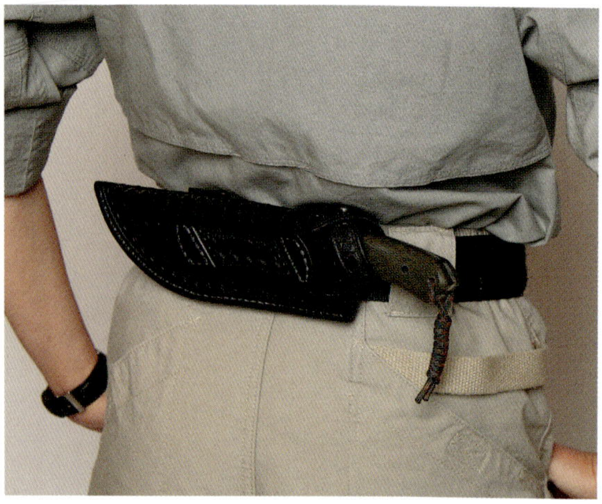

Sheath maker Stefan Kleinhuber created this leather sheath with perfect craftsmanship after an idea from Tom Brown for the Schanz USK.

As a consultant for the knives used in the movie, as well as for tracking in the forest, the well known tracker and survivalist Tom Brown (www.trackerschool.com) was called in. He was also responsible for the design of Hallam's combat knife. According to Brown, it took almost seven years and several prototypes until he developed the perfect survival knife. Long before the movie was made, Brown let former knifemaker Dave Beck manually produce the knife, which is also known under the names WSK (Wilderness Survival Knife) and Tracker Knife. And one of these knives can be seen in the hand of Hallam.

Beck made the knives in several versions distinguished by their different handle scales. At the time of the movie's release, the company TOPS entered the market with serial production of this model, which differs from the original in several points (serrations, handle scales, and coating). As blade steel TOPS uses 1095 carbon steel, which has an enormous edge retention and hardness. Since 2006, TOPS also offers a smaller version of the Tracker.

Besides Hallam's Tracker, several stone knives can be seen in the movie, which were made under the tutelage of Brown. Of course, these samples are mere props. The same goes for a makeshift knife of Hallam's that he forges from old leaf springs towards the end of the movie. Special attention was given to the leather sheaths carried horizontally on the back. Besides the Tracker, Hallam also packs a KA-BAR Next Generation in these sheaths. Their principle is similar to that of a kydex sheath that can be attached horizontally by means of a Tek-Lok. Although the Tracker was designed as a survival knife, it will be remembered as an impressive combat knife by many knife and film fans. Unfortunately, today Beck's original knives can only be purchased via the collector's market and are accordingly high in price. Nevertheless, whomever wants to have a handmade knife according to the design of Tom Brown will find a convincing model of D2 steel made by German knifemaker Jürgen Schanz, who produces the model licensed by Brown under its original name, WSK.

Tracker and Wilderness Survival Knife (WSK) models of TOPS Knives and German knifemaker Jürgen Schanz. From top: Schanz USK (Urban Survival Knife) and WSK and TOPS Knives Tracker Large and Tracker Small.
Photo Thomas Philippi

Another handmade variant of the Tracker model, here with black micarta coating as seen in the movie. The movie model, however, had no hole in the blade and was equipped with a black sheath without accompanying knife.
Photo Guy Curtis

CHAPTER 7
SELF-DEFENSE AGAINST DOGS
by Sohny

As a friend of dogs, I long thought about whether I ought to write anything about this topic at all because, on the basis of my experience gained on duty and privately, I can see that behind every dangerous dog ("problem dog") there is almost always a "problem human." The preventive approach with respect to one's qualification as a dog handler and checks on the characteristic traits of certain dogs make a good deal more sense to me than focusing on violent solutions to avoidable conflicts. But since the world isn't as good as we want it to be and severe dog attacks by dogs socialized the wrong way or purposely drilled for aggression happen just as often as "misunderstandings" between humans and dogs, I have assembled some knowledge on this topic. Especially for the use of knives in self-defense, it is important to me that no disproportionality exists between the "object of legal protection" endangered by the "dangerous animal" and the action of defense. Whoever kills a Yorkshire terrier with a machete does not understand what I mean.

7.1 Legal Basics

When acting defensively against an animal, various legal areas and regulations are touched on, the knowledge of which can protect you from prosecution according to criminal and civil law. In the United States, many of the laws regarding dangerous dogs are regulated by the states, rather than the federal government, and these laws can vary significantly.

In general, some states provide some provision for defending oneself against a dangerous canine that is either threatening your own life or is threatening the life of a domestic animal or livestock on your property. But other state penal codes only address self-defense against another person, and not against animals. In addition, most states also have detailed animal cruelty laws, protecting dogs from aggression. In addition, a federal law protects police dogs: the Federal Law Enforcement Animal Protection Act of 1999 sets penalties for willfully and maliciously harming a police animal.

Because there is so much variation in state laws, it is best to learn the laws in one's state or where one is traveling.

7.2 Psychological Aspects

Attitude towards dogs is decisive for the level of stress which is reached during a confrontation. Because humans and their ancestors during the course of evolution were "prey" for a much longer time than "hunters"—they were rather close to the bottom of the food chain—and were eaten by animals with teeth and claws for millions of years, a more or less pronounced primal fear is evoked when seeing a snarling dog with its teeth bared. The behavior in a life-threatening situation goes from simple "freezing" ("playing possum," practically being unable to act) to "running away," "threatening," and up to (counter-) "attacking." Here, our cognitive ability depends on the individual expectations of what may happen and the current stress level. Thus, it is important to get an adequate "stress injection," which means becoming acquainted with the situation in small doses beforehand so as to react if the real case occurs.

A dog basically sees humans as superior beings, but reacts to certain stimuli with instinctive or trained behavior. During this it evaluates optical, acoustical, and olfactory (smell) signals. The decisive stimulus for an attack can be triggered by the "prey" itself, or by a superior member of the pack (the dog handler). In addition, aggression caused by illness (for example, rabies or states of pain) can also trigger dog attacks.

The ability of a person to defend himself does not depend primarily on him being equipped with a suitable tool, but on the will to defend oneself and one's personal abilities. These derive basically from education and experience. People who are experienced handling dogs will generally be able to cope better with a dangerous situation than those who have never had any relationship with dogs, or have a fundamental aversion to them. Ultimately, it will be your concrete experiences with conflict, or even with being bitten that let you judge the risk correctly. The experience of how you felt after injuries in the past and to what extent you were still able to act at that time is also an important point. Even rarer are experiences with respect to using a knife for killing animate beings. In our culture, it is no longer self evident that somebody will be present when an animal is dying—for example, during slaughtering or dispatching a wounded or sick animal.

Both sides—dogs as well as humans—try to avoid real combat actions for as long as possible by threatening the opponent. Basically, each of the adversaries tries to show itself as bigger and stronger than they really are. Mock attacks are the maximum level of threatening and, of course, are also used for judging expected resistance. Dog attacks without previous threatening behavior are very rare.

To immediately destroy the illusion of people carrying knives: knives are not seen as a potential threat by dogs as long as they have not had any negative experience with respect to them. As long as a human stands upright and appears to be as big and self confident as

The most important rule when fighting against a dog is to protect the hand holding the weapon. It has to be kept away from the snapping jaws of the dog under all circumstances. Photo Frank Melzner

possible (for example, by means of open clothing in a spread-eagled position) and speaks with a firm and loud voice, an attack is less likely than if you run away with a shrill and fearful voice or fall to the ground. It is said that dogs can even smell fear.

7.3 Physiological Aspects

An attacking dog's perception of pain is reduced to almost zero. Thus, injuries which ought to lead to an immediate end of the attack have to effectively reduce or inhibit the use of its fangs and/or its locomotor system. In practice, this is only possible with a knife at the risk of being bitten or seriously injuring the dog.

Like all mammals, a dog is dependent on breathing, blood circulation, and the function of its central nervous system. Death due to external violence is caused by:

1. shock after large blood loss when large blood vessels have been damaged,
2. breathing arrest after suspension of lung function,
3. destruction / damage of the central nervous system.

But death is only an unwanted side effect of the goal, which is "immediate inability to attack." Unfortunately, when using a knife, the latter quite often can't be achieved without accepting the former. For sake of completeness, it has to be mentioned that this descendant of the wolf has developed a killing technique of its own: small prey are paralyzed by biting with the fangs (perforating/squashing the lung and blood vessels, as well as inhibiting the ability to breathe), with subsequent "shaking to death" (breaking the spine, quite often in the area of the neck). Large prey are pulled down by biting their neck/windpipe and subsequently suffocating them.

7.4 The Right Knife

In the realm of hunting, for killing animals prepared to defend themselves, a "cold weapon" with a blade length of at least six inches (15 centimeters) is recommended. For all other cases, the blade length should not be much below four inches (ten centimeters). This doesn't mean you won't be able to kill an animal with a shorter blade: 1.25 inches (three centimeters) of sharp steel is sufficient to open the carotid artery. But under stress and with the goal of quickly causing an inability to attack, a short knife is not recommended. Because of the possible loss of grip due to blood or other fluids, a sufficiently large handle with a rough surface and a secure finger guard towards the blade edge is an advantage. To keep the option of striking with the handle butt, a stable, pointed end is especially favorable.

Because the used techniques are mostly stabs, the blade should taper towards a stable point. It does not matter whether this point lies centrally or is slightly on top of the center line. In order to create the largest possible wound channel, the blade should not be too narrow. It can be useful for the blade to have an edge ground on both sides, at least partially. From a certain length onwards, a knife can also be used for dealing effective blows. Thus, the center of gravity of such a knife should be quite far to the front. Although cuts are a rather rarely used technique—especially for short knives—a high sharpness is of advantage. Whoever has already tried to cut "real fur" off a living animal may have realized that the skin glides over the muscles at many places and doesn't give necessary resistance to such a cut. In addition, the dense hair coat keeps the edge busy for quite a while until it can get to the skin and then further on. It is self evident that a blade should not bend or break. The way you carry your knife should allow you secure access to the knife with both the right and left hand, and while lying on

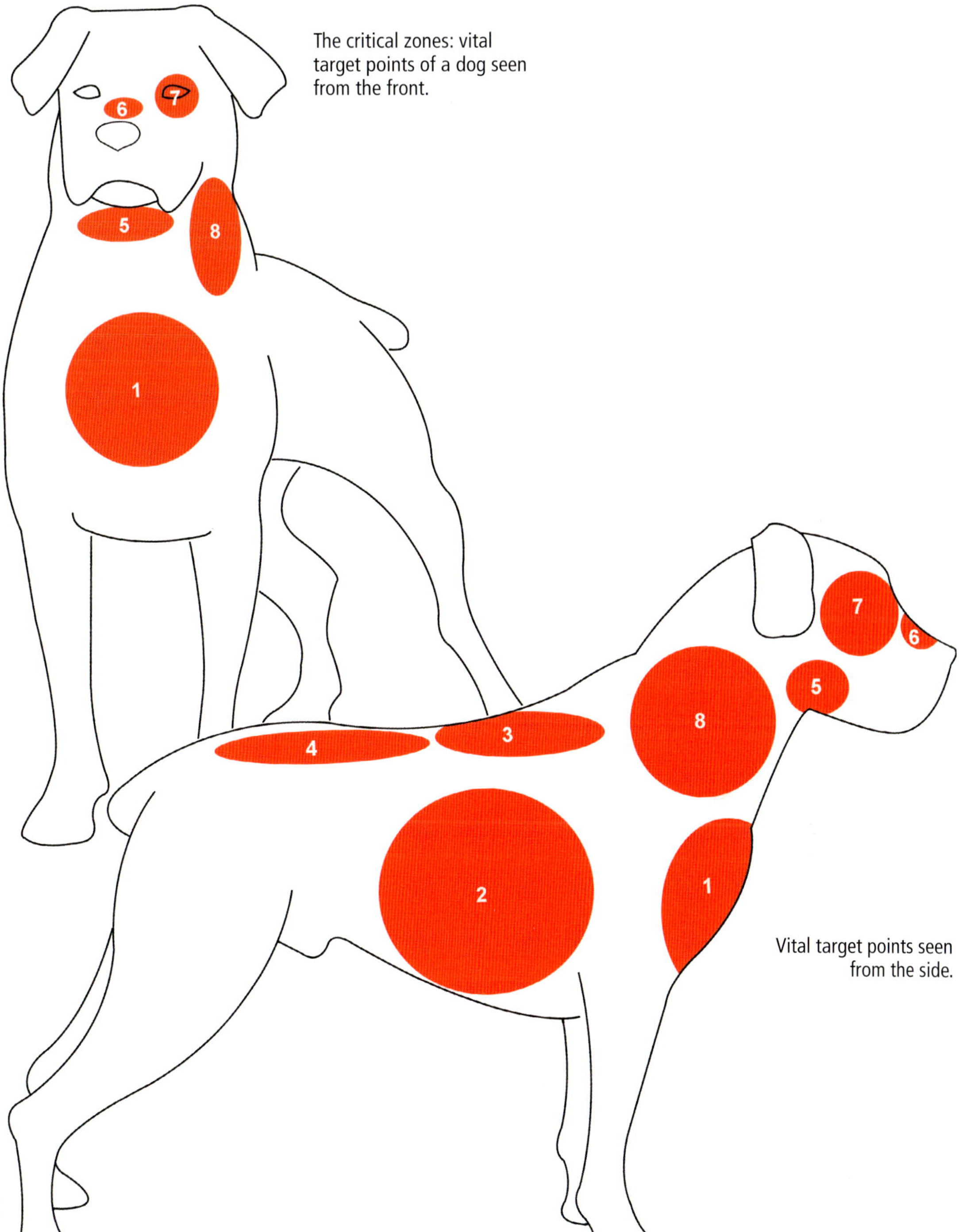

The critical zones: vital target points of a dog seen from the front.

Vital target points seen from the side.

the ground. The knife must not be lost during dynamic sequences. Folders have to be able to be opened with either hand. To enable quick action, closed pouches are less suitable than a clip or a sheath that can be opened single-handedly.

7.5 The Right Tactics

It is said that attack is the best form of defense. The advantage is that you are the one who determines the time and type of attack. You don't get surprised, but have surprise on your side. In reality, this tactic comes into consideration mainly in case you help another person against an attacking dog. If the dog locks jaws on its victim, forceful, deep stabs have to be made into the ribcage from the side to damage the lungs and heart as severely as possible. Depending on the animal's position, you can try to pull it away from its victim at either its legs, tail, or genitals as soon as it becomes aware of its own injuries and turns towards its attacker. The danger of being bitten while doing so is quite high, so you have to protect your hand bearing the weapon!

If you are attacked by a dog, if possible, you ought to offer an object (backpack, bag, jacket, chair), or at least a solid boot or a protected arm as an item to first bite at. It is especially important to not fall down if a big dog jumps at you and to protect your neck, face, and genitals! Regardless of how the first bite turns out, it is unrealistic to think that one bite will be all and external rescue will surely come. Flight will rarely be possible if the attack was a serious one. A dog is far superior in running compared to humans.

To protect your own life, a knife should be used as resolutely and confidently as possible. Depending on your position, you immediately ought to make deep stabs towards the lungs, the big blood vessels, and the central nervous system. This means you have to stab into the chest from the front, the sides, or from above with attacks towards the back, giving the additional advantage of hitting the spine, which in turn may lead to quick paralysis in case you hit the spinal cord. Another option is diagonal, lateral stabs through the lip into the jaw and throat; but here, the danger exists of injuring yourself. With respect to the head, hard blows on the root of the nose with the pommel or deep stabs into the eye sockets or neck are effective, too. As soon as the dog is isolated and no other persons are endangered, immediately retreat into a safe area. Now you have to call for help for all injured parties as quickly as possible. Bites—even if they don't look very dramatic at first glance—always carry a high risk of infection and complications and require medical treatment! For the sake of completeness, it has to be mentioned that quite often dog owners or other people take part in the conflict—and not necessarily in favor of the human!

A fight between a human and a dangerous dog is not a desirable situation. Just the opposite: when using our superior intelligence, it is usually avoidable. But in any case, for dog owner as well as defender against attack, it will be critically examined in court.

Sohny is the pseudonym of an experienced hunter and policeman who was a member of a SWAT team for almost twenty years and thus does not want his real name.

The blade tip of the Brent Beshara model Custom XSF-1 is designed for maximum penetration and doesn't yield to humans or animals.
Photo Brent Beshara, Point Seven Photos

CHAPTER 8
JIM WAGNER'S THEORY OF KNIFE COMBAT

If a person has never used their knife for defense or offense in an actual conflict situation, then everything they have learned, and have practiced, is "theory," mainly because it has never been put to the test. On the other hand, if a person has actually fought someone in a knife situation (successfully or unsuccessfully), or has fended off a knife-wielding attacker, then their experience is "reality"; they have actually put their fighting skills to the test. The person fortunate enough to run away in a knife fight, or who was tragically the victim of a stabbing, indeed has real practical experience, but such experience is limited in value, because they were not actual combatants.

Being in a knife fight alone does not mean a person is adequately trained. Likewise, a person who has studied traditional martial arts may have the skills to protect themselves in "come-at-me-this-way" knife training attacks common in most schools, but may be totally unprepared for an unmerciful criminal knife attack. There are a wide variety of potential conflict scenarios and mitigating factors that make it difficult to train for all possible scenarios. Thus, anything not experienced is theory.

For military police, corrections, bodyguards, security, or civilian protection training dealing with edged weapons, one must train as realistically as possible. There must be the inclusion of Pre-Conflict, Conflict, and Post-Conflict training to have a complete conflict training package. If you come as close as you safely can to real conflict through Conflict Rehearsal (scenario training using actors, realistic training knives, and a realistic training environment), then that is as good as it gets. Short of that, you will only be cheating yourself, and even worse, develop a false sense of security. If you're practicing for a real fight but are coming up to your opponent, bowing, then waiting for the command to start, such as is done in many traditional schools, then that is practice that is conditioning you for an unrealistic situation. Real knife attacks are close, fast, and over before most realize what has happened.

In a real conflict, there will not be such preparatory preludes. Not only is any such training "theory," but it is theory that flies in the face of reality. Even if a student has never experienced a real conflict before, common sense will at least dictate that fights do not start out the way many traditional schools make them. At minimum, one should start by coming up to an opponent during training and start pushing them while yelling, "What is your #@!# problem!," then out comes the rubber or plastic training knife and the attack is violently launched. Such training not only gets theory closer to reality, but it also helps you deal with compressed decision time, which is essential preparation for real-life conflict.

Theory and Practice: Even the most realistic training scenario (here with a color-marking knife) doesn't replace real combat experience.

In a real knife fight, you will only use a few simple techniques. As a police and military defensive tactics instructor for over a decade, I have had the opportunity to talk with at least a hundred officers and military personnel about their personal experiences in edged weapons attack. All of them have stated the same two underlying principles:

- The attack happened quickly, at extremely close range, and their instinct was to get away.
- They did not take unnecessary chances, such as complex moves, performing only simple reactive techniques.

For those of you with a martial arts background, the key to knowing what knife techniques and training methods to keep and which ones to throw out is a matter of prioritization. For example, since I am most likely to experience a simple frontal knife attack in a real self-defense situation when I am unarmed, I will spend most of my time learning to shield my body, move away from the attack, do a tactical "L" if I am pursued, and either escape at this point or launch a counterattack. A counterattack means deploying my own weapon or striking the opponent to stop him. This is all known as Knife Avoidance, and is the first drill in my Knife Survival course.

To have an effective counterattack, you have to stick to simple stopping techniques: a finger thrust to the eye or a bone-breaking kick to the knee. Keep in mind, this is someone who is going to rip you open with a knife. By having only a few core skills to work on, I can keep them fresh.

You have a limited amount of time to train in order to prepare yourself for not only a potential knife fight, but all of the conflict situations you may encounter. Since all conflict skills are perishable, you must prioritize your time and devote yourself to those knife techniques that will contribute to your survival. In other words, do techniques that you are most likely to actually use in conflict.

8.1 The Adequate Reaction

Most martial arts instructors teach their students to defend themselves the moment the attacker attempts a stab or cut with a knife. In other words, you must block the incoming knife and then launch a counterattack. I say that waiting for a stab or cut could be too late; rather, the moment you feel your life is in immediate danger you should launch your attack. In a potential knife attack situation, is waiting for the suspect to make the first move really the best course of action? Is it legal, or moral, to launch a preemptive strike on a potentially hostile subject? Isn't the best defense a good offense?

According to United States and international law, a person has the right to defend themselves

JIM WAGNER REALITY-BASED PERSONAL PROTECTION

The Elements of Attack

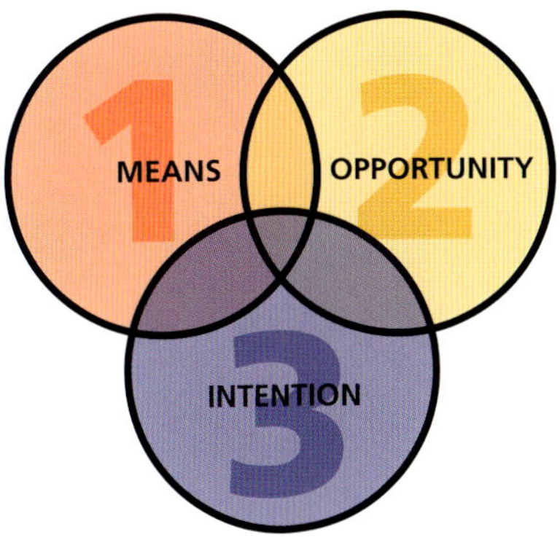

1. **MEANS:** The tools or immediately available capabilities to commit a crime.

2. **OPPORTUNITY:** The Circumstances which make committing a crime look like a profitable things to do.

3. **INTENTION:** The state of mind at the time of the crime. (indicated intention)

Graphic jw

against physical harm intended by another. Like any legal issue dealing with the use of force, it depends on three factors:

- The totality of circumstances
- Means, opportunity, and intent of the attacker
- The "reasonableness" of the force used

Unfortunately, there is no secret formula or equation to determine if defending yourself will be viewed as justified or unjustified in the eyes of the law. The court will first look at the "totality of circumstances." For example, a person may come up and start a fight with you by saying they are going to cut or stab you, but that doesn't necessarily mean you can legally use your self-defense skills on them. The introduction of a knife changes the totality of circumstances dramatically. The aggressor must have conditions immediately favorable to commit the crime. If a man threatens with a knife, but he is in a wheel chair because he is a paraplegic, I cannot start pounding on him if all I have to do is walk to an area he cannot get to.

We cannot know what a person is thinking; however, we can make an educated guess at what a person is thinking (implied intent) based upon the totality of circumstances. For example, if I am at an ATM machine withdrawing some money and a man walks up to me with a knife in his hand, I can reasonably assume he is about to rob me. In situations where the likelihood of minor injuries may occur, one must use *reasonable force*. For example, a ten year old child is throwing a temper tantrum and is flailing away with a knife. Perhaps a good kick might be a better solution than killing him.

No matter what techniques you decide to use to defend yourself in a knife fight, anything you do will be scrutinized, second guessed, torn apart, and cross examined. You're going to have to justify your actions verbally to law enforcement or the courts.

8.2 The Use-of-Force Ladder

It is imperative that you know what you can and cannot do in any conflict situation. This is why I created the Use-of-Force Ladder for Civilian Self-defense™. Although "the ladder" is similar in concept to what military and civilian law enforcement agencies must follow, my ladder is specifically designed for civilians. Like a real ladder you would lean up against a building, the most stable place to be is not on the ladder at all. Once you get on, there are risks—even from one step off the ground you can get injured. Likewise, in daily life you are always safest when you avoid conflict.

Before we go up or down the ladder, you will notice that to the left of the ladder are the subject's actions (your attacker), indicated with a gray triangle, and a vertical arrow next to it with a gradient of colors. The arrow corresponds to the conflict color code system that I developed: secure (white), caution (yellow), danger (orange), and conflict (red).

Secure (White) – staying off the ladder altogether. At this level you are in a secure place: home, work, social events, etc. Conflict is not anticipated.

Caution (Yellow) – This is the level you must always maintain when you are in public. You should always be aware of your environment: people, vehicles, behind large objects, dark areas, etc. This is not a state of paranoia, but prudent caution known as Situational Awareness; that's why the arrow extends below the ladder and into the white area. You should be alert long before you are about to get into conflict. You should look at people's hands because hands are what pull out knives.

Danger (Orange) – At this level there is a real possibility of danger, since the subject is giving verbal indicators: direct threats, suspicious words, etc. The intensity of this Pre-Conflict phase can escalate or dissipate.

Conflict (Red) – At this level you are in physical conflict. Does this mean you can use whatever self-defense techniques you like? No. There are many levels of conflict. Someone who pushes you because they are rude should not be treated like someone who is trying to stab you with a knife.

JIM WAGNER REALITY-BASED PERSONAL PROTECTION

THE USE-OF-FORCE-LADDER

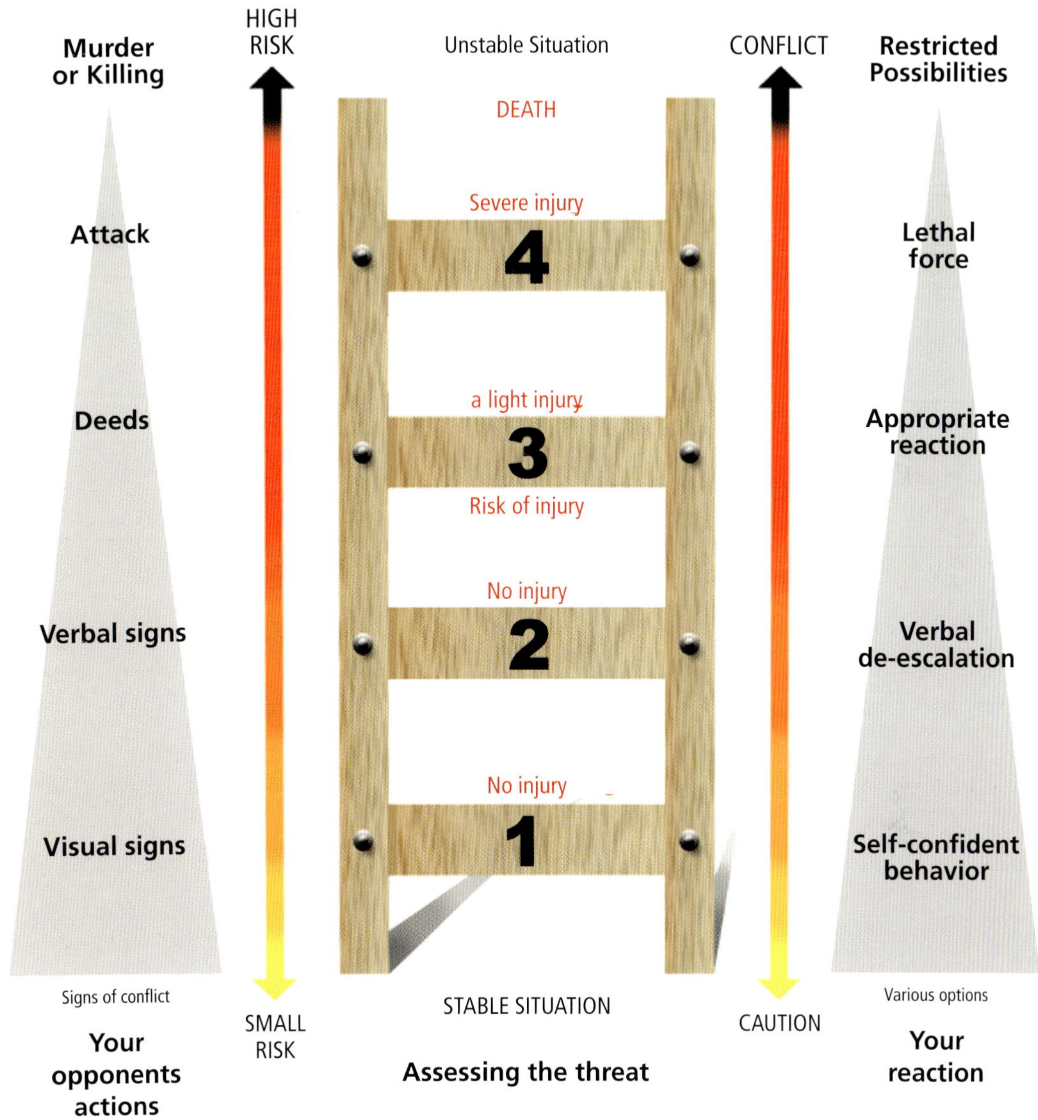

APPROPRIATE FORCE: The kind of force used by a sensible person in a similar situation.
APPROPRIATE REACTION: The way a sensible person would react in a similar situation.
VERBAL DE-ESCALATION: Words or silence used to calm down the situation, not make it worse.
SELF-CONFIDENT BEHAVIOR: Bodily expression of self-confidence and resolution.
THREAT ASSESSMENT: Avoiding conflict situations before they arise.

Graphic jw

Notice that the left arrow of the graph starts at the bottom of the ladder as a low risk situation, then escalates to a high risk situation, while the arrow to the right starts from being cautious to being engaged in physical conflict.

There is good reason why the two arrows in the graph both point upward and downward. That's because a conflict situation may start at any level, at any time. You may find yourself in Code Red without going through all of the previous rungs first. For example: if you're standing on a street corner, making a phone call, and all of a sudden a street person comes up to you waving a knife in front of your face asking for your wallet, you're in the Red zone instantly.

The Jim Wagner Reality-Based Personal Protection Use-of-Force Ladder has four rungs to make use-of-force levels easy to remember. Rung 1 (Level 1) starts at the base of stability and ends at Rung 4, which is an unstable and unpredictable height. Remember this rule: *The suspect's actions will always dictate your actions.*

Level 1

At Level 1, a subject uses visual indicators. In other words, you will feel there is possible danger based on things that you see: a suspicious subject approaching you, somebody who is looking around nervously, or a car slowing next to you. At that moment no laws are being broken by the subject—none that you are aware of—but

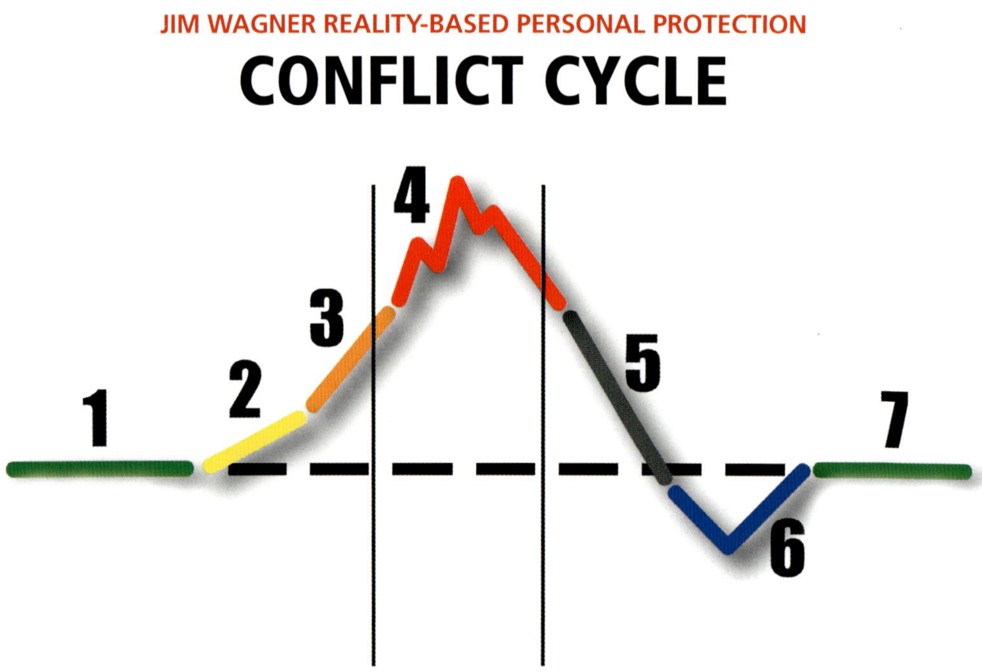

1. **PERCEPTION** The knowledge about the potential risks (preparation by training).
2. **INITIATION** The incident which started the conflict.
3. **ESCALATION** Sudden or stepwise increase of danger.
4. **CONFRONTATION** Preserving the proportionality of means.
5. **STABILIZATION** Escape or arrest, first aid/self-helpf, calling the police.
6. **NORMALIZING** Possible hospitalization, coping with events.
7. **ANALYSIS** Review, learning from experience, adapting into training.

Graffic jw

you know something is wrong, so you prepare yourself mentally for all possibilities. First you take on a confident demeanor (see your reaction under the right gray triangle). This means you look confident and not afraid. Your facial expressions indicate you are aware of your environment and know how to use it to your advantage. Confident demeanor also means you look like you are prepared for an encounter, or you are aware of the danger and you are making a "tactical retreat."

Level 2

At Level 2 things start to heat up. The subject is actively engaging you, or others around you, through verbal indicators. This can be anything warning you that an attack is about to happen, but short of direct threats. The conflict cues can be anything from the subject's tone of voice to implied threats, or even things you overhear, such as suspicious passengers in a train whispering about how "this is going to be a short trip." Those are not alarming words in and of themselves, but with some visual indicators, one might suspect a possible terrorist attack. If a subject is trying to start a fight with you, the best thing to do is to try to calm that person down or ignore them altogether. This is known as verbal deflection. By reacting in this manner, you will not incite the situation any further. However, in some situations, you may have to use a firm, confident voice to talk some subjects down. You may have no choice but to try to intimidate them and try to resolve the conflict in this manner. Words will not hurt you physically, but words will be a good indicator that it may escalate to a physical confrontation.

Level 3

At Level 3 we enter into actual physical contact with the subject or multiple subjects. It may be a precursor push, or a punch to the nose, or it could even be a sexual touch (sexual battery). If someone simply pushes you to intimidate you, or to get you to swing first, you cannot deploy your knife and "go medieval" on the person. If you do, even though you have a right to defend yourself, you would go to jail for excessive force and use of a deadly weapon. This would be "unreasonable force" for the situation.

At Level 3 you can get injured: a broken nose, cuts, bruises, scrapes, soreness, etc., but they are neither serious nor life threatening. If the subject throws a few swings at you because you're throwing him out of your party, you can't cut or stab him—the law won't allow you to do that, even if you did sustain minor injuries from his blows.

Level 4

At Level 4 death or serious bodily injury is likely to result, whether the suspect's, or yours, or someone you are trying to protect. If a suspect does attack you and death or serious bodily injury is likely to result (felony or serious assault), then you have the right to use deadly force. This not only applies to felony or serious assaults against you, but concerns those you choose to protect, as well who are in your immediate presence. If someone is trying to harm a family member or co-worker in your presence, you may (but are not required to) use deadly force. However, if the case goes to court, you will still be judged based on reasonableness of the force. In other words—and remember these words very carefully—you must have fear for your life, or the life of another. If someone is attacking you with a knife and you fear for your life or the life of another, you can use deadly force to stop the attacker.

Notice that the gray triangles start off with broad bases, then taper off to mere points. The right triangle represents the options you have in a conflict situation. When we start off with Level 1, there are multiple options: you can walk away, call the police, yell for help, etc. However, by the time you are engaged in a life-and-death conflict like a knife fight, there are limited options. If someone is trying to stab you, you have basically one option: control the weapon or get far from it. If you don't block the knife or grab the hand that controls it, or even run away, you could be dead.

Realistic knife combat training ought to be practiced under unfavorable light conditions, too.

CHAPTER 9
REALISTIC KNIFE COMBAT TRAINING

One of the most important components of Reality-Based Knife Survival is the concept of "A to Z training." What this means is that all conflict drills and exercises have three stages:

1. a realistic starting point
2. technique performance
3. a reasonable finishing point.

This concept can best be illustrated with an actual incident that occurred in Canada several years ago. A uniformed Canadian police constable was on patrol and he was an avid martial artist. A criminal came up to him and pointed a live pistol in the constable's face. Before the suspect could pull the trigger, the officer flawlessly did a gun disarm technique and safely pulled the weapon from the suspect's hand. Tragically, without even thinking, the constable handed the loaded pistol back to the suspect a few moments later, just as he had done hundreds of times before with his training partners. Without a word, the suspect gladly took the weapon back. When the constable realized what he had done, he immediately tried again to retake the weapon. Unfortunately, the second time around the suspect pulled the trigger and sent a bullet smashing into the constable's shoulder. Luckily, the constable had the will to survive and keep fighting, despite his injury, and he managed to once again pry the pistol from the suspect's hand and take him into custody.

So, why did the constable give the pistol back to the suspect after a successful gun disarm? That's right, you guessed it. The constable had made this move repeatedly during training and ended up falling back on his training in a real incident. He properly conditioned himself to disarm someone pointing a gun at him, but unfortunately, he also conditioned himself to hand it back to his training partner immediately after the technique was performed. His muscle memory (repetition that commits a movement to be a conditioned response) inadvertently conditioned him to give a dangerous gun back to a suspect.

Whenever you practice any conflict technique, you should always perform it from start to finish—from A to Z. Rather than stopping the technique during training and handing the training knife back to the "suspect" (your training partner), you must complete the action to a "reasonable" conclusion. In a real situation, you would not intentionally hand the weapon back to the suspect. In any real situation, you are going to take self-preserving action: running away, using the disarmed weapon against the criminal if he is still coming at you, using the handle of the knife as a weapon, or discarding the weapon in a safe direction.

You must not develop bad habits in training. You must think about what the final moves should be to end up in a safe position.

9.1 Compressed Decision Time

You've heard it said that "90% of a fight is mental and 10% is physical." I agree with this proverb. It's comparable to driving a car. The actual physical movements of steering, braking, and accelerating are easy movements to learn and master. The hard part of driving is the constant scanning for dangers, obeying traffic rules, and reacting instantly to constantly changing road conditions. Plus, it's one thing to drive on a quite rural road with little to no traffic, but exactly the same skills can become quite a daunting task if one is immersed in the bustling traffic of a major city.

When it comes to conflict training, it's important for the participant to get off the "rural road," so to speak, and to test one's skills in the "fast lane." In a real conflict a bar fight, a single mugger, or an aggressive pan handler represent the proverbial rural road. Conflict involving weapons, multiple aggressors, or acts of terrorism are situations that induce what we in the Special Operations world call compressed decision time. This is the fast lane of martial arts. These are information overload conflicts where things happen fast and furious, and where there is no single focus luxury, but rather multi-tasking.

The reality-based method for simulating compressed decision time is done through an exercise called the Conflict Immersion Exercise. The wonderful thing about this exercise is that anyone studying self-defense can duplicate it any place at any time. All you need is a paper bag, a cord, a puller (a trainer), and a little creative conflict rehearsal (role playing).

You start by taking an ordinary paper bag and punching a hole in the bottom. Next, you run a cord into the hole and duct tape the end of the cord to the bottom of the bag. You then place the bag on top of the trainee's head and the rest of the cord runs to the puller (a trainer who pulls the bag from the trainee's head when the signal is given by the instructor).

While the trainee has the bag over his/her head, a scenario begins in close proximity while the trainee is "blind." The scenario can be whatever one wants it to be. For civilian training scenarios, the trainee can be in the middle of a knife fight. The point is that the trainee has no idea what they are going to face and what they are going to have to immediately deal with, unless there are some audio cues. More importantly, the trainee has no idea exactly where the threat will be or at what distance.

The puller, who is directly behind the trainee, immediately yanks on the cord and pulls the bag off the trainee's head at the instructor's hand signal. In a split second, the trainee must find the threat and take action. This requires scanning the area and identifying the immediate threat, yet not forgetting there may be other threats. This is compressed decision time.

The scenarios can also be set up to allow for more reaction time or less, attacks that require distance coverage, or people who are right in the trainee's face when the bag is removed.

For those already employing reality-based training, the scenarios can include "shock factors" when the bag is removed, such as gruesome wounds (stage blood and moulage), fog from a fog machine, and actors who have been hidden and then reveal themselves looking like the real thing: gang members, bikers, terrorists, etc. Ultimately, the more involved and realistic the scenarios are the more accustomed the trainee will become to the bombardment of stimuli in complex conflict situations, because that is exactly what a knife fight is—a fast-moving complex situation.

How will you perform at the moment of truth in a knife attack? What's going to happen to you emotionally when you're facing the real possibility of injury or even death? Will you have the will to survive, or will you be so paralyzed with fear that you hesitate during the first few critical seconds of the fight—or worse yet, you can't move at all? The answer is, you won't know until you can say, "Been there, done that."

To properly deal with a potential knife attack, training is the only way to properly condition oneself. When the human body is subjected to extremely cold temperatures there are predictable physiological conditions that occur: the body pulls blood from the limbs and concentrates it in the inner core, giving warmth to vital organs. This makes digits go numb, reaction time slows, fine motor skills are reduced, and the thinking process is dulled.

In an actual knife fight, the body can experience similar stresses like those of cold: fine motor skills give way to gross motor skills, breathing becomes rapid and shallow, and reaction time may be slowed. To simulate this stress in training takes nothing more than cold water. In the privacy of your own shower, turn on the cold water and let it run down your entire body while holding onto a rubber training knife. The sudden shock to the body is close to the shock you'll experience when you're in a knife fight, or any high risk conflict situation for that matter. The shock of the cold water, like conflict stress, makes the body take shallow, rapid breaths. Under such conditions it's hard to carry on normally, but that's exactly what you have to train yourself to do.

When you're standing in the stream of cold water, the key to mind and body control is to slow down your breathing by taking deep, controlled breaths and exhaling in a rhythmic pattern. Warriors and many martial arts masters have known this for centuries. The better you control your breathing, the more relaxed your muscles will be and the clearer your thinking will be. Depending on how cold the water can get, you may have to build up your tolerance a little each time. Your reward will be a warm shower afterward.

Fatigue, like cold, is a demoralizer. When you are extremely tired even simple tasks become difficult. In a knife fight, it is easy to become exhausted very rapidly, especially in a prolonged conflict, or if injured and losing blood. Most fights that I have been in have ended in a matter of seconds. The average knife fight lasts only five seconds, but there is a possibility that energy was expended prior to the blade coming out, such as in a situation where an escape was attempted, running a fair distance. Depriving yourself of sleep and forcing yourself to do knife defense techniques is another way to prepare you for conflict stress.

9.2 Training Conditions

A Reality-Based Personal Protection Training Facility looks nothing like a traditional martial arts school. The walls are bare and they are painted flat black. Every inch of the room is painted black: the walls, the ceiling, and even the floor. The reason for this is simple. We treat our training area more as a theater stage than a display case. Once the training room is completely black, all light leaks must be sealed. The room should be like a cave when the instructor turns out the lights. A blacked out training area is much more conducive to low-light scenarios and space manipulation, and can even give the feeling of infinite space if spot lighting is done correctly.

You must not only think of the floor as an area to stand on, but as another element to enhance your scenarios. The best type of training surface for the Knife Survival course is concrete. However, when it comes to any type of ground training—and there are a few exercises in the Knife Survival course that require participants to practice on the ground—mats are an absolute must for safety. The roll-out type or puzzle fitting mats work best. Traditional martial arts schools usually have permanent mats fastened to the floor and in many cases they are too spongy, and thus not acceptable. Fixed mats can easily be damaged in Conflict Rehearsal, because participants usually wear shoes during scenarios or use props that can tear the surface.

When you are doing your Conflict Rehearsal, or even your basic knife techniques, throw some cardboard boxes, newspapers, boxing gloves, striking gloves, or other "soft" materials down on the floor. We call these items "clean debris," because there are no sharp edges to fall onto and no biohazards (rotten food) or chemical hazards (detergent residue) on them. This will simulate an obstacle-filled environment. Such training helps you learn to maintain balance should you step on something or trip. This will also make you more aware of your surroundings in a conflict situation.

Proper attire is an important element in creating realistic Conflict Rehearsal scenarios. For the trainee, the proper clothing to wear is whatever clothes they would normally wear for a given situation. If the scenario calls for the trainee to be walking down the street, then street clothes would be the proper attire. Plus, the season and the time of day or night must also be established. If the training facility is cold and you are simulating night or winter, then warm clothing should be worn. This will help the trainee learn how to deal with bulky and restrictive clothing during a knife fight. If the scenario calls for a warm spring day, then light clothing should be worn—even sandals and shorts if need be.

The whole point is for the trainee to feel like they would in a real situation. If I'm training soldiers or SWAT operators in Knife Survival, I would not have them practice in comfortable workout clothes, but in their actual duty gear. I expect no less from my civilian students. Of course, safety gear can be worn under the "costume" or over it. Even if you wear a full protection suit, oversized clothes can still be slipped over it to give visual realism. Plus, when the conflict training gets a little rough and clothing is torn, the sound of ripping cloth is a sound that participants want to get used to and not be distracted by it.

For the attacker, the clothing has to be more creative. If a scenario calls for three gang bangers (trainers) to jump the trainee and stab him with a knife, then the trainers need to look the part. Let's face it, we all judge people by their clothes and the accessories they wear. If I see three clean-cut men in business suits holding briefcases as I'm about to pass them, I may not have my guard up as much as I would if three skinheads were about to pass me.

9.3 Simulated Wounds

One of the greatest training aids for injuries is stage blood; the same type used in theatrical productions and Hollywood movies. I started using stage blood in self-defense training back in 1991, while training law enforcement and military personnel. Later on, when I began teaching civilian seminars, I carried the concept over with tremendous results. For anyone who has gone through my Reality-Based Personal Protection Knife Survival course, they know firsthand the physical and mental impact that stage blood has on training.

In one drill that I created, I have students stand in the corner of a room and I pour stage blood all over their hands. Then I have an attacker trap them in the corner and start pumping a hard plastic, rounded training knife into them like a criminal would straight out of prison. The defending student is shocked at just how hard it is to grab onto the attacker's wrist and arms when slippery blood is present. Of course, that is exactly what it will be like in a real knife fight. Blood will be present, and most likely it will be your blood.

The purpose of using the stage blood—whether in knife defense training or other forms of training—is twofold:

1. Students learn how to deal with the physical properties of blood, which is slippery when wet and sticky when drying.
2. Students get used to the sight of blood, which will reduce the shock factor when they see it all over themselves in a real conflict.

One of my New York instructors that I trained named Fernando Figueroa taught me a clever trick that I now use often in my Defensive Tactics course. It is called the Foot Injury Simulation. This may be in a situation where you tried to kick the knife out of the attacker's hand, or you're on the ground, trying to keep the knife-wielding attacker away while bicycle kicking, and your foot or toes get cut. What I do is place a small rock in a student's shoe at the bottom of the sole (I train only with shoes and boots for realism, never barefoot) and make them fight with the discomfort of the rock digging into the bottom of their foot. The students are very much aware of the pain and avoid putting pressure on it, just as one would do in a real situation had their foot been cut. Needless to say, kicks and stance stabilization have to be modified.

The reason I include such graphic props like stage blood in my training is not to make my students think they are seeing real blood, but to get them used to the idea of seeing such sights—to make it routine. After all, in a real knife fight there will be torn flesh and blood everywhere. God forbid one of my students actually does experience a knife fight, but if he or she does and they see the blood everywhere, they will think, "It looks like stage blood." The carnage won't be such a shock to them and they can get on with the business of survival.

Another trick I do in wound simulation is to tie a student's hand to their belt. That's right—a belt (in the reality-based martial arts we wear street clothes in training). By tying the hand in place it immobilizes it, simulating the paralysis that could occur as a result of a deep knife cut into the tendons or muscles. A student learns very quickly how to compensate for the loss or they end up getting pumped or cut to ribbons.

It is imperative that you not only accept the fact that you may be hurt in a real knife fight, but it is prudent to include practical applications into your own training as I have described. If you don't do it and the real event takes you by surprise, it will be too late to learn what you need to learn. Training for injuries now will help you reduce conflict technique times and prepare you psychologically for the trauma that may come upon you. This kind of training is standard fare for law enforcement and combat military training, and it should be a part of your knife training as well to help you become more reality based.

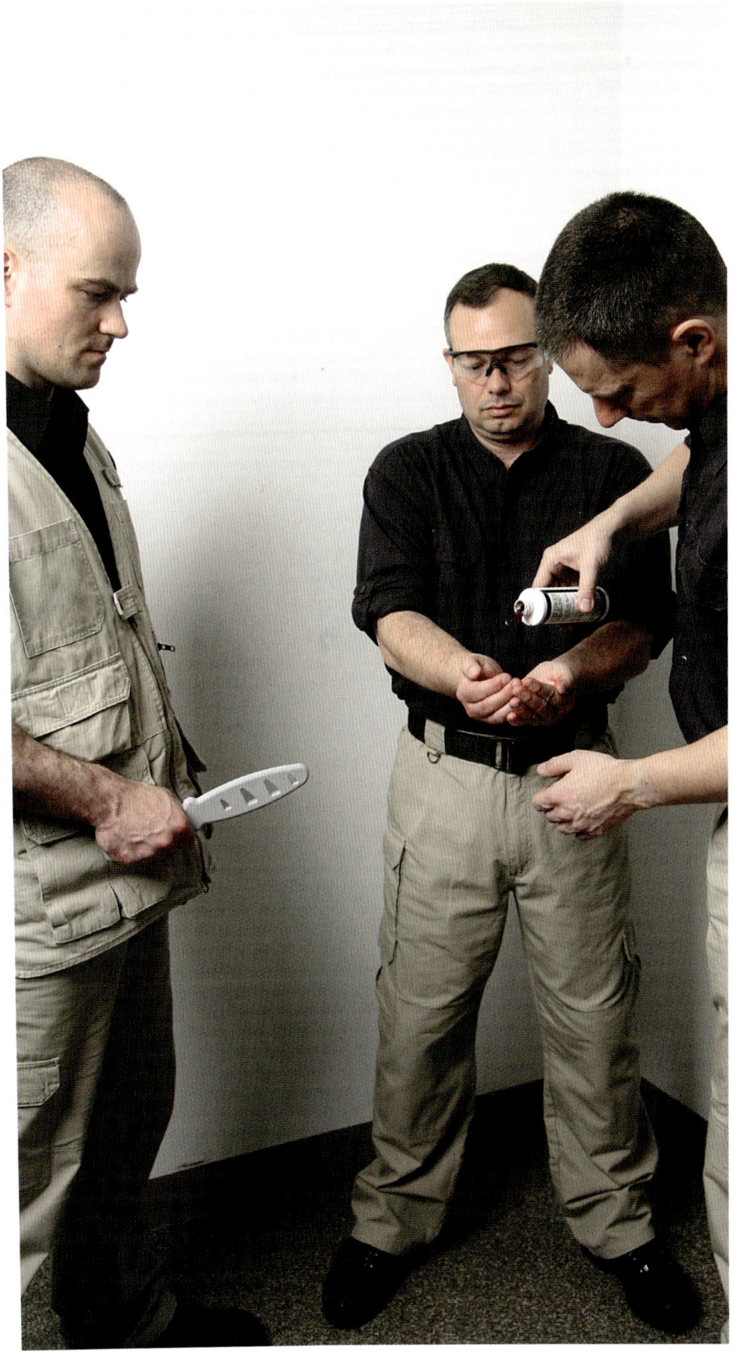

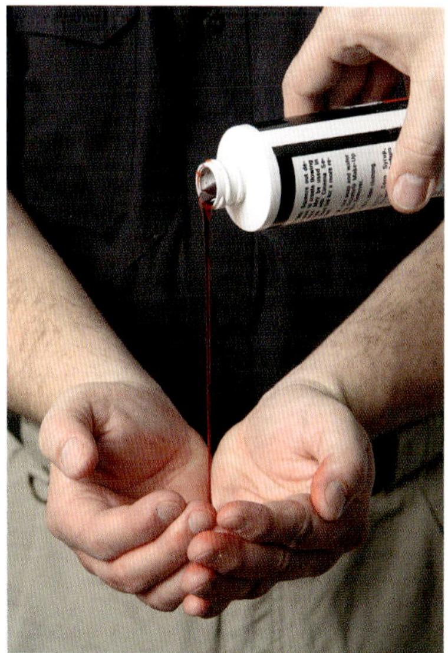

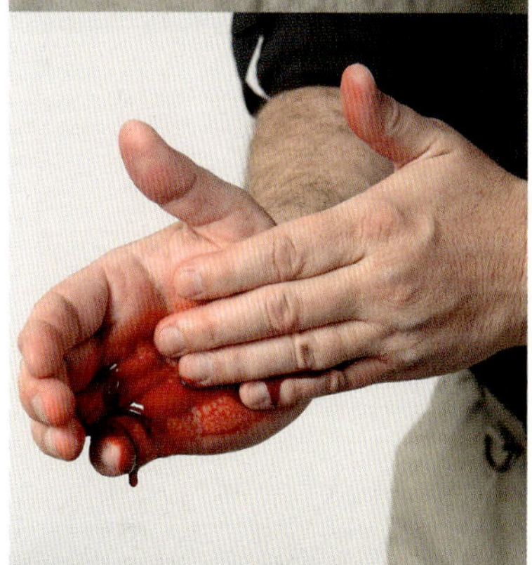

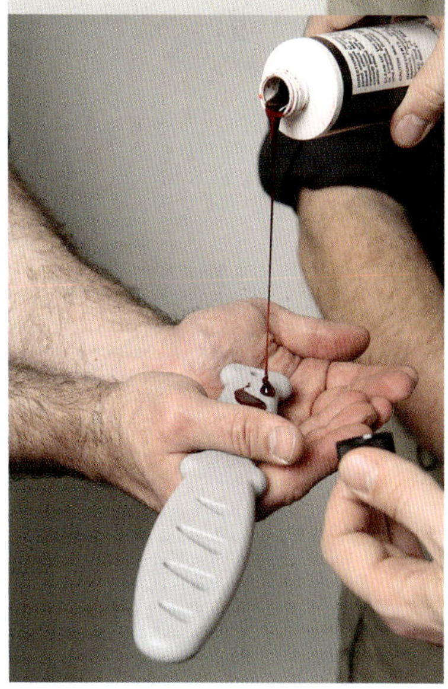

Stage blood is applied to the hands of the trainee. It represents the blood you have on your hands after coming into contact with the blade in a real fight. Your hands are sticky with blood, which doesn't run all over the place. The hands of the trainer are also covered with blood. After all, he probably also will come into contact with blood in a knife combat.

Preparing the color-marking knife: lipstick is rubbed onto the edges and tip of the felt. It represents the blood in case the marked area hits the body of the trainee.

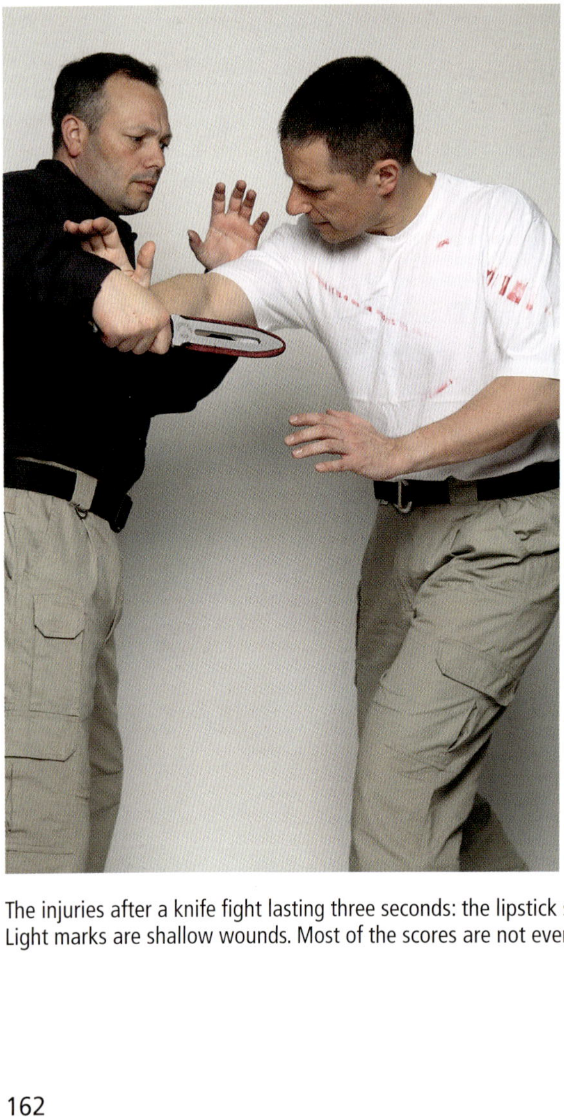

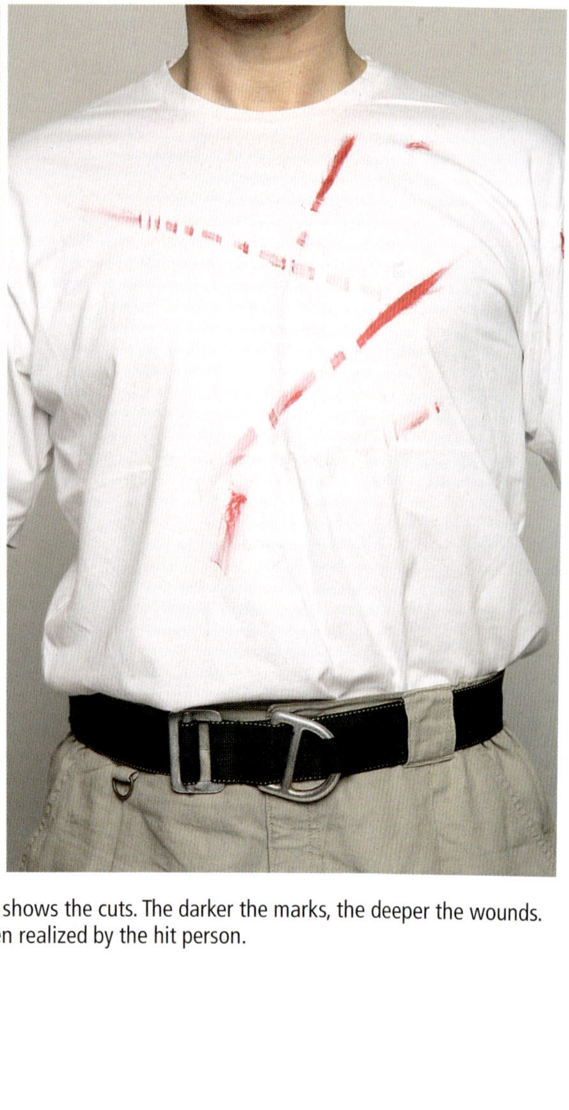

The injuries after a knife fight lasting three seconds: the lipstick shows the cuts. The darker the marks, the deeper the wounds. Light marks are shallow wounds. Most of the scores are not even realized by the hit person.

TRAINING SAFETY TIPS

Knife Survival training can be dangerous if you do not take the proper safety precautions:

1. Never use live blades (weapons that can actually cut or puncture)!

2. Use the right training knives for the right exercises. For example, I have my students use soft rubber training knives for exercises requiring a lot of repetition. This will prevent blunt trauma on stabbing techniques and prevents arms from getting beaten up on slashing and blocking moves.

3. For disarm training, a ridged, thick plastic knife (rounded edges and tip) works best. Both the attacker and the defender will know by feel the exact placement of the knife as the technique is performed. Soft rubber knives bend too much to know if a technique is truly effective.

4. For any training involving your training partner's face as a target, eye protection is mandatory. A pair of inexpensive protective goggles found at any hardware store work well for this purpose, providing full wrap-around protection.

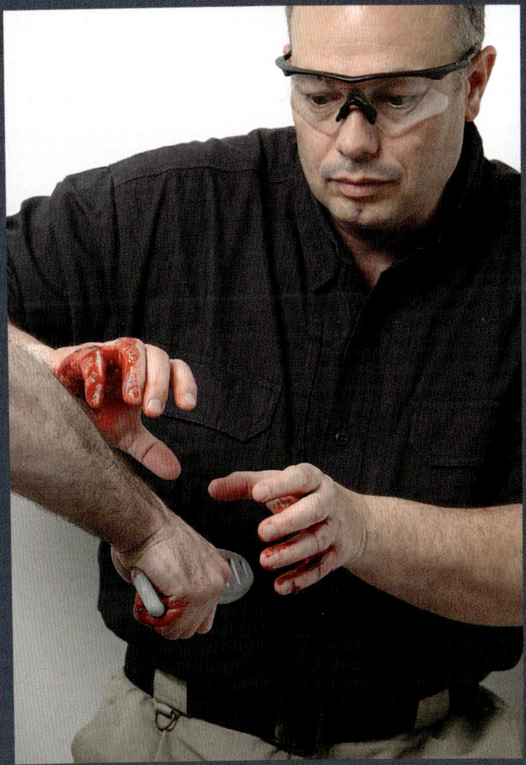

The right gear is a must: head protection or at least protective goggles are imperative.

Soft or not? Depending on the exercise, the training knife has to be more or less flexible.

CHAPTER 10

KNIFE COMBAT TECHNIQUES

Knife combat techniques also include protection with improvised cutting and stabbing weapons, such as a broken bottle.

10.1 The Ten Directions

There are ten primary striking and blocking directions: forward, backward, vertical, horizontal, and diagonal on both sides (see pages 168 and 169). Of course, circular movement has its place in the Jim Wagner Reality-Based Personal Protection system as far as movement and delivery, but an actual impact on the target will make contact in a primary direction line. The ten directions cover every conceivable way to come at the human body. In a knife attack, your attacker is going to send his blade your way on one of these planes or directions. Likewise, if you are armed with an edged weapon yourself, then you will follow these primary angles of attack (the physics term for attack is used here).

We assign each primary direction a number. A numbering system is put in place to make it easier for the instructor to instruct. It's a lot easier to say, "Come at me with a number nine" than to say, "Come at me with a diagonal strike, from down to up, from right to left" during a demonstration.

To understand the numbering concept I created my own numbering system and designed my own graph. Similar graphs have been in print for approximately 500 years in one form or another, and references to these same angles have been made by many cultures: the Roman army, Apache Indian warriors, European fencers, ancient Filipinos, and others. To use the Primary Knife Striking Directions graph, all you have to do is face the graph with your training knife in hand and follow the directions of the arrows with the corresponding numbers. There is a graph for right hand usage and one for left hand usage.

Direction 1, making sure you are holding the knife with a good fist grip, point up (the preferred grip of the Reality-Based system), is a straight stab—the forward direction. The target you penetrate can be the opponent's neck, chest, stomach, or wherever, as long as it is a forward thrusting movement.

Direction 2 is a strike backwards, if someone is behind you and you don't have the time or space to turn around as human nature dictates to you. Therefore, the striking surface is the butt end of the handle of the knife, or if you happen to be using the fist grip, point down, the point is already pointing rearward as the strike is made.

Directions 3 and **4** are horizontal cutting movements, or jamming the point into the target if the point is intended to be used that way.

Directions 5 and **6** follow the vertical plane—up and down—and can be a slicing action or a stabbing move, depending on the position of the blade.

Directions 7 and **8** are diagonal strikes coming downward on the "X," and **directions 9** and **10** are upward diagonal strikes using cutting actions, or sticking the point into the intended target.

It takes knowing how to strike someone with a knife using the ten primary directions to know how to defend against such attacks. The good news is that there are only ten directions a person can throw at you. With a little practice, no attack coming your way will be a surprise to you, and you will at least know how to deal with it.

2
3
4
5
6
7
8
9
10

JIM WAGNER REALITY-BASED PERSONAL PROTECTION SYSTEM
Basic Stabbing-, Cutting- and Blocking Directions
RIGHT HAND
BACKHAND
5
FOREHAND
8
7
4
1
3
2
10
9
6

Graphic jw

JIM WAGNER REALITY-BASED PERSONAL PROTECTION SYSTEM
Basic Stabbing-, Cutting- and Blocking Directions
LEFT HAND
BACKHAND
5
FOREHAND
7
8
3
4
1
2
9
10
6
Graphic jw

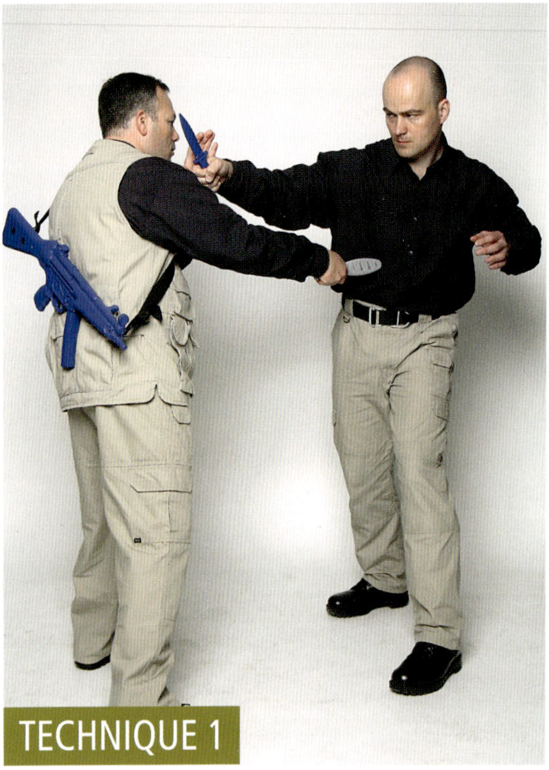

Technique No. 1 (on all photos executed with the right hand by Jim Wagner, grey training knife) is a straightforward stab. Target can be the eye, throat, chest, abdomen, or any other body part in a straightforward line.

Technique No. 2 is a backwards stab. It aims at the head of the opponent and uses the knife handle as a baton for hitting.

Technique No. 2 can also aim at the ribs or the body's center. Definition: every stab backwards is a type-2 technique.

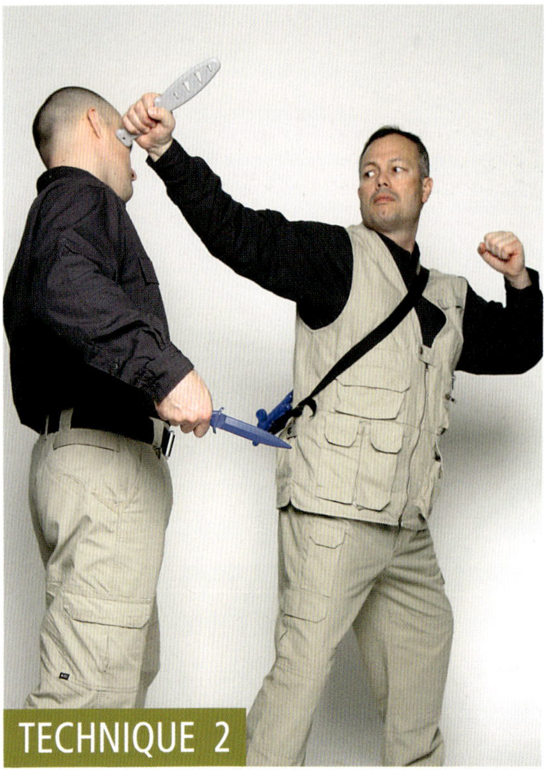

Technique No. 3 is a horizontal move from right to left. It can be executed cutting or stabbing.

Technique No. 4, too, is a horizontal move, but from left to right. You can use it for cutting (as shown in the photo below) or penetrating the target with the blade tip.

TECHNIQUE 5

Technique No. 5 is a vertical cut downwards. It can aim for the head or the shoulders or, as shown here, block the attacker's arm.

Technique No. 6, too, is a vertical movement, but is executed as a straight upwards hit.

Technique No. 7 is a diagonal movement from the upper right to the lower left. Depending on the desired effect, you can use it for cutting or stabbing.

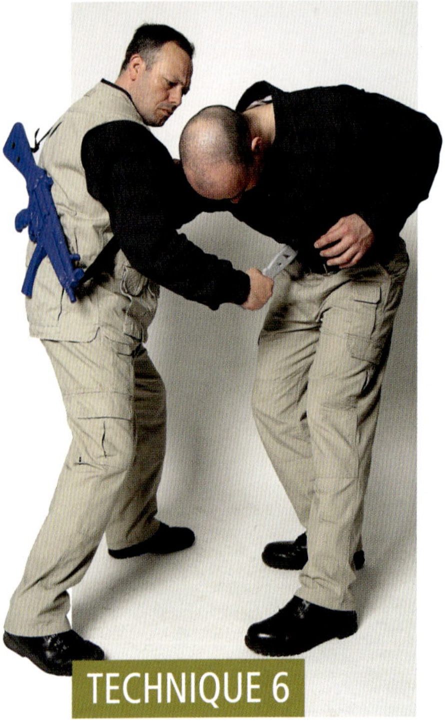

TECHNIQUE 6

TECHNIQUE 7

TECHNIQUE 8

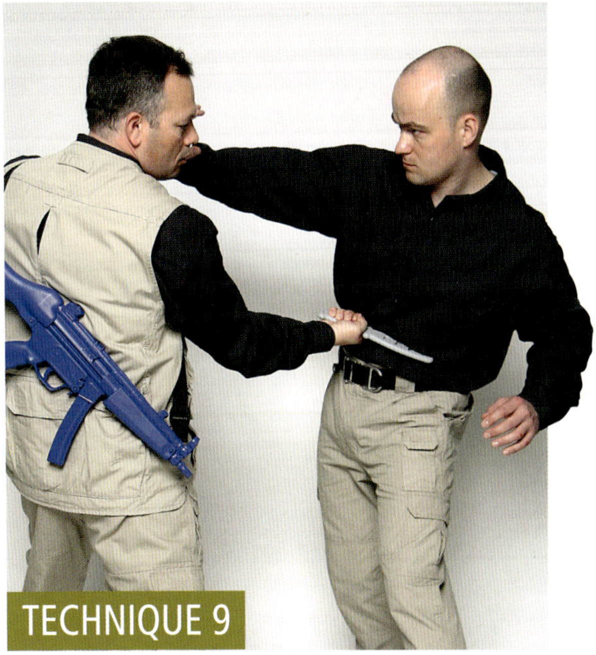

TECHNIQUE 9

Technique No. 8 is also a diagonal movement, but from the upper left to the lower right. You can use any part of the knife for hitting or cutting.

Technique No. 9 is a diagonal cut from the lower right to the upper left. All diagonal cuts follow the "X-pattern."

Technique No. 10 again is a diagonal cut, but from the lower left to the upper right. You can use the blade edge or tip. In the photo, the cut leads directly to the arm of the attacking opponent.

TECHNIQUE 10

10.2 Theory of Combat Techniques

In order for knife strikes to be truly effective in actual conflict, there are three principles that must be applied: technique train, stopping power, and target acquisition.

Technique Train

This term refers to the step-by-step order, or "train," that every technique follows. In the case of closed-fist arm strikes, the train is as follows:

Conflict Position: For any technique to work properly, it must be initiated from the proper position. We use the term "conflict position" instead of "fighting stance," because the word "fighting" indicates premeditation towards physical contact, whereas "conflict" does not necessarily indicate a physical altercation, but also refers to lower levels of the Use-of-Force Ladder, such as confident demeanor or verbal deflection. As always, we must remain cognizant of the words we use, since we will inevitably end up facing law enforcement officials and the judicial system when we use our martial arts skills for actual self-defense. With that stated, the body's weight is distributed 50/50, the body is bladed, and the arms are up (the lead hand on the center line just below the chin, like the sights of a firearm, and the rear hand floats around the cheek).

Hand Position: The fist is closed tight by curling in the fingers and thumb over the handle of the knife. The tip of the knife is for penetrating and the edge of the knife is for cutting.

Line of Trajectory: The knife travels in a straight line from Point A (the launch point) to Point B (the impact point).

Recovery Phase: After contact with the target, the striking arm is retracted and cocked again for the follow through technique (combinations until the threat is stopped).

Stopping Power

In the world of firearms, the bigger a bullet is, and the more grains of smokeless powder it has to propel it, the more "stopping power" it has when it slams into body tissue; so too for knife strikes. The goal in any conflict is to "stop" the aggressor, not kill him or injure him (although knife strikes may be the consequence of such an attempt). Therefore, if you want to guarantee your knife strikes will stop a hostile opponent, you must strike him hard. In other words, it is better to stop the aggressor with one or two good cuts or slashes than to give him the opportunity to continue fighting.

A concept that I developed for thrusting knife strikes, and one which all of my students easily adapt to, is the Piston Concept. If one were to take an honest look at the art of striking, the ten strikes all utilize one main mechanical function—a straight line path, just like the powerful piston of an engine. Whether the knife strike is on a horizontal path or coming straight up into the lower ribs (Vertical Knife Strike), the Piston Concept simplifies the motion and emphasizes the power stroke.

Target Acquisition

Target acquisition is a military term that means accurate detection and locking on to a target. It does little good to strike an area of the body with an edged weapon that is not likely to stop an aggressor. In a knife fight, the primary targets are in the "red zone." The human body is divided into zones based on targets that inflict the most serious injuries upon contact. The red zone is the head, neck, torso, and front pelvic area. The orange zone is the inner arms and inner thighs, where the arteries are likely to get cut. The yellow zone is the outer part, including the limbs and fingers. Cutting or stabbing in the yellow zone is not likely to stop an attacker.

The right target is decisive as well: striking the surface of any target does little good. The goal of any knife strike is to drive through, or penetrate, the target. This requires an aim point beyond the visual part of the target. This is why it is important that the stance is close to the opponent. Knife fighting is "up close and personal."

A word of caution: it is not safe to strike your training partner with a training knife using full contact, because injuries are likely to happen. I never let my students go beyond 75% force, especially if the training knife is rigid, such as a hard plastic or marking blade.

So, how does one learn to develop stopping power and target acquisition with a knife? The

Fist grip with the blade facing upwards: the recommended grip type for Jim Wagner's Reality-Based Personal Protection System.

Fist grip with the blade facing downward: a recommended alternative which is used by many armed forces worldwide.

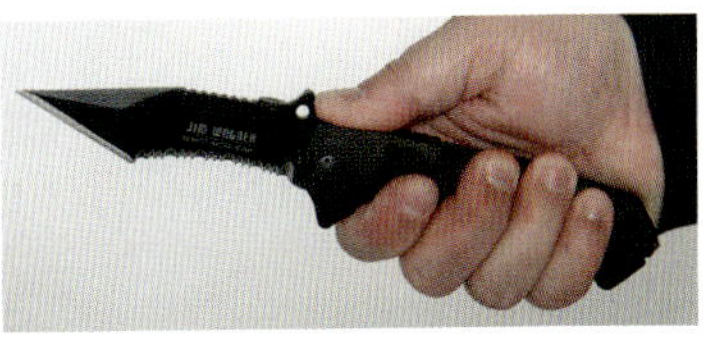

The fencing grip or Hollywood-style grip is the most popular, but is not recommended, because every free piece of the grip is a weak point.

This position for the upcoming conflict is the one recommended in Jim Wagner's system. The body side with the weapon is withdrawn in order to protect the knife.

The position for the upcoming conflict is like a boxing stance; the feet are shoulder width apart. This gives optimal mobility as well as ease.

During the combat, the defender may move the knife forward. It ought to be up high enough to protect the body, in case the opponent hits with a knife.

answer is in properly using a heavy bag or training mannequin. Rather than going up to the bag or mannequin and practicing your knife strikes, like a boxer does when he is practicing punches, it is best to approach the training device as a real confrontation. Create a conflict scenario in your head (Conflict Rehearsal) by deploying the knife and striking the bag or mannequin as if it were a real knife fight, and only as long as a real conflict would actually last (typically under five seconds). Then, once you have your pause in conflict, simulate taking this person down, making a citizen's arrest, or escaping, but don't just stand there playing with the training knife. You are conditioning yourself not just for the striking phase, but the complete A to Z conflict phases. In other words, never get "comfortable" around your bag or mannequin, but always treat it like a real person who is an actual threat. That way you condition both mind and body.

10.3 Automatic/Instinctive Blocks

If I took a swing at your head with a broken beer bottle, your natural instincts would force you to raise your arm in order to try to block it, whether it is your free arm or weapon arm. It doesn't matter which angle I would come at you, your abilities to block would suddenly be excellent.

As we discovered with knife strikes, there are only a few strike planes; an attacker is going to strike you with a forward strike, a horizontal strike, or a diagonal strike if he or she is facing you. Blocking an incoming object or knife is a natural reaction. In my courses, I'll pick a student and start trying to hit him with a rubber baton or plastic baseball bat. I don't tell them how to block it, they just naturally do it in order to avoid being hit. Of course, every student I do this to ends up using simple forearm blocks. They don't ever try anything fancy.

Let's face it, in a real knife fight you are only going to block once or twice, if at all. You cannot win a fight being defensive. Sure, you may have to block if you find yourself in a sudden attack, but in order to survive, you must switch to an offensive mode or an escape mode.

In blocking—whether against arm strikes or weapons—you are going to follow the exact same planes as the striking planes: forward/back blocks, vertical blocks (up and down blocks), horizontal blocks (left and right blocks), and diagonal blocks ("X" blocks). These fundamental blocks are also known as primary blocks. If you count them, there are ten, thus the Jim Wagner Metric Striking and Blocking System. Your blocks will either be inside blocks (movement toward your center line or center mass) or outside blocks (movement away from your center line or center mass).

Whether I'm instructing soldiers, police officers, or civilians, it takes less than an hour to practice and perfect the blocks. There is no such thing as "advanced blocks," just as there is no such thing as "advanced knife strikes." If you try to do some fancy block in a real knife fight, you're going to be stabbed or cut. It's that simple.

Jim Wagner in a defending stance with raised knife.

1 An attacker can be blocked by going up against him frontally (direction 1) and braking him. But this is no real blocking.

2 Direction 2 moves backwards away from the attacker. Here, too, he is not blocked. But sometimes moving backwards is the best method to avoid injury.

3 The defender blocks horizontally inwards (direction 3). Each blocking movement towards the center line is seen as blocking inwards. In the situation shown, the knife itself is providing the block.

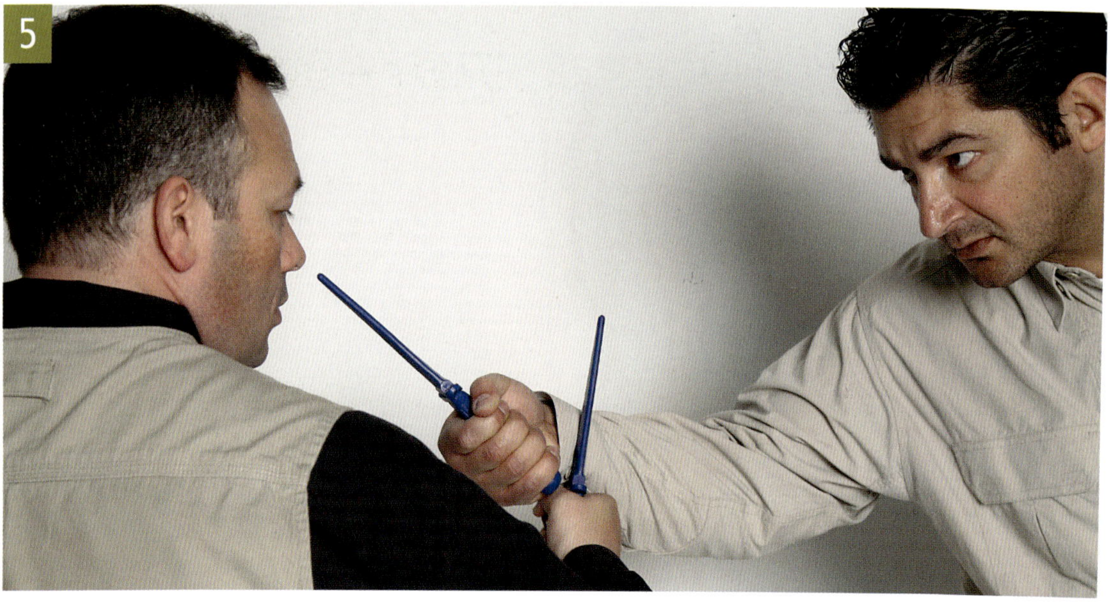

4 For horizontal outwards blocking the movement goes away from the center line. Here the opponent attacks at angle no. 4 and is blocked by technique no. 4 (horizontal from inside left to outwards right).

5 The same technique, but from right to left (direction no. 3). Here, too, the block is done away from the body's center and horizontally outwards.

6 To block a vertical attack from above, the defender blocks upwards with technique no. 10. The blade is held at a slight angle so the attacker's blade will slip off in case it hits one's own blade.

7 The attacker thrusts upwards with his knife. The defender blocks him in direction no. 5 (vertically downwards).

8 If the opponent attacks with a diagonal movement, the defender also has to block diagonally. Here, he blocks upwards from the inside outward (direction no. 10).

6

7

8

9 The attacker thrusts diagonally, but with a fist grip and the blade is facing downward. The defender blocks in direction no. 8 (from above left to the lower right).

10 There are four diagonal directions of thrusting. Here, the attacker thrusts from direction 7 (upper right to lower left) and the defender is urged to block in direction 10 (from lower left to upper right).

11 The attacker uses a diagonal inward hit (direction no. 3) and the defender blocks him diagonally downward in direction 7 (from upper right to lower left).

9

10

11

10.4 Ground Knife Survival

In most knife conflict situations, the ground is the last place you want to be. You can end up on the ground because an opponent forces you there (a takedown), or you inadvertently trip and fall. Either way, once committed to *terra firma*, you're forced to give up several key tactical advantages that you would normally have in a standing position: loss of mobility, loss of retreat and escape, loss of long range striking capabilities, and almost always the loss of the conflict element of offense. Since many conflict situations do end up going to the ground—whether intentionally or unintentionally—you ought to devote time and energy in order to learn how to fight from the ground.

Establishing a ground survival program is more than just a matter of taking your current ground fighting training and putting a training knife in your hand, but rather, adhering to elements that make the training truly reality-based. I've listed ten elements that will help achieve this goal:

1. Although in a real knife fight you're probably going to be fighting on a hard surface, you still need to train on mats or other soft surfaces for safety. However, instead of always laying the training mats out flat, build a plywood slope or put items under the mat (such as kicking shields, boxing gloves, etc.) to make a bumpy, uneven surface. Another suggestion would be to cover your mat with sandbox sand, party ice, or other clean debris (clean empty plastic bottles, newspapers, used clothes, etc.). By adding "garnish" to your mat, you provide a greater degree of realism, and it will condition you to fighting on "contaminated surfaces." Plus, the clean up afterwards is minimal.

2. Military operators and police officers are always training in "low-light" scenarios. You should do the same, since most violent crimes against persons occur during darkness. When practicing your ground knife survival techniques, try turning the lights completely out from time to time, or dimming them to low levels. This will simulate a dark alley, bar, nightclub, or even your home when awakened by an armed intruder.

3. Wear what you'll fight in. If you're a police officer, security guard, soldier, ambulance driver, or another type of professional who is subject to a knife attack, practice your ground knife defense in full gear: ballistics vest, gun belt, boots, etc. If you're a civilian who lives in a cold climate, try out your knife techniques wearing a winter coat, gloves, and a hat. If you're only training in comfortable workout clothes, then you're going to possibly be handicapped when a real situation arises. By wearing the clothing that you will most likely have on in a physical conflict, you will discover real quick what part of your gear gets caught and what restricts your movement. The purpose is to find these things out during training, not in an actual knife fight.

4. Practicing knife strikes from the ground is just as important as learning them from a standing fighting position. Learn to strike from your back and sides. Use striking gloves, kicking shields, and other striking devices. The key to striking with a knife from the ground is to rotate or torque the body into each strike.

5. Incorporate arm and leg strikes into your conflict rehearsal along with the knife techniques. Whenever your training is on the ground, do not limit your striking techniques. Obviously, contact should be light to medium, but it needs to be done in order to promote muscle memory (a law enforcement term that means developing automatic responses through repetitive movement during training). Protective gear must be worn to protect the "attacker" when practicing strikes to the face with a training knife.

6. Incorporate fight-for-the-same-weapon training into your ground survival training using a rubber, plastic, foam, or marking training knife. I start my students out on the ground, having them place their hands on the same knife handle, and on the command of "go" they are to take the knife from one another and try to use it against one another.

7. How do you simulate someone who is under the influence of a mind altering drug or violent from ingesting alcohol? It's simple: make sure the "attacker" (your workout partner) is fresh and rested before a match, while you've done some calisthenics or have taken a run

until exhausted. Then you return to the mat to grapple with your energized opponent, who is armed with a training knife. This simulates the strength and energy that a person will have when they are under the influence—especially hallucinogenic drugs. Sure, it's unfair, but that's reality. It's this kind of knife training exercise that is going to save your life one day, because you'll be able to go the extra distance even when you feel you have no more strength.

8. Try multiple attackers while you're on the ground. The thought is scary, but you have to train for it. If you want to see if your ground tactics are capable of getting you out of a bad situation or not, go up against two opponents, where one or both of them are armed. What ends up happening is that one attacker will be able to hold onto the victim while the other stabs the victim (a situation you may find yourself in when attacked by gang members, since they jump their prey in packs). The key to survival is to use fast and effective techniques and to get to your feet as soon as possible (ground recovery). In a real knife fight, you cannot afford to roll around on the ground.

9. I have one training drill that I teach in my Ground Survival seminar that actually makes the training feel "life threatening," but it is a fairly safe exercise. The name of the exercise is Freestyle Ground Knife Attack. The trainee is lying on his back, wearing eye protection and completely unarmed. The trainer is mounted on top of the trainee and is armed with a rubber training knife. The trainer then starts stabbing and cutting violently. The trainee does nothing more than try to disarm the opponent, except this is performed on the ground. The main goal of the trainee is to control the weapon hand and then get the attacker off and escape.

10. In a real knife fight you can get seriously hurt, so how does one go about simulating injuries in order to learn how to keep pressing on in spite of them? The way I do it is rather crude, but effective. As fighters are grappling on the ground we will suddenly pour a bucket of ice water over them when they least expect it. The sudden shock to the body due to the extreme cold simulates the instantaneous shock one would experience when wounded: the breathing becomes rapid and shallow, clothes get wet (just like they would from blood and sweat), and muscles of the body tense. Sometimes I will simulate injuries by shooting the students with paintballs or plastic air gun pellets while they are on the ground grappling. The students wear only eye protection, a T-shirt, and workout pants.

The instructor will take aim and shoot each student once from across the room (never shoot someone with these training devices at distances of ten feet or less); he tries to aim for a limb. The sudden sting of the projectile as it impacts accurately simulates the instantaneous pain associated with a stab wound. Although the sudden shock is enough to make anyone want to writhe in pain, students learn to override their natural instincts and continue the fight until they are victorious, or are able to escape. In both training exercises, learning breathing control and how to keep the mind focused are the keys to overcoming pain in combat. Such realistic training reinforces what we peace officers call "The Will to Survive."

1

1 The attacker approaches the "victim" rapidly, draws his concealed knife, and attacks. Here, the trainee has to learn to fall backwards the right way.

2 For this purpose, the trainer pushes the trainee so that he loses balance. He ought to go down to the ground as if he had stumbled.

3 To fall backwards the right way, the trainee sits on the ground behind him, pulls his knees up to his chest to not fall onto the back of his head, and prepares himself for the fight.

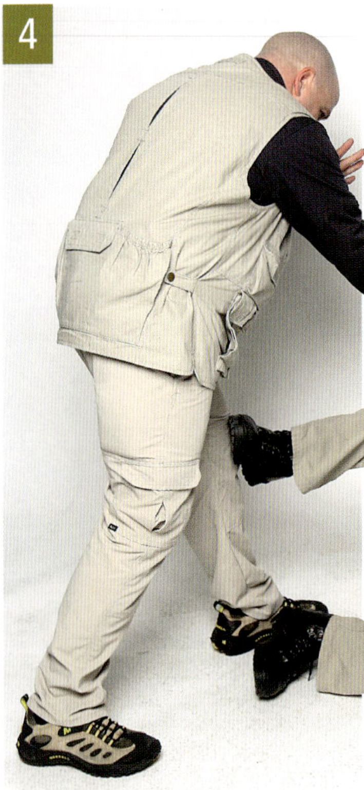

4 To keep the attacker away, the defender has to kick as hard as possible against his knee and shin. During training, only light contact is made while wearing protective gear.

5 A hard kick against the knee can already be enough to immobilize the attacker.

6

6 Even when the attacker wants to step behind the defender, the defender has to continue kicking against the knee and shin to stop the attack.

7 By kicks against the lower extremities, you keep the attacker at a distance.

8 If you are lying on the ground and are attacked with a knife, the "bicycle kick" with both legs is also recommended.

7

8

9 If you are armed, you have to keep the attacker away from you as long as you need to draw the weapon for self-defense.

10 The defender on the ground (in a real situation) wants to break the knee or shin in order to win time to stand up (get up from the ground).

11 Standing up during a knife fight looks easy, but is extremely difficult unless the opponent stumbles or is injured.

9

10

11

10.5 Surmounting Barriers

Let me ask you a question—is everyone an expert with a knife? The answer is yes. Everyone, from every culture, is a knife expert. As children, all of us learned growing up how to cut our food and we knew how much force it took to spear it before putting it into our mouths. Knives belong to our everyday life. They are tools that all of us are very familiar and comfortable with.

Knowing that everyone is an expert with a knife means that you never, and I repeat *never*, underestimate someone who is armed with an edged weapon. Although everyone is a knife expert, not everyone is a knife fighting expert. Learning to be a knife fighting expert in order to protect yourself and others is not difficult, but it does require you to overcome some psychological obstacles.

By nature, human beings are reluctant to pierce the body of another person in combat. This "psychological block" in a self-defense situation can be disastrous. The ancient Romans were aware of this reluctance, and it was well documented by the Roman historian Vegetius. Early on in the empire's history, it was observed that most of the soldiers engaging in close quarters battle were slashing with their short swords, rather than thrusting. Enemy soldiers were being wounded but not "stopped." Cuts and slashes seldom kill, but penetrating thrusts are often fatal. The Romans began an aggressive training program emphasizing a quick thrusting technique. The re-education paid off, and the Roman army's military exploits are now legendary.

In 1787, fencing Master Domenico Angelo (considered the first instructor of modern fencing) wrote: "You cannot practice the thrust too much, it being the most essential and the most superior technique that is made in fencing."

Why do human beings find it difficult to stab someone? One reason may be that stabbing is up close and personal. Lieutenant Colonel Dave Grossman, author of the world famous book *On Killing*, called it "intimate brutality." For the average person, knowing that there is a natural resistance to stabbing a fellow human being is the first step in overcoming the "problem." Greater effectiveness in self-defense situations can be achieved through proper training.

One exercise I have my students perform in my Knife Survival course is an exercise I call the Multiple Stabbing Exercise. Student A is armed with a rubber training knife. Student B holds a kicking shield in an upright position. Upon command, Student A "pumps" the knife into the shield without stopping, pushing Student B backward (the manifestation of aggression and dominance). Student B slowly walks back, absorbing the blows with the shield. As Student A has Student B "on the run," Student A continues to thrust and retract the training knife, all the time giving a fierce "war cry." The students will move both forward and backward (tactical retreat), covering a total distance of twenty-one feet seven meters). Not only does this exercise instill the idea of multiple thrusting moves, but it also helps develop endurance and the "warrior spirit."

Another exercise (one that best simulates lethal force conflict) is called the Standing Free Style Drill. Two students are each armed with rubber training knives (a knife-to-knife fight), and each is equipped with wrap-around eye protection. The goal is to "fatally" strike the opponent with a thrust to the torso area, or inflict a slash to the jugular of the neck (the one sure fatal slash). When the command to start is given, the students must defend themselves from each other freestyle. In order for a student to "win," the student must successfully thrust the weapon into the opponent's torso, making the rubber blade bend.

Upon retraction of the weapon, the student must get out of the "kill zone" before becoming a casualty himself; in other words, "a mutual kill" will eliminate both fighters. If a student loses his or her fight, or they both lose due to a mutual kill, I always punish the loser(s). Losing is unacceptable, because losing in the streets, jails, or on the battlefield means losing your life. Thus, I have the losers go to the left side of the room, where they are required to do a few strenuous exercises. Once punished, they are "forgiven" and able to rejoin the class. This may sound a little bit strange, but it immensely supports the learning process.

When my students do the Standing Free Style Drill, I never stop the conflict when a fatal blow occurs; I let the students continue to engage each other for approximately five seconds longer after I first see the fatal blow. I do this for three reasons:

Reason One: if you stop students every time there is a fatal blow, they will end up doing the same thing in a real life situation. You fight like you train. You don't ever want to stop and give up in a real encounter, and you learn this only through proper training. Even if you think you may be mortally wounded, whether it is because of pain or fear, you never stop. A strike to a fatal area does not mean it will be fatal. However, giving up will definitely turn fatal. If you stop in training every time you're on the losing end, the same may happen in a real encounter.

If your attacker sees you hesitate, stop, or give up, another natural human phenomenon kicks in called the chase instinct. It is the instinct to take down anyone who runs. A good example of this is when a mean dog threatens you. Most of the time you can intimidate the animal and it will back down. Start running, and even the smallest dog will chase you. The same holds true for humans. Most killing done on ancient battlefields occurred while the enemy was in retreat (a sure sign of weakness and defeat).

Reason Two: Immediately stopping a fight after "scoring a point" gives the student a false sense of security, leading them to believe that "it is all over" just because the opponent got a good hit.

Reason Three: In a real life situation, an attacker is still capable of fighting even after sustaining fatal wounds. For example, if the jugular (one of two large veins in the neck) is severed, the attacker may still have five seconds or more of blood supply to the brain and keep attacking; just enough time to seriously injure you or take your life. Therefore, stopping a training match immediately after a fatal blow would negatively condition the fighter. Anyone who mortally wounds another must be prepared for the possibility of an extended fight. It's never over until the attacker is rendered unable to fight.

10.6 Correct Avoidance

The first defensive move you should employ in a surprise edged weapons attack, where you have some distance to work with, will be to evade the knife. To best learn how this is done I created a special avoidance exercise several years ago. As the name implies, your intentions are to avoid this gruesome weapon altogether. The further you can get away from it, the better off you are. Of course, when performing this exercise safety is paramount. Both the trainer and the trainee must wear wrap-around eye protection, since even rubber or plastic training knives can damage the eyes. I know that many schools train with wooden or non-pointed, non-cutting metal training knives, which is good, but they should not be used in this exercise, because this exercise is done at full speed and with full contact. Full contact means making the rubber blade bend backward. When you are suddenly attacked by a suspect wielding a knife, the first thing you want to do is back off and bring both of your hands

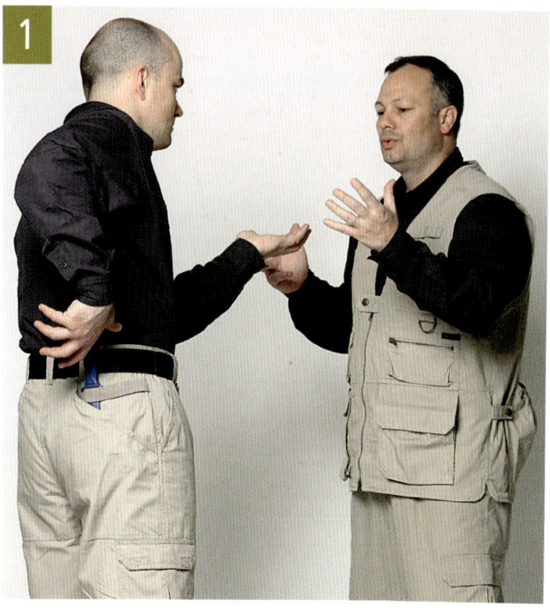

1 Hands kill. Always look at the hands of a suspicious person. Be prepared if they reach for a weapon quickly or even gradually.

2 If the opponent attacks with a knife, the defender first uses a shielding technique and withdraws his body from the line of attack.

3 The defender steps sideways away from the attacker. This is the so-called "tactical-L-move." This is especially important if you are followed.

4 If the defender can't escape immediately, he has to strike the opponent with impeding force; for example, by a kick towards the knee or by stabbing his eye with a finger.

directly in front of you to guard your center line (the imaginary line that runs down the center of the body from the top of the head to the groin). This technique is called "shielding." Your arms should be extended out in front of you and your elbows slightly bent.

In a real fight, if your hands and arms get cut (known as "defensive wounds"), so what; you can always get sewn up in the hospital after the fight is over. In a knife fight you will get cut. Cuts to the hands and fingers are not critical. However, you can't afford to take any slashes or stabs to the torso (head, neck, chest, and back). Tip penetration over 1¼ inches (approximately three centimeters), although not always fatal, can induce instantaneous shock that can weaken you, or even render you unconscious.

The problem with most law enforcement officers (who have little or no training in edged weapons) is that the first thing they go for when attacked with a knife at close range is their pistol. I've heard many officers joke when I invited them to my Knife Survival course: "If someone pulls a knife on me I'll just shoot them. Don't come to a gunfight with a knife, ha! ha!"

Unfortunately, the facts tell a different story. At the Costa Mesa Police Department, we had a young police officer stabbed in the arm with a screwdriver by an auto theft suspect. I spoke with this police officer later, who told me he was unable to unholster his weapon at the moment of the assault. Afterward, I offered to train my fellow officers (on my own time and at my own expense) how to survive edged weapons incidents such as these. The Training Bureau—those in charge of officer safety training—didn't think the training I offered was needed, even after the stabbing incident, and they declined my offer.

However, after the demonstration I give, police officers in my Knife Survival course become firm believers that a knife can win in a "gunfight." This again illustrates my point. If armed officers have difficulty surviving knife attacks if not properly trained, how much more vulnerable are civilians when victimized at knife point? The key to surviving an edged weapons attack is to get distance between yourself and the knife. You do this by aggressively slapping the incoming weapon away with both hands and sidestepping. This technique is known as a "Tactical L," and is used in order to get your body out of the line of attack. It's harder for the attacker to move laterally than to pursue you straight back. If you do have to retreat backwards, don't go too far without sidestepping or the attacker will easily catch up with you.

Once you have put some space between you and the attacker in those few moments and you still find that you can't draw your gun or get to another type of weapon, strike the attacker with a rapid kick to the knee, or attempt an eye poke with a finger. Your goal is to stop the pursuing attacker, or at least slow him down. If, after this, you still can't get your own weapon deployed—be it a gun, knife, or even a writing pen—get your hands back in front of your centerline and go through another cycle. In a situation where you have no weapon at all, immediately grab a nearby object and use it as an improvised weapon, such as dirt, a lamp, a jacket, or whatever will work. Remember, the longer the fight goes on, your chances of survival diminish rapidly. Few people can survive a knife fight while unarmed more than ten seconds without launching a damaging counterattack or successfully running away. That's why knife fights are so scary.

10.7 Teamwork in a Knife Fight

In military and law enforcement circles, teamwork is an essential element to operational success. To have effective teamwork requires clear and concise communications between members of the team. It doesn't matter if the team is made up of two police officers making a car stop on a country road or a 150-man counterterrorist team hitting a compound in a foreign country to rescue hostages.

Good communication is just as important as using the proper tactics and techniques. Right from the start, be it in Basic Combat Training or the police academy, recruits are taught how to communicate with each other in routine and crisis situations, and it continues throughout their careers.

Most civilian self-defense programs fall short in the area of team communications and teamwork. There is an assumption that the defender will be a sole defender. This mindset is evident when we take a close look at traditional and sport-based schools in activities such as sparring (contact matches), katas (choreographed conflict), and the tournament environment (which is based on sporting rules). These activities focus on one-on-one situations or one vs. multiple attackers. There are very few civilian schools that teach multiple defenders who must work together for mutual survival, be it against one dedicated attacker or many.

There are many instances where you could find yourself "teamed up" with a partner, by choice or unwittingly. Examples of this include a group of employees huddled together during an office shooting incident, a classroom full of students in yet another school shooting, you're with your family that gets car-jacked, or you're with a group of friends enjoying an evening out when the group is jumped by several gang members and one or two of them pull a knife on you.

If you train only to protect yourself and you do not train to work and communicate with those engaged in the conflict with you, then the odds of failure increase. Abandoning persons you are with may not be an acceptable or moral option. Since it is likely you may be fighting alongside others in a real knife conflict situation, you must incorporate techniques and scenarios dealing with such eventualities into your training regime.

Having a firearm doesn't necessarily mean that you have the superior weapon in close combat. A knife can win the fight.

Teamwork in training: coordinated combat ought to be trained with one or several partners to be prepared for such situations.

Regardless whether as a professional SWAT team advancing in a building or as civilians during a knife fight in a self-defense situation, in both cases, not only the tactics and techniques have to work well, but the communication, too.

During a real conflict you'll surely get cut. Nevertheless, continue fighting!

CHAPTER 11
CONFLICT FIRST AID

Anybody who has ever served in the military or has worn a badge has received mandatory first aid training. And I don't just mean bandaging up minor cuts or putting on text book splints, but actual combat first aid: CPR (cardiopulmonary resuscitation), sucking chest wounds, gunshot wounds, lacerated arteries, punctured eyeball, and many other unpleasant injuries resulting from conflict. The reason that a first aid curriculum is mandatory in these professions is because there is a strong likelihood of coming across injuries or becoming a casualty.

Although you may have little concern about the damage you inflict upon your attacker, you should be concerned for your own well being, or someone you are trying to protect if they ever become a victim. In a knife fight you will get cut or stabbed, and you need to know what to do during the post-conflict phase of the fight.

When I train fellow law enforcement officers or military personnel—with edged weapons, for example—I always tell them, "You're going to get cut." It's obviously not a popular statement, but it prepares them mentally for the "real world." And the truth of the matter is, if you are attacked with a knife at close range you will most likely get cut. This doesn't mean you can't go on to win the fight, but at least you won't be surprised and paralyzed with fear should an injury occur. In like manner, when I train my police and military students in Close Quarters Battle (CQB) involving firearms, I give them similar advice, "Only ten percent of those who are shot end up fatal, so keep fighting."

When faced with an actual crisis, these truths may be the only thing that a person hangs onto for strength. In fact, I remember while going through sniper school a few years ago a quote painted on the supporting beam of a classroom of the 1st Marine Division Scout/Sniper School at Camp Pendleton that has inspired me on several occasions since. It read: "Sweat dries, blood clots, bones heal. Positive mental attitude." Powerful statements like that really help in time of need. That's why the military and law enforcement have hundreds of sayings and mottos.

But such bravado cannot be limited to mere words only. Your own personal protection training must not only reflect the "will to survive" mentality if you are injured during a knife fight, but practical application in self first aid as well. This training should also extend to administering first aid to others.

To incorporate beneficial first aid training into your own schedule, you need to designate a person to be "wounded" during a training exercise. Assign them a specific injury as a result of a knife attack. To help you imagine how this would work, let's assume that I am the martial arts instructor for a moment. I select two students. One is armed with a rubber knife and the other is empty-handed. If during the exercise the unarmed student is "cut" I will yell out to him, "You have a deep cut to the forearm" or "a stab to the chest," or whatever the case may be. Once the fight is over, I tell the "wounded" student to immediately tend to the injuries: direct pressure to stop the bleeding, request help, prevent shock, or whatever it takes.

Now, if you are the one selected to be "stabbed" in a training exercise, you must visualize the actual trauma. It does little good if you are not training as if it were the real thing. Remember, you perform only as well as you train. Of course, if you use props and stage blood as I mentioned before, it will enhance this type of training.

As a police officer, I've seen many people survive their knife wounds, but I have also seen a few who have not. The student who trains for this possibility has a better chance of survival if he or she has visualized the trauma on his or her own body caused by the knife. Should a real incident ever occur, the student will be better off mentally than those who don't contemplate these things, or actually see them with moulage and stage blood. I can tell you from my own experiences on the streets as a police officer that a lot of people go into shock or hysteria for relatively minor injuries, and others are totally calm under the same circumstances. The same holds true for serious injuries.

A lot of it is mental. If you get injured in a fight you can't afford to panic. Even though you may be hurt, you must try to keep on fighting until the danger is over. This is especially true if you are protecting others. Yes, you may have just got your throat cut, and it was fatal, but you still have a minimum of three seconds of blood left in your brain to continue to function. Just enough time to neutralize your attacker before he can get to your family member behind you.

11.1 Self Triage / Self First Aid

In my Knife Survival course, I set up a scenario where someone has a close call with a knife; the knife came close, but there was no decisive victory for the attacker. Once the immediate danger has passed and the student is in a "safe" area, I ask them if they were injured. In the case of the knife attack, I told the attacker to get close to the victim's body with some stabs and slices, but not to actually make contact for the purpose of the drill. I tell the student who was the victim, "What are you going to do now?" The typical answer is, "I'm going to call the police." I bark at them, "No, wrong! You must check yourself for injuries, even if you don't think you got hit."

After a knife attack, you must never assume you were not hit. In fact, it is quite the opposite. You must assume that you were hit, and you have to find where the object penetrated your body. In a real conflict, especially when you are thankful you survived it, you are going to be so pumped up with adrenalin and your mind is racing about that you may not notice any injuries. In reality, you could be bleeding to death and not even know it. This has happened to many people who thought they were all right.

Since sustaining unknown injuries is a very real phenomenon in a knife conflict, you must perform what I call Self Triage / Self First Aid once you are no longer in immediate danger. once you are in a secure area you need to do a self pat down. A pat down is where you touch and squeeze with your hands on your own body, or the body of a victim. You start at the top of your head and work your way down to the neck with both hands. Then you check your hands for any signs of blood. As you are doing the pat down, you may also feel tenderness or pain if you come across an injury. Once you are finished with the neck, you will radiate out from your body and along your left arm. It is especially important to check under the arm pit to see if your artery was severed. You will continue to grab and squeeze until you reach your left hand. Then you will start at your right shoulder. As you can see, we are doing this triage in a systematic manner.

Once the arms are checked you will feel the chest, back, and move down to the waist. Every few seconds you will check your hands for blood. You will then carefully examine the pelvic area, especially along the inner thighs where the arteries to the leg go down into the legs. You will then pat down the left leg, then move over to the right leg and do the same. If you come across any injury in the course of the self triage, then you will determine the severity of the wound. If it is not life threatening, you will continue your pat down until the whole body has been searched. You can subsequently go back to the injury you found. If you do come across a serious injury, you will apply direct pressure and stop the bleeding. You will then call for help.

You can find more information about the military-based self-defense training of Jim Wagner on the internet at www.jimwagnerrealitybased.com or www.realitybased.de

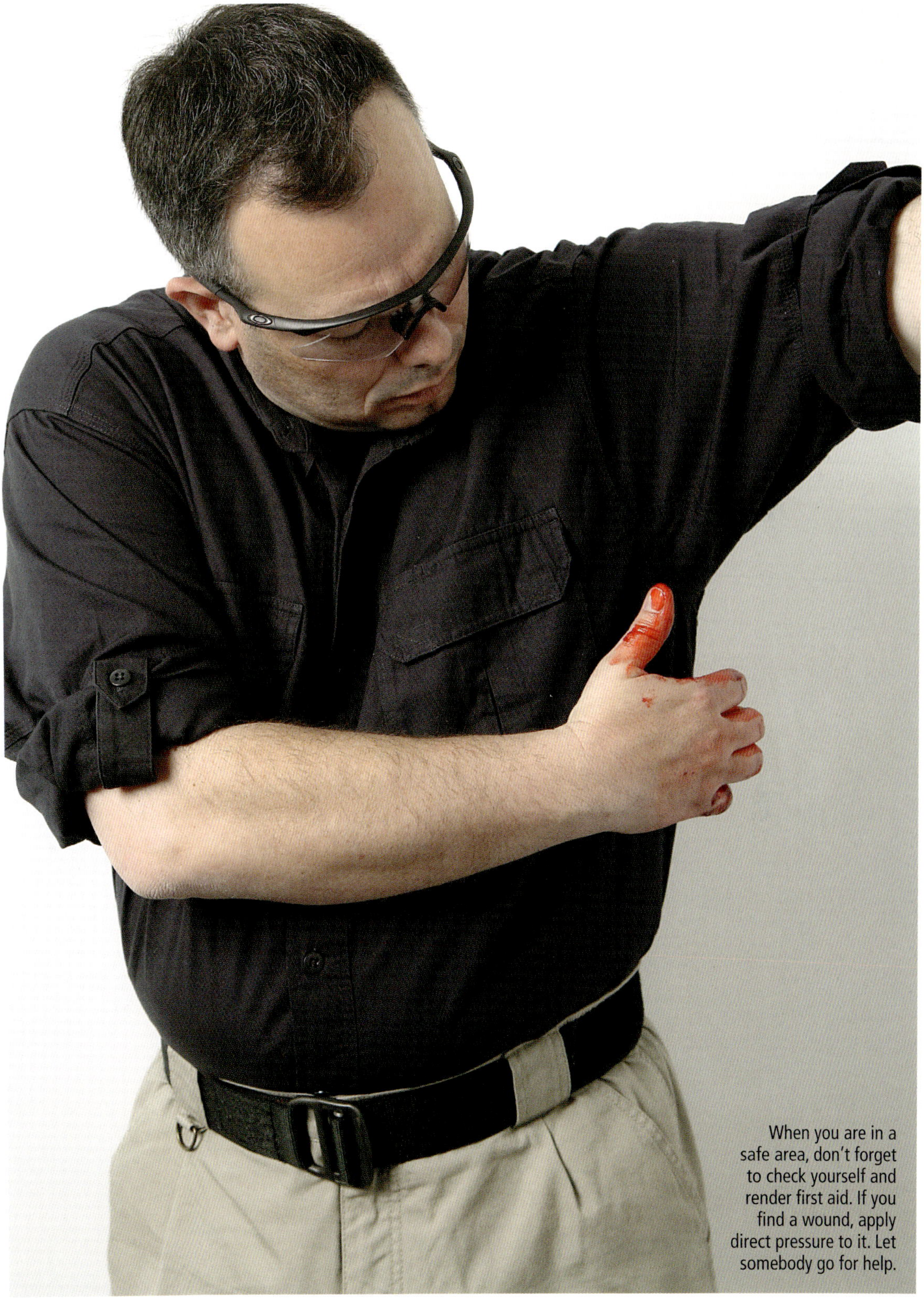

When you are in a safe area, don't forget to check yourself and render first aid. If you find a wound, apply direct pressure to it. Let somebody go for help.

Combat knife prototypes and special runs made by the company Böker, Solingen. Author Dietmar Pohl played an important role in their development.

Photo Thomas Ruhl

APPENDIX

Acknowledgment

The authors want to thank the following persons and companies for their support during the creation of this book:

Persons

Beshara, Brent
Brüggendick, Dirk
Buerlein, Robert
Constantinidis, Mike
Cronstedt, Einar
Curtis, Guy
Deus, Reiner
Dräger, Björn
Draper, Olive
Elishewitz, Allan
Fronteddu, Peter
Fuller, Mike
Götzmann, Marc
Grabosch, Nicole
Harsey, Bill
Hartsfield, Phill & Phil
Hayes, Wally
Hibben, Gil
Homann, K.
Kleinhuber, Stefan
Kittel, Hans-Peter
Klein, Rainer
Knoche, Peter
Koll, Natalie
Leckebusch, Tobias
Lehner, Helmut
Lüttecken, Werner
Malloy, William
Martin, R.J.
Mück, Helmut
Nealy, Bud
Peiniger, Christian
Perey, Stefan
Philippi, Thomas
Piorek, James
Randall, Gary
Raschke, Siegfried
Reeve, Chris & Anne
Ruhl, Thomas
Schanz, Jürgen
Scharlach, Martin
Sweeny, Mike
Weidner, Dan
Wolfsdorf, Peter
Wydeau, Caroline

Companies

AASW (www.aasw.de)
Abanico (www.abanico.de)
ACMA Reus (www.acma-reus.de)
Besh Knives (www.beshknives.com)
Blackhawk (www.blackhawk.com)
Bladerigger (www.bladerigger.com)
Caliber (www.caliber.de)
Der Messerkönig (www.messerkoenig.at)
Eickhorn Solingen Limited (www.eickhorn-solingen.com)
Ek Knives (www.ekknife.com)
Feinste Stahlwaren (www.feinstestahlwaren.de)
Fehlschärfe (www.fehlschaerfe.de)
Frank Soens Photo (www.franksoens.de)
Hayes Knives (www.hayesknives.com)
Heinr. Böker (www.boker.de)
Helmut Hofmann (www.helmuthofmann.de)
Herbertz (www.herbertz-messerclub.de)
Knoche Werbung (www.knoche.de)
Kytac (www.kytac.de)
Mastersmiths (www.beautifulblades.com)
Mehler Law Enforcement (www.mehler-law-enforcement.de)
Microtech Knives (www.microtechknives.com)
Old West Leather (www.oldwestleather.de)
Philippi Fotografie (www.foto3003.de)
Policeland (www.policeland.de)
Recon Company (www.5Punkt11.com)
Reeve Knives (www.chrisreeveknives.com)
Ruhl Studios (www.ruhl-studios.de)
R.J. Martin Knives (www.martinsite.com)
Sinn Spezialuhren (www.sinn.de)
Spydercon (www.spyderco.com)
TOPS Knives (www.topsknives.com)
VVA (www.vva.de)

BLADE STEELS

Name	Carbon	Chromium	Molybdenum	Vanadium	Silicon	Nickel	Sulfur	Phosphor	Manganese	Tungsten	Cobalt	Nitrogen	Hardness HRC
	Alloying Elements in Percent												
1.4034	0.43-0.50	12.50-14.50	–	–	1.00	–	0.02	0.04	1.00	–	–	–	52-55
1.4109	0.65-0.75	14.00-16.00	0.40-0.80	–	0.70	–	0.02	0.04	1.00	–	–	–	55-57
1.4110	0.48-0.60	13.00-15.00	–	0.05-0.15	1.00	–	0.02	0.04	1.00	–	–	–	54-56
1.4112	0.85-0.95	17.00-19.00	090-1.30	0.07-0.12	1.00	–	0.02	0.04	1.00	–	–	–	57-59
1.4116	0.45-0.55	14.00-15.00	0.50-0.80	0.10-0.20	1.00	–	0.02	0.04	1.00	–	–	–	56-58
1.4125	0.95-1.20	16.00-18.00	0.40-0.80	–	1.00	–	0.02	0.04	1.00	–	–	–	58-60
1.2003 (75Cr1)	0.70-0.80	0.30-0.40	–	–	0.25-0.50	–	0.03	0.03	0.60-0.80	–	–	–	56-59
1.2235 (80CrV2)	0.75-0.85	0.40-0.70	–	0.10-0.25	0.25-0.40	–	0.03	0.03	0.30-0.50	–	–	–	57-59
1.1625 (C80W2)	0.75-0.85	–	–	–	0.10-0.30	–	0.03	0.03	0.10-0.35	–	–	–	57-59
C30 (Bessemer)	0.27-0.34	–	–	–	0.40	–	0.05	0.05	0.50-0.70	–	–	–	52-54
420 (=420 J2)	0.40-0.50	12.00-14.00	–	–	1.00	–	0.01	0.02	1.00	–	–	–	52-55
420 HC	0.50-0.70	12.00-14.00	–	–	1.00	–	0.01	0.02	1.00	–	–	–	54-56
425 Modified	0.40-0.55	13.50-15.00	0.60-1.00	0.10	0.80	–	0.03	0.04	0.50	–	–	–	56-58
440 A	0.60-0.75	16.00-18.00	0.75	–	1.00	–	0.03	0.04	1.00	–	–	–	55-57
440 B	0.75-0.95	16.00-18.00	0.75	–	1.00	–	0.03	0.04	1.00	–	–	–	56-59
440 C	0.95-1.20	16.00-18.00	0.75	–	1.00	–	0.03	0.04	1.00	–	–	–	58-60
440XH	1.60	16.00	0.80	0.45	0.40	0.35	–	–	0.50	–	–	–	58-62
154 CM	1.05	14.00	4.00	–	0.30	–	–	–	0.50	–	–	–	58-61
S30V *	1.45	14.00	2.00	4.00	–	–	–	–	–	–	–	0.20	58-61
S60V (440V)*	2.15	17.00	0.40	5.50	0.40	–	–	–	0.40	–	–	–	56-58
S90V (420V)*	2.30	14.00	1.00	9.00	–	–	–	–	–	–	–	–	56-58
CPM-10V*	2.45	5.25	1.30	9.75	–	–	–	–	–	–	–	–	56-58
CPM-125V*	3.20-3.40	14.00	2.50	11.50-12.25	0.40-0.60	0.40	0.03	0.03	0.40-0.60	0.50	0.50	0.10-0.50	59-64
CPM-15V*	3.40	5.25	1.30	14.50	–	–	–	–	–	–	–	–	58-62
CPM-3V*	0.80	7.50	1.30	2.75	–	–	–	–	–	–	–	–	55-57
CPM-9V*	1.80	5.25	1.30	9.00	–	–	–	–	–	–	–	–	57-60
CPM-M4*	1.40	4.00	5.25	4.00	0.55	–	0.06	–	0.30	5.50	–	–	56-59
20CV*	1.90	20.00	1.00	4.00	0.30	–	–	–	0.30	0.60	–	–	58-62
ZDP-189*	3.00	20.00	–	–	–	–	–	–	–	–	–	–	57-62
K190*	2.30	12.50	1.10	4.00	0.40	–	–	–	0.40	–	–	–	60-64
K390*	2.45	4.15	3.75	9.00	0.55	–	–	–	–	1.00	2.00	–	61-65
BG-42	1.15	14.50	4.00	1.20	0.30	–	–	–	0.50	–	–	–	57-60
D2	1.40-1.60	11.00-13.00	0.90	0.80	0.60	–	–	–	0.60	–	–	–	58-61
M2	0.95-1.05	3.75-4.50	4.75-6.50	1.95-2.75	0.20-0.45	0.30	–	0.03	0.15-0.40	5.00-6.75	–	–	59-64
A2	0.95-1.05	4.75-5.50	0.90	1.40	0.50	0.30	–	–	1.00	–	–	–	57-61
W-1	0.70-1.50	0.15	0.10	0.10	0.10-0.40	0.20	–	–	0.10-0.40	0.50	–	–	57-63
W-2	0.85-1.50	0.15	0.10	0.10	0.10-0.40	0.20	–	–	0.10-0.40	0.15	–	–	57-63
LV04	0.90	18.00	1.15	0.10	–	–	–	–	0.07	–	–	–	55-58
SK-5 (1.1830)	0.90-1.00	–	0.30	–	0.30	–	–	–	–	–	–	–	57-60
0170-6C (50100B)	0.95	0.45	–	0.20	–	–	–	–	0.45	–	–	–	57-60
MBS-26	0.85-1.00	13.00-15.00	0.15-0.25	–	0.65	–	0.01	0.04	0.30-0.60	–	–	–	56-59
MRS-30	1.12	14.00	0.60	0.25	1.00	–	–	–	0.50	–	–	–	58-61
Vascowear	1.12	7.75	1.60	2.40	1.20	–	–	–	0.30	1.10	–	–	58-61
INFI M	0.60	8.00	1.40	0.50	1.00	0.30	0.01	0.02	0.40	0.10	0.03	–	56-58
0-1	0.85-1.00	0.40-0.60	–	0.30	0.50	–	–	–	1.00-1.40	–	–	–	57-61
1050	0.47-0.55	–	–	–	–	–	0.50	0.40	0.60-0.90	–	–	–	55-57
1055	0.52-0.60	–	–	–	–	–	0.50	0.40	0.60-0.90	–	–	–	56-58

BLADE STEELS

Name	Carbon	Chromium	Molybdenum	Vanadium	Silicon	Nickel	Sulfur	Phosphor	Manganese	Tungsten	Cobalt	Nitrogen	Hardness HRC
1065	0.59-0.70	–	–	–	–	–	0.50	0.40	0.60-0.90	–	–	–	56-59
1085	0.80-0.94	–	–	–	–	–	0.50	0.40	0.60-0.90	–	–	–	57-60
1095	0.90-1.04	–	–	–	–	–	0.50	0.40	0.60-0.90	–	–	–	58-61
5160	0.55-0.65	–	–	–	0.15-0.30	–	–	0.04	0.75-1.00	–	–	–	56-59
52100	0.95-1.10	–	–	–	0.15-0.30	–	0.03	0.03	0.25-0.45	–	–	–	58-61
Carbon V	1.05	0.45	–	0.15-0.20	0.20	–	–	0.01	0.50	–	–	–	56-59
8Cr13MoV	0.80	13.00	0.15	0.10	0.50	0.20	0.01	0.02	0.40	–	–	–	56-58
AUS-4	0.40-0.45	13.00-14.50	–	–	1.00	0.49	0.03	0.04	1.00	–	–	–	52-55
AUS-6	0.55-0.65	13.00-14.50	–	0.10-0.25	1.00	0.49	0.03	0.04	1.00	–	–	–	55-57
AUS-8	0.70-0.75	13.00-14.50	0.10-0.30	0.10-0.26	1.00	0.49	0.03	0.04	0.50	–	–	–	57-59
AUS-10	0.95-1.10	13.00-14.50	0.10-0.31	0.10-0.27	1.00	0.49	0.03	0.04	0.50	–	–	–	58-60
AUS-118	0.90-0.95	17.00-18.00	1.30-1.50	0.10-0.25	0.50	–	0.03	0.04	0.50	–	–	–	58-60
VG-10	0.95-1.05	14.50-15.50	0.90-1.20	0.10-0.30	0.60	–	–	0.30	0.50	–	1.30-1.50	–	58-61
VG-1	0.95-1.05	13.00-15.00	0.20-0.40	–	–	0.25	–	–	–	–	–	–	58-61
Shirogami 1)	1.20	–	–	–	0.20	–	0.03	0.02	0.20	–	–	–	59-63
Aogami 2)	1.20	0.20-0.50	–	–	0.20	–	–	–	0.30	1.00-1.50	–	–	60-63
GIN-1	0.90	15.50	0.30	–	0.37	–	0.03	0.02	0.60	–	–	–	58-60
SGPS*	1.40	15.00	2.80	–	0.50	–	0.03	0.03	0.40	–	–	–	59-62
ATS-34	1.05	14.00	4.00	–	0.35	–	0.02	0.03	0.40	–	–	–	58-61
RWL-34*	1.05	14.00	4.00	–	0.50	–	–	–	0.50	–	–	–	58-61
ATS-55	1.00	14.00	0.60	–	0.40	–	–	–	0.50	–	–	–	58-61
PMC-27*	0.60	13.50	–	–	0.50	–	–	–	0.50	–	–	–	54-56
12C27	0.60	13.50	–	–	0.40	–	0.01	0.03	0.40	–	–	–	54-56
12C27 Mod.	0.52	14.50	–	–	0.40	–	0.01	0.03	0.60	–	–	–	54-56
13C26	0.65	13.00	–	–	0.40	–	0.01	0.03	0.65	–	–	–	55-57
19C27	0.95	13.50	–	–	0.40	–	0.01	0.03	0.65	–	–	–	57-60
Elmax Supercl.*	1.70	17.00	1.00	3.00	0.40	–	–	–	0.30	–	–	–	58-62
N 690	1.05	17.00	0.50	–	0.40	–	–	–	0.40	–	1.50	–	59-62
N 695	1.05	17.00	0.50	–	0.40	–	–	–	0.40	–	–	–	57-60
X15-T.N.	0.40	15.50	2.00	0.30	0.20	–	–	0.02	0.40	–	–	0.20	57-60
H-1	0.15	14.00-16.00	0.50-1.50	–	3.00-4.50	6.00-8.00	0.03	0.04	2.00	–	–	0.10	54-56
40X13	0.35-0.45	13.00	–	–	0.30	–	0.03	0.03	0.35	–	–	–	54-58
65X13	0.60-0.75	13.00	0.75	–	1.00	–	0.03	0.04	1.00	–	–	–	56-58
95X18	0.95-1.00	17.00-19.00	–	–	0.80	0.60	0.03	0.03	0.80	–	–	–	58-60
110X18	1.10	17.00-18.00	0.30	–	–	0.50	0.03	0.03	0.50	–	–	–	58-61
Z60	0.60-0.65	14.00	0.55-0.60	0.15-0.20	–	0.15	–	–	0.45	–	–	–	56-58
Z70CD15	0.70	15.00	0.75	–	1.0	–	0.03	0.04	1.00	–	–	–	55-57
XC 70	0.65-0.75	–	–	–	0.10-0.30	–	0.03	0.03	0.10-0.35	–	–	–	56-58
MVS-8	0.85	14.00	2.50	0.15	0.50	–	–	–	0.50	–	–	–	58-61
CRB-7	1.10	14.00	2.00	1.00	0.30	–	–	–	0.40	–	–	–	58-61

(Alloying elements in percent)

* type of steel metallurgically produced by powder
1) = "White paper steel" (Hitachi)
2) = "Blue paper steel" (Hitachi)